THE GLOBAL INFORMATION SOCIETY

Aslib, The Association for Information Management, has some two thousand corporate members worldwide. It actively promotes better management of information resources.

Aslib lobbies on all aspects of the management of and legislation concerning information. It provides consultancy and information services, professional development training, specialist recruitment, and publishes primary and secondary journals, conference proceedings, directories and monographs.

Further information about Aslib can be obtained from:
Aslib, The Association for Information Management
Information House, 20–24 Old Street, London ECIV 9AP
Tel: +(44) 0171 253 4488 Fax: +(44) 0171 430 0514

THE GLOBAL INFORMATION SOCIETY

William J Martin

Published by
Aslib Gower
Gower House
Croft Road
Aldershot
Hampshire GU11 3HR
England

Gower
Old Post Road
Brookfield
Vermont 05036
USA

British Library Cataloguing in Publication Data
Martin, William J.
   Global Information Society. – 2Rev. ed
   I. Title
   303.4833

   ISBN 0–566–07715–9

Library of Congress Cataloging-in-Publication Data
Martin, William J., 1938–
      The global information society / William J. Martin.
         p.   cm.
      Includes bibliographical references and index.
      ISBN 0–566-07715-9
      1. Information society. 2. Information technology—Social aspects. 3. Information technology—Management. I. Title.
   HM221.M292   1995
   303.48'33—dc20   95–9309
                                                                 CIP

Typeset in Cheltenham and Fenice by Bournemouth Colour Press and printed in Great Britain by Biddles Ltd. Guildford

Contents

Abbreviations

ABI	Applications Binary Interface
ACP	Acceptable Use Policy
ADE	application development environment
ADSL	Asymmetrical Digital Subscriber Line
AI	artificial intelligence
AMPS	analog cellular radio
ANSI	American National Standards Institute
API	Applications Programming Interface
APP	Applications Portability Profile
ASPA	Account Service Planning and Analysis
ATM	Asynchronous Transfer Mode
BOSTID	(US) Board on Science and Technology for International Development
BPR	Business Process Reengineering
CASE	Computer-Assisted Software Engineering
CCIR	International Radio Consultative Committee
CDMA	Code Division Multiple Access
CDPD	Cellular Digital Packet Data
CIO	Chief Information Officer
CISC	Complex Instruction Set Computing
COS	Corporation for Open Systems
CPU	central processing unit
CT2	digital cordless telephone
DBS	direct broadcast satellite
DRAMS	Dynamic Random Access Chips
DSP	digital signal processor

DSRR	digital short range radio
ECL	emitter controlled logic
EDI	electronic data interchange
EDIFACT	Electronic Data Interchange for Administration, Commerce and Transport
EFT	electronic funds transfer
ETSI	European Information Technology Standards Institute
Eutelsat	European Telecommunications Satellite Organization
GATS	General Agreement on Trade in Services
GATT	General Agreement on Trade and Tariffs
GNS	Group of Negotiations on Services
GUI	Graphical User Interface
HDTV	higher definition television
IBS	International Business Satellite
ICT	information and communication technology
Immarsat	International Maritime Satellite Organization
Intelsat	International Telecommunications Satellite Consortium
ISDN	Integrated Services Digital Network
ISO	International Standards Organization
IT	information technology
ITU	International Telecommunications Union
IVM	information value management
LEO	low earth orbiting satellite
MAC standard	Multiplexed Analog Component standard
MDNS	managed data network service
MHS	Message Handling Service
MIMD	multiple-instruction, multiple data mode
MIPS	million instructions per millisecond
MPEG-2	Motion Picture Experts Group
MRCI	Microsoft Realtime Compression Interface
MVP	multimedia video processor
NWICO	New World Information and Communication Order
OCS	Open Computer Systems
OECD	Organization for Economic Co-operation and Development
OOPS	Object-Oriented Programming Systems
OSI	Open Systems Interconnection
PC	personal computer
PCN	Personal Communication Network
PCS	personal communications services
PDA	Personal Digital Assistant
PHS	Personal Handy Phone
PMR	private mobile radio

POSIX	Portable Operating System Interface for Computer Environments
RBOC	Regional Bell Operating Company
RISC	Reduced Instruction Set Computing
ROI	return on investment
SHF	super high frequency
SIMD	single-instruction, multiple data mode
SMATV	Satellite Master Antenna Television
SMS	Satellite Multi Service (Eutelsat)
SNA	Systems Network Architecture
SNMP	Simple Network Management Protocol
SPC	Software Publishing Corporation (US)
SPOT	Satellite pour l'Observation de la Terre
TAPI	Windows Telephony API
TBMS	text based management system
TCP/IP	Transmission Control Protocol/Internet Protocol
TQM	Total Quality Management
TRIMS	Trade-Related Investment Measures
TRIPS	Trade-Related Intellectual Property Rights
TSAPI	NetWare Telephony Services API
TSS	Telecommunications Standardization Sector
TVRO	television receive only
UHF	ultra high frequency
UN	United Nations
UPS	uninterruptible power supply
VADS	value added and data services
VLSI	very large scale integration
VLWI	very long word instruction
VMS	voice messaging system
XIWT	Cross Industry Working Team

Acknowledgements

This book would not have been written were it not for the help and support of librarians at Dublin City University, University College Dublin and the Royal Melbourne Institute of Technology. I am grateful to them for all their many kindnesses. It would certainly have been much harder to do had I not had the assistance of Denise Oh, my indefatigable research assistant. However, without the help and encouragement of Clara I would have given the whole thing up long since.

Bill Martin
Melbourne
October 1994

Preface: Information Society Revisited

This book started out as a second edition of a previous volume and has become much more than that. *The Information Society* was published by Aslib in 1988, and since that time, and indeed during the writing of the present book, much has happened to change perceptions of the central subject matter, the information society. In a sense it is a curious combination of *déja vu* and *plus ça change*: those people still interested in the idea are still debating the same topics – does the information society exist, how do we know, what does its presence or absence portend for the future? Does it matter anyway? Now there is a question which has haunted this writer on occasions too numerous to mention!

At one level, whether or not we are living in an information society or are likely to do so in the future, is really of little consequence. This is easily apparent when one considers those events and trends which are of transparent and demonstrable significance, those truly global phenomena that are already casting their shadow on the future. As graphically depicted by historian Paul Kennedy, these trends include:

- Demographic crisis: the current world population of over five billion could reach beyond 10 billion by the mid-21st century. As this population growth will occur in the developing world, which lacks the resources to cope with it, there is the prospect of famines, wars and uncontrolled mass migration from the poorer countries to the richer ones.
- Environmental challenges: drastic ecological damage resulting from the pressures of population and economic activity on the world's natural resources, and the spectre of global warming which

threatens major climatic change, forced relocation of habitats and radical shifts in the nature and location of economic activity.

- Biotechnology: where the ability of scientists to engage in genetic engineering raises ethical, health, environmental and economic questions of truly fundamental proportions. In the agricultural sector, for example, while biotechnology holds out the promise of new seeds, new crops and the potential to eradicate food shortages, it also threatens the livelihoods of farmers in both rich and poor countries through the *in vitro* cultivation of crops which, in many cases, form the mainstay of national economies.
- North–South tensions: where the combined impact of imbalances in population growth and resource levels, the increasing technology gap between rich and poor countries, and the role of western multinational corporations could seriously exacerbate existing tensions between North and South.[1]

When viewed in such a context, the issue of whether or not we are moving towards an information society suddenly seems rather less than critical. Nevertheless, as a focus for the examination of what is happening within society, developments which are inextricably linked to those other, truly epochal trends, the subject is well worth further examination.

One of the weaknesses attending the study of information society to date, has been that much of it has entailed reaction to various forecasts or predictions by futurologists. Quite apart from the, at times, outrageous claims appearing in some of these forecasts, their less than impressive record of success has scarcely added to the credibility of notions of an information society. Tom Forester has attributed the lack of success of these forecasters to the fact that they were driven by utopian visions of technological change, rather than by practicalities and hard realities. Not only were forecasts for the uptake of leading edge technologies such as robotics found to be out by factors of hundreds, but there was really no evidence that the forecasters had any idea of what the technological future would look like.[2] Although such forecasts continue to appear, indeed, to proliferate, there are also encouraging signs of a new reality in some quarters, and it relates directly to the kinds of crisis identified by Kennedy. Examples would include:

- Realization that our view of technology has been essentially an unsophisticated one, being perceived in terms of *tools* rather than as a *social process*, with costs as well as benefits.
- Growing awareness of the need for sustainability on a planet faced

with dire choices, the need for shifts from quantitative and material emphases on growth towards qualitative and non-material growth.[3]

● Recognition of the meta crisis caused by the break-up of an old order based on East–West confrontation and the emergence of a new order full of threats and uncertainties.[4]

These and other issues form a backcloth against which matters pertaining to the development of an information society can be examined. More than this they share an arena in which information and its related technologies, their characteristics, impacts and implications can be observed and assessed. As such they are the focus and the essential purpose of this volume.

REFERENCES

1.   Paul Kennedy (1993) *Preparing for the 21st* Century. London: Harper Collins.

2.   Tom Forester (1992) Megatrends or megamistakes? What ever happened to the information society? *The Information Society*, **8**, pp. 133–46.

3.   Richard A. Slaughter (1993) Looking for the real 'megatrends'. *Futures*, **25**, (8), pp. 827–49.

4.   William E. Halal (1993) World 2000: an international planning dialogue to help shape the new global system. *Futures*, **25**, (1), pp. 5–21.

1 The Information Society

Although the term *information society* was in widespread use by the time that the first edition of this book appeared, its currency denoted neither the existence of a broad consensus on any associated constructs or concepts, nor indeed on their legitimacy. Writing some six years later, it has to be admitted that little has changed in the interim. In essence, therefore, while people all over the world continue to talk about the information society, and some would even claim to be living in it, there seems to have been little, if any, real progress made in establishing either some form of metrics for this phenomenon or in amassing the kind of evidence that would result in credibility. Indeed, the very absence of such criteria might well indicate that the information society has remained little more than a catchphrase or a slogan, more a matter of rhetoric than of reality.

There was always an element of symbolism about the term, with information serving as a talisman for a new kind of society, a society in which reason and consensus set the tone rather than raw power and materialism. Nevertheless, by the 1980s, it became clear that within certain advanced, western-type societies, a series of social, economic and technological changes had been set in train which marked them off, not just from developing nations, but from less advanced industrial societies. In such circumstances the concept acquired considerable substance, whether in the form of infrastructure developments or the emergence of information trade and the well-nigh pervasive influence of information and communication technologies in economic and social life.

Today, the *informatization* of such societies has proceeded to the point at which structures and institutions are affected, and the so-called *information revolution* is global in its extent and influence. Nevertheless, the same criticisms as were being voiced a decade ago, can be levelled against the concept today. Is the so-called information society really little more than the product of technological determinism, initially as the result of developments in computing but increasingly affected by those in telecommunications? Rather than information society would it not be more appropriate to label it a *broadband society*, one in which telecommunications has become the true catalyst for change? In such a society, it is claimed, everyone will have access to virtually unlimited information and universal telephone service will be replaced by universal information services.[1] Or alternatively, are such changes which have occurred not more representative of the emergence of an *information economy* than an information society? It is clear that fundamental questions still need to be answered as to the true nature of these changes, as to what has caused them and what they really mean for society. In the event, the label which we put upon such developments is a relatively minor issue. Much more important are the lessons that need to be learned from such developments and their implications for the future of all societies. Before turning to these issues, however, let us pause to reconsider the concept itself and its evolution from social construct to vernacular catchphrase.

INFORMATION SOCIETY, EVOLUTION OF THE CONCEPT

The concept of information society emerged in the 1970s and throughout the 1980s, and it rapidly gained widespread currency. It has a broad provenance, its proponents ranging from scholarly and academic authors to the best-selling popularists. Prominent in the first group of writers were Masuda, who perceived an eventual transition to the point at which the production of information values became the formative force for the development of society[2] and Stonier, who perceived the dawning of a new age for western society, one as different from the industrial period as that period was from the Middle Ages.[3] Although apparently uncomfortable with the term information society, Daniel Bell did much to sustain it through his work on what he termed *postindustrial society*. Postindustrial society was characterized by a shift from goods producing to service industry, and by the codification of theoretical knowledge, with knowledge and innovation serving as the strategic and transforming resources of society, just as capital and labour had been in earlier industrial society.[4]

Although Marc Porat and before him, Fritz Machlup did much to focus attention on its economic implications, few writers have done so much to popularize the concept of information society as have Alvin Toffler and John Naisbett. Naisbett, for example, argued that the United States made the transition from an industrial to an information society as early as the 1960s and 1970s and that in this process the computer played the role of liberator.[5] Toffler talked of an *information bomb* exploding in our midst and of a power shift in society, consequent upon the extent to which it had come to depend on knowledge.[6]

The inherent attraction of these ideas and the confidence and vigour with which they were expressed, fired the public imagination, and no doubt helped sustain that sizeable body of writing on the information society which ensued. Perhaps significantly, not a great deal of effort went into definitions of the phenomenon or detailed categorizations of what was involved. The focus tended to be on broad trends and on their implications for the way of life in information society. Before going on to consider some of the arguments for and against the concept, let us return to a definition of the information society coined by the present author in 1988:

> ...a society in which the quality of life, as well as prospects for social change and economic development, depend increasingly upon information and its exploitation. In such a society, living standards, patterns of work and leisure, the education system and the marketplace are all influenced markedly by advances in information and knowledge. This is evidenced by an increasing array of information-intensive products and services, communicated through a wide range of media, many of them electronic in nature.[7]

In this definition, the intention was to broaden the focus from the merely technological or economic, and to portray the information society *as society*. Although no attempt will be made to repeat the definitional exercise six years later, it is clear that the need for this broader basis of assessment is just as great today as it was at the end of the 1980s. It is still unclear what people mean when they talk about information society. The criteria for information society status are by no means obvious, nor are the characteristics which would set information societies apart from industrial societies. In his attempt to synthesize existing writings on the subject, Ian Miles did much to widen perspectives on the information society. Indeed, he argued that there is not simply one information society but many possible information societies.[8]

In seeking a synthesis between the views of those who saw information society as something that was fundamentally new and those who regarded it as largely a continuation of what had gone before, and between those who were optimistic about such

3

developments and those who viewed them with concern, Miles came up with a structuralist perspective. The structuralist approach was a synthesis of extremes, which sought to introduce some sense of the complexity of the impact of social and technological change, and the likelihood that a diversity of interests, actors and social structures would produce a variety of outcomes or, as he put it, many possible information societies.[8]

CRITIQUE OF THE INFORMATION SOCIETY CONCEPT

The best-selling status of populist accounts of the information society stemmed from more than just the skill and passion of their authors. While critics could complain of the excessive hyperbole employed and an undue acceptance of both technological wizardry and free market individualism, it was clear from even the most detached accounts that major information-related change had been occurring in certain advanced societies from at least the 1970s.

By the 1980s, the evidence for such change was all around us. People were beginning to use computers at home as well as at work; most advanced economies had an information sector and realtime, 24 hour global trading on highspeed communications networks, was a fact of life. Along with such developments, society was beginning to face up to the threat of information related crime and to invasions of personal and corporate privacy. To that underclass which has always existed in all developed countries, was being added a new group known as the *information poor*, while the plight of the emerging world was aggravated by a new form of outside interference, dubbed *electronic colonialism*. Moreover, whether or not there was any general consensus on what was meant by it, the term information society was in common use throughout the world. So it was easy enough to be caught up in the excitement of what seemed to be the dawning of a new age, an information age.

The key question of course, was the extent to which society had actually changed. Leaving aside the matter of nomenclature, had the environment in which the events listed in the foregoing paragraph itself undergone dramatic and fundamental transformation? For this to be the case, there would have to be evidence not only of increased information or information-related activity within society, but also of the kind of changes involved in the transition from first, agricultural to industrial society and then from industrial to information society.

Although our definition of the information society does not specifically mention the mode of production, it is implicitly couched in relation to western, capitalist societies. Socialist states on the old totalitarian model would not have commended themselves as candidates for information society status. Indeed, it has been argued elsewhere that it was the very presence of information and its dissemination by means of communication technologies that served to break up the former Soviet and Eastern European monolith.[9] Following the Industrial Revolution, first in 18th-century Britain and then in other parts of the globe, the nature of production became a metaphor for society itself, as the factory system and the capitalist mode of industrial organization spread throughout much of the modern world. Information had always played a major role in such developments and was to become even more important with the adoption of modern management practices at the turn of the 19th and 20th centuries. However, as writers like Schement have pointed out, the United States was already a capitalist society before the onset of the factory system. The commoditization of information, such a prominent feature today, was well entrenched in the United States before 1877, as indeed was a marketplace for information workers such as printers and journalists.[10]

David Lyon was one of many writers to question whether or not the sum of the changes inherent in what people refer to as the information society in fact amounted to a shift beyond industrial capitalism. As Lyon pointed out, many of the anticipated benefits of an information society have failed to materialize so far as the majority of people in advanced countries are concerned, for example, a leisured lifestyle in a culture of self-expression, political participation and an emphasis on the quality of life.[11] A similar conclusion was reached by Tom Forester, originally an enthusiastic proponent of the information society concept. In fact, observed Forester, by the 1990s, people were working longer rather than shorter hours and the paperless office, like the so-called *electronic cottage* was little more than a myth.[12]

None of this would have come as any great surprise to those commentators who had consistently taken a less sanguine view, perceiving the information society as characterized by the presence of all-powerful multinational corporations, mass unemployment and economic and information inequities.[13] Such critics dismissed the possibility of real social progress in a society which, to them, was tightly constrained by the forces and values of monopoly capitalism. Hence, nothing had changed. All that had happened was that the dominant forces in capitalist society had found new avenues of exploitation and new technological means by which to pursue them.

Mindful of the dangers of unbridled late 20th-century capitalism, Lyon focused on the locus of power within information societies, aware of the fact that control of the new technologies could prove crucial.[11] Moreover, like Gershuny and Miles, Lyon was sceptical about claims for the development of an *information sector* within modern economies. Gershuny and Miles challenged the so-called 'march through the sectors', which had been popularized by, among others, Machlup, Bell and Porat. Rather than economic development occurring in a series of sequential and discrete movements between first agricultural and industrial societies and then, industrial and information societies, they perceived a more heterogeneous transition, with continued growth in manufacturing within the so-called service-based economies of the information age.[14] Lyon also voiced widespread unhappiness with those attempts in the Machlup–Porat–Rubin tradition to separate information activities and occupations from the general run of economic activity. Not only was the designation of many such occupations as *informational* a highly contentious affair, but also all manner of activities were clearly becoming much more information-intensive and, in the process, rendering the breakdown of occupations into information and non-information categories both difficult and suspect.[11]

In the previous edition, certain criteria were suggested to assist in identifying likely candidates for information society status. Although intended only as guidelines, these proved useful and they continue to be employed, if less formally, in the relevant chapters of the present volume. They are reintroduced at this point in order to help lend a more holistic dimension to our assessment of progress towards the evolution of information society. The list is short and includes: economic criteria, technological criteria, social criteria, political criteria, and cultural criteria.

Economic criteria

Although there is much more to the information society than the means by which it earns its living, it is clear that any successful challenge to the credibility of the information sector would inevitably call into question the entire concept. It is equally clear that the case for an information sector in modern economies has not been helped by the at times, bizarre attempts at occupational and industrial reclassification. Not only are many of these classifications questionable in themselves, but the end result of such quantification may well be of little real meaning in terms of its contribution to economic and social life. Simply aggregating occupations and counting totals, for instance, tells us nothing about the really significant information workers in society, nor does it enable us to differentiate the most important dimensions of information work.[15]

This is not to say that all efforts at measurement should be abandoned, rather that the limitations of existing methods need to be addressed. Such obstacles notwithstanding, there are well established national and international channels and structures for trade in information goods and services. In attempting to locate such activities within formal reporting and accounting structures, bodies such as the Organization for Economic Co-operation and Development (OECD), continue to find it useful to group them within national information sectors. The same is true of this book, where the information sector is regarded primarily as a device for scrutinizing progress towards the information society, and only after that as an entity within modern economies.

Technological criteria

Not unexpectedly, the technological case for information society development is a strong one. The convergence of computing and telecommunications continues to make itself felt in just about every area of life in modern societies. This has resulted in the automation not just of entire industries like banking and automobiles, but at times of what appears like whole societies with tax, social security vehicle registration, credit card and medical information all held in digital form, and with national and international security inescapably linked to computerization, be this in the form of satellite-based defence and early warning systems or weather and navigation systems. Indeed, the world can have had few more dramatic illustrations of the wider social impacts of information technology than in the command and control systems, and the so-called 'smart' weapons, employed by the allies in the Gulf War. Fact and fantasy, the ultimate reality of war and the excitement of the arcade videogame blended seamlessly and ceaselessly in both space and cyberspace, revolutionizing the reporting of the conflict as much as its conduct.

This aspect of the information revolution is not just international but global. It would not be possible for global markets to function effectively without the power of computers and telecommunications systems. This is as true for manufacturing industry with its globally networked groups of executives, engineers and production workers, as it is for financial services companies engaged in foreign exchange dealing or futures trading. In describing such activities, therefore, and the environment within which they are performed, is one in fact talking about information societies?

The question is not unreasonable, although the answer may be somewhat different than expected. If one takes those countries which qualify for membership of the OECD as representative of the more advanced nations in the world, it is clear that in most cases they are 7 heavy users of a wide range of information and communications technologies. On this basis alone it could be argued that they are already information societies, in that they rely upon sophisticated information and communications technologies to perform a wide range of functions and processes, most notably in the area of decision making. However, technological sophistication is not in itself a sufficient condition for the attainment of information society status, although it may well be a necessary prerequisite. The key to such developments lies in the extent to which these technologies have become an integral part of the everyday life of the citizen and the uses to which they are put.

Research undertaken by Halal in the United States has shed valuable light upon the relationship between technological progress and social change, and in particular, the lag which commonly occurs between the availability of a technology and its adoption by the community at large.[16] The research indicated that soon after the year 2000 there would be widespread use of very sophisticated technology including optical computers, very advanced expert and knowledge-based systems and those enabling access to computerized libraries. However, it would not be until later in the that decade, that those information services involving sensitive social consequences are likely to be adopted, such as electronic education, teleconferencing, electronic shopping and telework. It will take time before these information systems are sufficiently sophisticated and user-friendly to attract enough users as to change entrenched social patterns. In time, however, this will produce not just a dramatic shift in the technological base of modern societies but a dramatic social revolution as well.

One does not have to agree with each and every example given by Halal to see the plausibility of his findings. Even in the United States, this is a matter of developing trends rather than established social practice. Even in the narrower technological sense it is somewhat premature to be talking about information societies, because the technologies are neither sophisticated enough nor sufficiently embedded in the social fabric as to be, in any significant sense, representative or typical of society.

Social criteria

One problem with such lists is that of overlap between categories, with criteria being at once social and political, for example. This is particularly the case with social criteria which, almost by definition could embrace just about anything to do with information-led social change. It could include the impact of Freedom of Information legislation, or of its absence, for example; or that possibility, envisaged by Halal, where networking and electronic communication could lead to a resurgence of family and community life.[16] Miles has anticipated the possibility that the interactivity made possible by new information technology-based consumer technologies, could usher in changes in ways of life, including the emergence of new sexual divisions of labour and of new private modes of goods and service provision.[8] There is obviously also the potential for adverse effects, for instance the danger of alienation of an underclass of information poor from the general electronic community, or the re-emergence of a form of sweated labour in so-called telecottages, exploited by employers and denied the benefits of employee protection and full time contracts.

These and similar issues are discussed in later chapters; at this point the emphasis is on major information-led change of the kind that clearly signals significant social dislocation. This would entail changes in general social behaviour or attitudes, along the lines of those foreseen by Masuda well over a decade ago. Masuda envisaged an information society of which the axis would comprise information values rather than material values, and an economy in which knowledge capital would predominate over material capital.[17] Idealistic as this still sounds, it is interesting to find Halal coming up with very similar hypotheses in the light of his much more pragmatic enquiry, which anticipated a future focus on intellectual rather than material concerns, with, however, the likelihood of serious social and human costs.[16] It is significant that, in discussing such issues, the focus continues to be on events in the future rather than in the present.

Political criteria

Much of the focus on the political effects of information-generated change has traditionally been on the possibility and potential benefits of electronic polling. Although there has recently been a successful example of this phenomenon in Norway, it has had little impact elsewhere. Although this might perhaps suggest something of a failure to exploit the full potential of electronic democracy, the evidence from the United States is that such experiments tend to lose impact through being submerged in the overwhelming deluge of existing media messages.[12]

However, there is clear evidence of major political change consequent upon global television coverage of events in the former Soviet Union and the Eastern Bloc. The scandal of Chernobyl, the tragic events leading to the overthrow of Ceausescu in Romania and the massive political upheavals following first the Gorbachev affair and then the attempted overthrow of Yeltsin's fledgling democracy, these could all be directly linked to the free flow of information and the power of modern communications media. These developments, of course, may well have nothing to do with the emergence of the information society, being merely the product of the advanced communications technologies of the late 20th century. Be that as it may, some observers would perceive in such events the emergence of new electronically-mediated virtual communities, as a kind of global forum in which ordinary citizens around the globe can engage in direct interaction.[16] Were this to occur to any significant extent, then it clearly could point the way to a new kind of world politics and as such would provide powerful support for the case for the information society. Perhaps the information superhighway will eventually lead to this, but here again one is talking about the future.

Cultural criteria

Of all the criteria employed here, those which entail changes in cultural values and mores are the most difficult to identify. As a nation, Japan has a considerable history of what may be called *information consciousness*, reaching back to the Meiji period, and illustrated more recently in its censuses of information use and its drive towards a fully broadband communications infrastructure.[18] It is not surprising that Yoneji Masuda, the Japanese scholar, would be the most enthusiastic advocate of an information society premised on goals which maximized the common good and promised the attainment of synergy.[19]

Nevertheless, it would be to the United States that many observers would turn for evidence of a change in cultural values consequent upon the advance of the information society, and what would be more obvious than to look for signs of change in that vanguard of the computer revolution, Silicon Valley. The signs are not all that encouraging, with some observers suggesting that traditional values of home, family and community simply do not apply in the highly competitive and entrepreneurial environment of that part of southern California.[20] It should be remembered, however, that different societies show a propensity to respond differently to the presence of advanced technologies, and that even the emerging global electronic culture is susceptible to local and national influences. It is likely, in fact, that what is happening is the development and interaction of a wide range of cultures; not least the so-called youth culture which involves the exchange of food, music, fashion, software and information rights, of what have been termed *lifestyle images* right around the world.[21]

There is always the danger, identified in the previous edition, of the

10

dominance of one culture, for example, a *Coca Cola* culture heavily redolent of western materialist values, replacing indigenous cultures and thus leaving the world impoverished by the loss. Although the same CNN report, or indeed *soap opera*, may evoke different responses in different countries, it would be dangerous to underestimate the potentially deleterious effects of global information flows on cultural diversity and identity.[22]

So what does this tell us about the relationship between information-based change and established or emerging cultures? Well clearly, the sheer ubiquity and the well-nigh inescapable reach of the new information and communication technologies, carries serious implications for all cultures, be this through the promotion of political or commercial values or exposure to alien forms of entertainment. Much less clear is whether or not the world is witnessing the emergence of a new set of cultural values consequent upon the impact of these global information flows. In some of the more technologically advanced societies, there is clearly an increasing recognition of the global dimension not just to trade and commerce but to other aspects of life. This may result in cultures which place greater emphasis on immediacy and openness, and on increasingly information-mediated or at least information-intensive exchanges in social, political, economic and cultural life. It is simply too early to say, however, just as it is premature to predict whether the general tenor of such changes will be positive or negative. Change is a given in all of this, but whether or not it is the kind of change which denotes a major transformation in the ordering of social affairs, such as the emergence of an information society, is still open to question.

INFORMATION SOCIETY: IDEA OR ENTITY?

The idea of society as information society continues to exercise a certain amount of appeal. It somehow captures the feel of modernity and of society moving along exciting technological trajectories which are freeing humankind from the tyranny of time and distance. It is well to remember, however, that information society theory emerged either as social forecast or as a model of social possibilities, and that these have somehow been translated into views of reality and perceptions of actual societies.[23] Moreover, measured against conditions in the real world, nagging doubts remain as to the influence of technological determinism and the politico-economic nature of the so-called information society.

Today more than ever, the world can be described as an electronic global village where, through the mediation of information and *11* communications technologies, new patterns of social and cultural organization are emerging. Nevertheless, rather than viewing such developments as the result of advances in technology, there is merit in reversing the perspective to one where they are seen as outcomes of cultural and ideological influences within diverse societies. Apart from avoiding the more extreme manifestations of technological determinism, this allows for the possibility of there being more than one type of information society, depending upon the existence of different social and cultural milieux.[24]

Several writers have also questioned the extent to which the information society can in fact be differentiated from industrial society. Smart points to the increasing proletarianization of professional work and sees the growth of the services sector as, in fact, evidence of continuity in economic development rather than as marking a break between industrial and information society.[25] Aron has described such developments and the growth of automation as simply the signs of increased complexity in the process of industrialization.[25]

This book will argue the case for a more pluralistic approach to such issues. Technology in itself will not serve as an explanation for the kinds of changes we are trying to understand. Schoonmaker, for instance, has used the subject of transborder dataflows to show that while information technologies appear benign and in effect neutral, their legal definition has become the focus for intense political and economic debate.[24] However, it is not enough simply to take a more pluralistic and sociological approach to the study of these questions. The transfer of data between countries involves nothing less than the commoditization of information, and its sale and exchange under conditions of advanced capitalism.[24]

Among the more heroic assessments of life in the information society is that of Bankes and Builder, who talk of change driven above all by the nearly instantaneous mobility of information and ideas, leading to a diffusion of power among the population as a whole, rather than its concentration in the hands of elites.[26] Halal likewise predicts, around the turn of the century, an evolution to an *information age* characterized by a fluid, dynamic web of organic social-information networks spanning the globe.[16]

None of these writers is oblivious to the potentially negative impacts of such information-led development. Targowski has gone further to argue that existing differentials and inequities are likely to be exacerbated without sweeping change within dozens of nations.[21] In anticipating the growth of existing trends in networking and new interactive media, Miles foresaw not just increased demands for information and participation, but also the growth of new social movements and of dualism within society leading to continued alienation of the information have-nots from the mainstream.[8] Nevertheless, he did recognize that a sea change was underway, and with it the need to discuss different and, in some aspects, competing views of the information society.

In 1984, the European Commission drew attention to the dangers of alienation in an information society in a series of papers published under its FAST Programme.[27] It is fascinating to compare the tone of those earlier documents with that which prevails in the most recent European Union contribution to the debate, the recommendations of the High-level Group on the Information Society, chaired by Industry Commissioner Martin Bangemann.[28] Although this report to the European Council draws attention to the social challenge of pursuit of the information society – to the need for jobs partnerships within Europe and for education, training and promotional activities in order to improve the quality of life and reinforce social cohesion – it is very much a market-driven approach. In the quest for information society status, the vision is of private investment taking opportunities of deregulated and open markets and exploiting the multiplier effect of information in the production of new high value added services and applications. The role of governments and the European Union will be to facilitate such developments by the ending of monopolies, particularly in telecommunications; the enhancement of interoperability and standardization of equipment; the creation of an appropriate regulatory framework to ensure the protection of intellectual property rights, privacy and security of information; and the exploitation of key technologies including ISDN, broadband and multimedia, mobile and satellite communications.[28]

Emphasizing the need for attaining unambiguous standards and a critical mass of users for new basic services such as electronic mail, file transfer and interactive multimedia, the report identifies 10 key application areas which should be treated as priorities. These are:

- Teleworking
- Distance learning
- Network for universities and research centres
- Telematics services for small and medium-sized enterprises
- Road traffic management
- Air traffic control
- Healthcare networks
- Electronic tendering
- Trans-European public administration network
- City information highways[28]

This is an exciting and in many ways an imaginative approach, which combines the social with the economic dimension, and the practical with the visionary. However, while acknowledging the considerable investment effort required, the report assigns a largely supporting role to public expenditure, suggesting the need to refocus existing efforts and direct modest funding into awareness campaigns aimed mainly at small and medium-sized business and individual consumers. While there could be limited support from the European Commission for the development of services and applications, the group argues that the creation of the information society in Europe should be entrusted to the private sector and to market forces.[28] As to the outcome of this report and in particular the response of private investors, businesses and consumers, it remains to be seen. One's initial reaction is that, if implemented, the report has a better than even chance of exacerbating existing inequalities in access to information and to the high value added services which it depicts as central to life in an information society. The picture painted in the Bangemann report is one based on a particular perception of information society – an information market-based society in which the competitive survive and the consumer pays. Presumably, as is already the case in many technologically-advanced societies on the way to full information society status, if one is unable to pay or to operate effectively within the system, then social Darwinism takes its course and one joins the underclass.

In the final analysis, acceptance of the idea of society as information society is still largely a matter of faith, or at least of perception. Proponents of the concept appear to have taken the sheer volume of information in circulation, and its undoubted worth in economic terms, as evidence of *informatization*. Hence, says Webster, we have an assessment of information in nonsocial terms – *it just is* – but we must adjust to the social consequences. Therefore, if we are to understand the nature of information society and what makes it different from previous social systems, we need a much deeper understanding of the qualitative dimension to information. We also need the ability to recognize information society when we see it.[15] For the foreseeable future, therefore, it seems advisable to treat the information society as a concept rather than as an actuality. It serves a useful purpose both by helping to focus attention on the nature of social change and as a device by which such change can be assessed. It remains on the horizon, rather more idea than entity but, with these qualifications, it is none the less valuable for all that.

NOTES AND REFERENCES

1. William Marx (1993) Building the broadband society. In: *Globalization, technology and competition: the fusion of competition and telecommunications in the 1990s*, Stephen P. Bradley, Jerry A. Hausman and Richard L. Nolan (eds). Boston: Harvard Business School Press, pp. 359–70.

2. Yoneji Masuda (1985) Computopia. In: *The Information Technology Revolution*, Tom Forester (ed.), Oxford: Blackwell, p. 636.

3. Tom Stonier (1983) *The wealth of information*. London: Thames Methuen, 224 pp.

4. Daniel Bell (1973) *The coming of postindustrial society : a venture in social forecasting*. New York: Basic Books, 507 pp.

5. John Naisbitt (1982) *Megatrends: ten new directions transforming our lives*. New York: Warner Communications, 290 pp.

6. Alvin Toffler (1980) *The third wave*. London: Pan Books, 544 pp.

7. William J. Martin (1988) *The information society*. London: Aslib, 179 pp.

8. Ian Miles (1988) *Information technology and information society: options for the future*. London: ESRC, 31 pp.

9. Steve Bankes, Carl Builder *et al.* (1992) Seizing the moment: harnessing the information technologies. *The Information Society*, **8**, pp. 1–59.

10. Jorge Reina Schement (1989) The origins of the information society in the United States: competing visions. In: *The information society: economic, social and structural issues*, Lawrence Erlbaum Associates, pp. 29–50.

11. David Lyon (1988) *The information society: issues and illusions*. Cambridge, UK: Polity Press, 196 pp.

12. Tom Forester (1992) Megatrends or megamistakes? Whatever happened to the information society ? *The Information Society*, **8**, p. 3.

13. For example, Herbert Schiller, Kevin Robbins and Stephen Webster.

14. Jay Gershuny *and* Ian Miles (1983) *The new service economy*. London: Frances Pinter.

15. Frank Webster (1994) What information society?, *The Information Society*, **10**, pp. 1–23.

16. William E. Halal (1993) The Information technology revolution: computer hardware, software and services in the 21st century. *Technological Forecasting and Social Change*, **44**, p. 81.

17. Masuda (1985) *op. cit.*, p. 623.

18. Charles Steinfield and Jerry L. Salvaggio (1989) Towards a definition of the information society. In: *The information society: economic, social and structural issues*. Lawrence Erlbaum Associates, pp. 1–14.

19. Masuda (1985) *op. cit.*, p. 625.

20. Judith K. Larsen and Everett M. Rogers (1989) Silicon Valley: a scenario for the information society of tomorrow. In: *The information society: economic, social and structural issues*. Lawrence Erlbaum Associates, pp. 51–62.

21. Andrew S. Targowski (1990) Strategies and architecture of the electronic global village. *The Information Society*, **7**, pp. 187-201.

22. Bankes, Builder *et al.* (1992) *op. cit.*, p. 11.

23. Barry Smart (1992) *Modern conditions, postmodern controversies*. London: Routledge, 241 pp.

24. Sara Schoonmaker (1993) Trading on-line: information flows in advanced capitalism. *The Information Society*, **9**, p. 40.

25. Smart (1992) *op. cit.*, p. 39.

26. Bankes, Builder *et al.* (1992) *op. cit.*, p. 5.

27. Klaus Grewlich and Finn Pedersen (*eds*) (1984) *Power and participation in an information society*. Luxembourg: Commission of the European Communities, 289 pp.

28. High Level Group on the Information Society (1994) *Europe and the global information society: Recommendations to the European Council*. Brussels, 26th May, 35 pp. (The Bangemann Report).

2 Information and Communication

In this chapter aspects of the interrelated themes of information and communication will be considered together. This treatment is appropriate given both the symbiotic relationship of these two fields and the broader context of information-based society. This is, on the face of things, a somewhat ambitious undertaking and the reader is reminded that all that is intended in this chapter is to give an overview of these concepts central to the purpose of the book.

WHAT IS INFORMATION?

Although the question may appear rhetorical, there is a sense in which the answer is that nobody really knows. Definitions proliferate and interpretations multiply, but the answer to the question continues to elude the best minds in information science. As ever, of course, considerable importance attaches to the nature of the question and the manner in which it is posed. One is reminded of the story of the Irishman, who on being asked directions to a particular place, is said to have answered, 'Well if I were you I would not start from here.' In embarking on this particular journey, therefore, one does not intend to start, as is usual, with definitions of information, but rather with the sensible advice of T.D. Wilson, who observed that it was not so much the definition itself that mattered as the uses to which it was put.[1] By approaching the question of 'what is information?' from this direction, we shall undoubtedly pass one or two definitions of information, and such related concepts as data and knowledge, on the way.

EVERYDAY USES OF INFORMATION

The uses to which information is put are quite literally countless, hence the power of those metaphors which link the human and the social organisms in describing information as *the lifeblood of society*. Without an uninterrupted flow of this vital resource, society as we know it would quickly run into difficulties, with business and industry, education, leisure, travel and communications, national and international affairs all vulnerable to disruption. In more advanced societies, this vulnerability is heightened by an increasing dependence on the enabling powers of information and communications technologies. The extent of this dependence, and the degree to which information really has become the lifeblood of modern societies, has been described graphically by Toni Carbo Bearman as:

> ...how we make financial transactions, control the supply and movement of goods and services, educate people, communicate information entertain...work or shop from home; communicate from virtually anywhere to virtually anywhere...consult medical experts, sharing patient information, from remote areas...the list goes on...[2]

Furthermore, while the emphasis in this volume is to a considerable extent upon developments within advanced societies, this by no means implies that it is only in such environments that information is either used or valued. Information has been a significant element in the life of all societies, from those of the hunter-gatherers to the so-called *wired cities* of present-day Japan. Moreover, not only is it common for each culture or society to have its own characteristic information and knowledge base, but in the case of developing countries it may well be that indigenous knowledge rather than that contained in the *world's stores of information* is likely to be more relevant.[3]

This is an important point not just for our understanding of the development process, but also for an appreciation of what is really involved in our use of such categorizations as *information rich* and *information poor*. Viewed in the proper cultural context, the absence of formal information of the type contained in advanced information systems may not be the handicap in developing countries that it would be in advanced Western nations. Clearly the absence of formal information does not denote an absence of information *per se*, but rather the existence of more effective informal sources, which indeed are just as widespread in advanced societies in the shape of peer networks and invisible colleges.[3]

FOCUSED PERCEPTIONS OF INFORMATION

In a recent paper on the subject, Michael Buckland has attempted to expand on traditional perceptions of information and the uses to which it can be put. By focusing upon *information-as-thing* he brings into consideration such phenomena as objects and events, seeking in the process to widen our perception of what constitutes data and documents.[4] Buckland's approach is useful both for its breadth of vision and for the way it manages to weave together such key concepts as information, knowledge and communication. Moreover, by demonstrating that as *thing,* that is as embodied in objects or information systems, information can be tangible, as opposed to *knowledge* which is inherently intangible, he sheds fresh light on traditional perceptions of information, most notably that of Fritz Machlup who saw information as an intangible, involving either the telling of something or that which was being told. However, as Buckland points out, in order to communicate knowledge it must be expressed or represented in some physical way as a signal, text or communication. Any such expression would, therefore, constitute information-as-thing.[4]

Despite the very real difficulties of measurement involved, there has traditionally been an economic dimension to the perception and use of information, whether as a resource or as a commodity. The notion of *information-as-resource* is both inherently attractive and, in an age of global information and communication flows, intuitively plausible. Although the impact of these ideas is most evident within the field of information economics, and in that array of challenges to neoclassical economics reported elsewhere in this book, the notion of information-as-resource has spread to such diverse disciplines as communication studies and political science. It is a critical element in the emerging discipline of information management, with pioneers such as Horton extolling its virtues as a resource akin to oil and other raw materials.[5]

There are, however, difficulties with the treatment of information as a resource, not least those stemming from its inherently intangible nature, and the fact that, unlike physical matter, information *per se* is not subject to the kind of laws that would enable it to be treated in economic terms.[6] Some writers have also warned against the dangers of a premature acceptance of the arguments in favour of the resource characteristics of information. Among such critics, Michel Menou is sceptical of those claims which would portray information as a critical resource in all circumstances – individual, organizational and societal. Such claims, he argues, need to be supported by more than anecdotal evidence and a limited body of empirical research. In any case, says Menou, information is seldom identified to the level of specificity

19

required to demonstrate its impact on any given situation or problem; while continuing controversies over the size and composition of the information economy, merely reflect, at least to some extent, the discrepancy between the present level of understanding of micro level realities and their macro level representations.[3]

Although such criticisms are not to be taken lightly, they have to be balanced against the fact that the notion of information-as-resource is by now well-established in fact, most evidently in recognition of the related concept of a *marketplace of ideas*, as reflected in the profusion of national and international laws and policies relating to trade in information and its associated goods and services.[6] This serves to highlight another increasingly common practice, that of viewing information as a commodity.

The notion of *information-as-commodity* has gained considerable currency in the past decade, with *commodity* in this case, comprising all manner of information services, and including transborder data flows. The concept of information-as-commodity is wider than than that of information-as-resource, as it incorporates the exchanges of information among people and related activities, as well as its use.[6] The notion of information as a commodity is tied closely to the concept of value chains, with commoditized information gaining in value as it progresses through the various steps of creation, processing, storage, distribution and use.[6]

The problems which arise from the non-materiality of information when treating it as a resource are multiplied with the attempt to treat it as a commodity. The problems include those of measurement and appropriability, and with treating what many would regard as a public good as just one more free market commodity. There are also difficulties arising from the cultural and political implications of the information-as-commodity approach. One of the more controversial examples of the latter is international concern over the ability of the United States, both in the GATT and in bilateral trade negotiations, to exploit its competitive advantage in information commodities to the detriment of its trading partners, particularly those in the developing world.[7] One of the most durable definitions of information continues to be that which depicts it as the *reduction-of-uncertainty*. The origins of this definition lie both in economics and in communication theory. In the former case, research into the theory of risk, uncertainty and profit by Frank Knight in the 1940s, anticipated later work by Arrow who, in 1979, defined information as precisely a reduction in uncertainty.[7] However, the *mathematical theory of communication* devised by Claude Shannon in 1948, has been even more influential, and this despite the fact that the information to which it applied was a technical concept, totally devoid of any semantic connotations. In this narrow technical sense, information was the statistical probability of a sign or signal being selected from a given set of signs or signals.[8] Shannon applied the concept of entropy to the measurement of choice and uncertainty, where uncertainty was the measure of the statistical independence or degree of freedom of choice present in the selection of a message. The greater the freedom, the greater the uncertainty; the greater the degree of uncertainty the smaller the amount of information in a message.[9]

Information scientists in particular, have persevered with attempts to adapt syntactic communication theory to the circumstances of human communication. Recent efforts include the suggested revision of the Shannon–Weaver formula to take account of concepts, by presenting two views of uncertainty, one in relation to the selection of the message source and resulting in a complete reversal of the original theory by *equating information with uncertainty*, the other from the viewpoint of the receiver, with information being equated with the reduction of uncertainty from the signal.[9]

Although well-intentioned, it remains to be seen whether such attempted amendments can sufficiently impact upon the engineering perspective of the Shannon–Weaver approach, to overcome the fundamental incompatibility between the qualitative or semantic concept of information and the quantitative or syntactic concept. Indeed, even where the concepts derive from within the shared culture of economics, the link between information and the reduction of uncertainty is by no means immutable. In 1983, Fritz Machlup observed that countless numbers of messages are received by people without any effect on their uncertainty.[10] More recently, economists have dismissed as reductionist this equating of information with a lessening of uncertainty, pointing out that, for example, news of a hurricane *increases* uncertainty in the larger sense than merely answering the question 'will it be rainy tomorrow?'[7] Although it would be convenient to be able to equate information with the reduction in uncertainty, not least because it might bring the basic definition into line with that employed by Shannon, the fact is that some kinds of information will generate even more uncertainty than existed before.[11]

Those definitions which portray *information-as-a-constitutive-force-in-society* are seen as being of a higher order than those to do with the resource characteristics or commodity status of information. Definitions in this category grant information an active role in *shaping* context. Information is not just affected by its environment, but is itself an actor affecting other elements in its environment. Information is not just embedded within a social structure, but creates that structure itself.[6]

Of all the perceptions of information presented here, this one is the most politically and culturally laden. It constitutes a basic foundation for information policy making and has to be admitted as such. Policy decisions taken in the light of such perceptions of information, are inevitably coloured by a particular view of society and how it should operate. Unfortunately, it is even harder to quantify events and measure social, political and cultural impacts when working to this definition of information, than it is in the case of others.[6]

MEANING

When considering the nature and role of information, from whatever perspective, meaning becomes central. There is a clear and significant distinction between the two concepts. Information is an intrinsic property of various systems, which exists irrespective of whether any human or other forms of intelligence perceive it or utilize it. Information is something that one person communicates to another, the meaning of which can only be understood in a socio-cultural context.[11] Hence, as Stonier has observed, a word in a foreign language possesses information, but may have no meaning for the listener if the listener has no prior knowledge of that language.[12] Therefore, to be operative, information has to make sense and in order to do this, it has either to fit with pre-existing meanings or be capable of integrating with them and possibly transforming them.[3]

THE STUDY OF INFORMATION

The central importance of the Shannon–Weaver theory to the study of information has already been made clear, and this notwithstanding its highly specialized focus and purpose. Reference has also been made to the continuing attempts to revise and adapt the original work of Shannon and Weaver in order to make it more relevant to that semantic dimension of information, the meaning and contents-oriented perspective with which the majority of information scientists is likely to be concerned. There are of course, other theories of information, not least that of B.C. Brookes, and this too is subject to considerable reinterpretation and suggested revision. Hence, Michel Menou has taken Brookes' original proposition that information is that which adds to or modifies a knowledge structure, and on the assumption that the principal benefit of information is to be looked for in an enhancement of the paradigmatic structure of the knowledge base, has substituted the term *paradigmatic structure* for Brookes' original term, *knowledge structure*. This substitution leaves the fundamental equation unaltered, the only difference being that the knowledge structure has been relabelled as the paradigmatic structure.[3]

$\Delta I \rightarrow K (S + \text{delta } S) - K(S)$

where K(S) is the knowledge structure
ΔI is the increment of information
S is the effect of the modification.

However, in the event of a need to distinguish between the *superficial knowledge structure* – semantic and syntactic – and the *deep structure* – paradigmatic – Menou suggests a second equation based on the first and which may well be operated in combination with it:

$E = K(S + f(S, \Delta I) - K(s)$

where K(S) stands for the paradigmatic structure of the knowledge base.

The implication is that information should first present attributes that meet the requirements resulting from the paradigmatic structure of the knowledge base, and second, transform it in such a way that it becomes more able to cope with the kind of problem at hand, or is perceived as such.[3]

In referring to these emerging ideas, important as they may be, it is necessary to bear in mind those changes which have already taken place in approaches to the study of information. This is particularly the case with the challenge to traditional positivist epistemological paradigms from those grounded in what have been described respectively as the cognitive and pragmatic turn.[13] Whereas the traditional paradigms – representation, source–channel–receiver, and Platonistic – all considered the notion of a *knowing subject* in interaction with something in external reality known as information, the newer ones perceive human cognition as a necessary condition for the determination of information, and adhere to the complementary pragmatic view that information is a fundamental dimension of human existence.[13]

The so-called *cognitive turn* in information science dates from the 1970s and the work of Belkin and others on 'Anomalous States of Knowledge'. Henceforth, the focus was not simply on a knowing subject but on an anomalous state of knowedge, where the knower could also be a non-knower, an enquirer whose questions were based on a conceptual state of knowledge, that is, part of the user's image of the world. Instead of starting from an objectivist consideration of something called *information* and its interaction with a reductionist view of a *sender* or *receiver* common to all kinds of living and non-living systems, the *cognitive turn* asks for the intrinsic relationship between the human knower and his or her potential knowledge.[13]

This cognitive approach was strengthened by ideas from hermeneutics, particularly an emphasis on the holistic relationship between man and world; essentially the notion of our being in the world with others and sharing this world through communication. Hence, observes Capurro, herein lies the essential foundation of information science. Information in an existential–hermeneutical sense, means to thematically and situationally share a common world. Thus information is not the end product of a representation process, or something being transported from one mind to the other, or finally, something separated from a capsule-like subjectivity, but an existential dimension of our being-in-the-world-with-others.[13] The *pragmatic turn* emerged in the 1980s, with Roberts advocating a behaviouralist approach to *information man,* whereas Wersig looked at the *actors* within *problematic situations*, with information man being inseparable from specific social situations and the pressures of aesthetic and ethical functions.[13]

DATA, INFORMATION AND KNOWLEDGE

In everyday practice, knowledge is regarded as a higher order concept than information, as information that has somehow stood the test of time and has entered into the knowledge base. Drucker links knowledge with data and information in such a way that information is defined as *data* endowed with relevance and purpose, while the conversion of data into information requires knowledge. Knowledge, by definition, is specialized.[14] There is a tendency for the boundaries between some of these terms to overlap. While data, the raw material, is processed into information, in the form of summaries, totals and reports, and can therefore be regarded as a totally separate entity, information in turn can also serve as raw data in some future transformation. Hence, precise definition is difficult and, in practice, the terms information and data are used interchangeably.[15]

Frohmann is critical of the cognitive viewpoint, in which information is produced by *generators*, each with their own *world images* or *knowledge structures*, with the intention of changing the world images of the *recipients* who, for their part, pursue information as a result of a perceived gap in their own image-structure. What the generator knows is modified by beliefs, intentions, values, and this modified state of knowledge is, in fact, information. Information is a change of structure.[16]

Robert M. Hayes defines data as recorded symbols, in fact, just about anything from printed characters and the spoken word to DNA and RNA protein molecules. He insists, however, that data are not facts and that treating them as such can produce innumerable perversions. As recorded symbols, for example, propaganda or lies, data can be *things in themselves*, without any necessary real world referent.[17] Hayes defines information in a formal sense as that property of data, that is, recorded symbols, which represents, and measures, effects of processing them. Information denotes any stimulus that alters cognitive structure in the receiver. Something that the receiver already knows – that is, a stimulus that does not alter cognitive structure – is not information.[17]

Hayes identifies cognitive structure with knowledge, where the effect of information may indeed be a change in knowledge. He regards knowledge and information as mutually exclusive, where information is data and knowledge is inferred essence. He goes on to define knowledge as the result of the understanding of information that has been communicated and from integration of it with prior information. To an extent, it is a result of internalizing the information, but it is more than that, since it requires as an active process a restructuring of the cognitive process. This knowledge may reside in a wide range of entities, from individuals to society as a whole to institutions, such as libraries, and of course within machines.[17]

Knowledge systems have been reported by Soren Brier as being of three types:

- *Eigenwelt*, the understanding of self;
- *Mitwelt I*, the understanding of social relations, the social sciences; and
- *Umwelt*, the understanding of nature and the universe, the natural sciences.[11]

The role of knowledge within society can be seen to have undergone a major transformation, particularly since the 1960s, as the combined result of a proliferating and diversifying knowledge base and advances in information and communications technologies. More than just a matter of overload, this has resulted in problems of information credibility and concerns over technological determinism in relation to the broader directions in which society seems to be going.[18]

These key concepts then – data, information and knowledge – operate both interdependently and on a variety of levels. For present purposes it is sufficient that this diversity is appreciated and that the knowledge so gained can be applied to an understanding of the wider context of information-based societies. For a final illustration of why this is important, a further quotation from Toni Carbo Bearman is apposite, one that relates to the important socio-cultural changes in modern society:

> ... We have gone beyond the need for literacy and information literacy. Both of these are still needed but we also need what I call *mediacy* to denote the ability to find and use information in multimedia formats, and also to connote the sense of immediacy for instantaneous transmission and receipt of information in all formats.[19]

COMMUNICATION

There is widespread recognition of the confusion that attends the myriad attempts at defining *communication*, efforts which at least one scholar has declared not worth pursuing. Not so, however, the attempt to investigate the relationships between information as a phenomenon and communication as a process.[20] So far as definitions are concerned, one employed by Ruben has particular appeal. He described communication as:

> ...the process through which individuals in relationships, groups, organizations and societies create, transmit and use information to organize with the environment and one another.[21]

LINKS BETWEEN INFORMATION AND COMMUNICATION

Such is the commonality between these two disciplines, the scale of interaction at both practical and theoretical levels, that their defining concepts are frequently seen as being interchangable. Although denying that the two concepts are in fact interchangeable, Ruben has applied the General Systems Theory in an attempt to identify the more fundamental relationships between them. To Ruben, communication is the process by which living systems interact with their environment and other systems through information processing. Information is viewed as a vital link between a living system and its environment, and communication as the *transformation of information*. In this very close relationship, communication is an interactive process involving the transformation of information. Information is an artifact and a representation – for example, a text, a vocalization, a document or an image. Information arises out of communication; it is the product of communication. Communication occurs with respect to information. Process and product are inseparable. Moreover, rather than involving simply transportation, delivery, retrieval and intact use of information, interaction involves the creation of information that is appropriate and meaningful for the adaptive purposes of the system.[21]

Hayes too has highlighted the importance of *interactive communication* in his attempt to model and measure the information process. The need arises as a result of the differing perceptions of source and recipient in respect of the parameters of the processes of information selection, information analysis and information reduction. Specifically, this has to do with different interpretations of *a priori* probabilities, relevancies, definitions of fields and definitions of alternative bases for the data space. True interactive communication is seen to occur when the communication process results in changes to these parameters. Likewise, Hayes identified the presence of what he termed *intelligent communication* where, in the context of his same three models, the source of information has in some way enhanced the simple process of data transfer so that the recipient of the signal has received more information than would be implied by the mere number of bits transmitted.[17]

In his attempt to analyse the nature of the relationship between information and communication, Ruben has produced an interesting categorization of the information concept into respectively:

- *Information e*, which is raw data awaiting utilization in some fashion;
- *Information i*, which actually has been embodied in a living system, as for example, cognitive maps or personal constructs; and
- *Information s*, which has been socially and culturally validated and absorbed as the shared information-knowledge bases of social systems.

While being mutually defining, these categories are not interchangeable, they are different, and human beings must invent and internalize the messages: *Information e* and meanings; *Information i* and the need to relate to the environment and to each other by the use of symbolic language. However, as a consequence of the communication processes that give rise to each of the three categories of information, rules emerge over time in relation to the acquisition or otherwise of *Information e* and *Information i* and help to construct the information-knowledge bases – that is, *Information s* of relationships, groups, organizations and societies.[21]

Finally, as a way of looking at the nature of information use and communication, there is Dervin's *sense making* theory, which investigates the ways in which human beings make sense of their everyday experiences. This sense-making behaviour is in fact *27* communicating behaviour, while the search for, processing and use of information are all core sense-making activities.[22] The sense-making process includes knowledge and a range of other subjective factors, such as intuition and hunches, that would reflect an individual's interpretations of everyday situations. The essential contribution of this theory is that it treats information, not as a matter of *transmission*, but rather as a question of *construction*. It moves away from traditional mechanistic perceptions of information as something that is transmitted from a source through channels to passive recipients, towards those which view it as the product of human interaction, with users who are not mere robots but thinking people in control of their own destiny. Hence, all information is subjective, and information seeking and use are constructing activities – a personal creation of sense.[22]

INFORMATION QUALITY

One of the basic objectives of the sense-making approach is to effect a paradigm shift in library and information research into information needs and uses, from an institution and intermediary-centred approach to one which is essentially user-focused. In essence, this entails a move from user studies to studies of the uses to which the library is put. It evidences a concern with the nature and quality of the service provided, with its relationship to the purposes of the user and the extent to which the information provided actually was helpful.[22] This is a complex issue, however, and can involve more than simply the level of satisfaction of an individual user with the service provided. As Menou has observed, the question is not if the information obtained was useful and the users content with its attributes; rather it concerns whether or not the information was really instrumental in solving the problem for which it was sought, and the degree of value it contributed to the solution of the total problem.[3]

The issue of information quality is quite clearly one of fundamental concern to the information science community, as the design of systems and paradigms will well attest. However, outside the formal information science arena, interesting work is underway with the application of general 'Total Quality' concepts and methods to the study of information.[23] The aims and motivation are the same as in the general quality context, to address problems of uncertainty and quality in the handling of information – problems which have either gone unnoticed or have been tolerated as an inevitable consequence of the system. A good general example of this problem, which in fact relates to the information credibility question referred to previously, concerns the key issue of global warming. Not only are the issue and the prescribed solutions contentious in themselves, but there is also a major problem to do with the credibility of the data on which the contending claims are based, where, as Ravetz and Funtowicz have pointed out, the scientific issues cannot be discussed independently of methodological, ethical and political perspectives.[23]

To tackle such problems, Ravetz and Funtowicz have devised their NUSAP system for the management of uncertainty and quality in technical information. NUSAP is an acronym for the five basic categories employed in the system, which lend nuances of meaning to a notational scheme which displays the different sorts of uncertainty in data in an appropriate form. A qualitative dimension is embodied in the categories of *Assessment* and *Pedigree*. *Assessment* provides a place for the expression of salient qualitative judgements about the information; for example, in the case of statistics, this could be *significance level*, or in that of numerical estimates for policy purposes it could be the qualifier *optimistic* or *pessimistic*. In this case, *Pedigree* is an evaluative assessment of the mode of production and, where relevant, anticipated use of the information. The pedigree matrix embodies certain basic information skills obtained from practitioners by elucidation.[23]

The researchers envisage the possibility of NUSAP becoming an integral part of the total quality movement, owing to the centrality of information both to management and to its participation in total quality exercises. To date, the information factor has not received a great deal of attention in total quality circles, perhaps because the techniques for quality control are not sufficiently known. Ravetz and Funtowicz seek to change this situation through the adoption of their system as a means of empowerment of those who wish to be able to criticize technical information without necessarily being able to reproduce it.[23]

In attempting to tie together the various threads of information and communication theory in a way that is meaningful to the context of information-based societies, it is important to re-emphasize the essentially social nature of these concepts. The entire universe of human relations can be portrayed in terms of a vast complex of communication, involving nations and individuals, organizations and institutions in an endless process. Whatever the type or form of this communication, it can be regarded as a series of exchanges involving the sharing of experience or the attempt to learn from, or to exert influence on, the opinions or behaviour of others. These exchanges can be in written, oral or tactile form, or can find expression as nonverbal communication or *body language.*

Information is central to such processes, its critical presence the understandable, if erroneous, reason why some would portray the two distinct concepts of information and communication as being synonymous. Also important are the implications of an ever-expanding and increasingly sophisticated array of technologies, which not only serve to mediate the communication process, but to transform it through the creation of new media and the facilitation of new relationships.

Some observers have portrayed these developments as leading to more open and rational societies. Others see them as characteristic not of a more participative society, but of one where information users will be forced to become information consumers through the privatization and commercialization of information. Already, it is argued, much of the information and communication that takes place today is far from rational and uplifting, having a high level of symbolic, mythical content and passive entertainment value.[24]

Whatever point of view one takes on such matters, it is clear that issues of fundamental importance for society and its people are involved. As the 20th century approaches its close, questions of access to, and exploitation and control of, information are of increasing significance for governments and citizens alike. It may not exactly be a matter of life or death, but when one thinks about it, neither liberty nor the pursuit of happiness seem assured in a society which fails to maintain proper stewardship of its information resources.

REFERENCES

1. T.D. Wilson (1981) On user studies and information needs. *Journal of Documentation*, **37**, (1), pp. 3–15.

2. Toni Carbo Bearman (1992) Information transforming society: challenges for the year 2000. *Information Services & Use*, **12**, pp. 217–23.

3. Michel Menou (1994) *The impact of information: definitions and measurements* (pre-print, accepted for IP&M, 1994).

4. Michael Buckland (1991) Information as thing. *Journal of the American Society for Information Science*, **42**, (5), pp. 351–360.

5. Forrest Woody Horton (1979) *Information resource management: concept and cases*. Cleveland, Ohio: Association for Systems Management, 343 pp.

6. Sandra Braman (1989) Defining information: an approach for policymakers. *Telecommunications Policy*, **13**, (3), pp. 233–42.

7. Robert E. Babe (1994) The place of information in economics.

In: *Information and communication in economics*, Robert E. Babe (ed.). Boston: Kluwer Academic Publishers, pp. 41–67.

8. Claude E. Shannon (1948) A mathematical theory of communication. *Bell System Technical Journal*, **27**, (July), pp. 379–423.

9. Charles Cole (1993) Shannon revisited: information in terms of uncertainty. *Journal of the American Society for Information Science*, **44**, (4), pp. 204–11.

10. Fritz Machlup and Una Mansfield (eds) (1983) *The study of information*. New York: Wiley, pp. 641–71.

11. Soren Brier (1992) A philosophy of science perspective on the idea of a unifying information science. In: *Conceptions of library and information science*, Pertti Vakkari and Blaise Cronin (eds). London: Taylor Graham, pp. 97–108.

12. Tom Stonier (1991) Towards a new theory of information. *Journal of the American Society for Information Science*, **17**, pp. 257–63.

13. Rafael Capurro (1992) What is information science for? In: Vakkari and Cronin, *op.cit.*, pp. 82–96.

14. Peter F. Drucker (1988) The coming of the new organisation, *Harvard Business Review*, **66**, (1), January–February, pp. 39–48.

15. Alan Freedman (1989), *The computer glossary*, 4th ed. Pittsburgh: AMACOM, American Management Association, p. 358.

16. Bernd Frohmann (1992) Knowledge and power in library and information science: towards a discourse analysis of the cognitive viewpoint. In Vakkari and Cronin, *op.cit.*, pp. 135–48.

17. Robert Hayes (1992) The measurement of information. In: Vakkari and Cronin, *op.cit.*, pp. 268–85.

18. Gernot Wersig (1992) Information science and theory: a weaver bird's perspective. In: Vakkari and Cronin, *op.cit.*, pp. 201–17.

19. Bearman (1992) *op.cit.*, p. 220.

20. Tefko Saracevic (1992) Information Science: origin, evolution and relations. In: Vakkari and Cronin, *op.cit.*, pp. 5–27.

21. Brent D. Ruben (1992) The communication–information relationship in system-theoretic perspective. *Journal of the American Society for Information Science*, **43**, (1), pp. 15–27.

22.   Reijo Savolainen (1992) The sense-making theory: an alternative to intermediary-centred approaches in library and information science? In: Vakkari and Cronin, *op.cit.*, pp. 149–64.

23.   J.R. Ravetz and S.O. Funtowicz (1992) *Total information quality.* (Pre-publication draft of paper circulated at a seminar).

24.   Philip Elliott (1986) Intellectuals, the information society and the disappearance of the public sphere. In: *Media, culture and society: a critical reader*, Richard Collins *et al.*, (eds). London: Sage, pp. 105–15.

3   Developments in Computing

Although the corresponding chapter in the previous edition referred to information technology (IT) and this one to information and communication technology (ICT), the focus is still on converging developments in computers and telecommunications. This chapter looks at developments in computing and, as before, the emphasis will be on developments and trends which on current showing would seem to be significant for the future. In most cases, the technologies covered here were included in some form or other in the previous edition. Some will be seen to have advanced impressively in the intervening period, and this would be obvious in the case of computer chips and optical storage devices. In the case of technologies such as, for example, voice interface and artificial intelligence, the pace of change has been less spectacular, and the anticipated breakthroughs in performance slower to materialize.

A REVOLUTION IN TECHNOLOGY?

Writing some six years on, it is still appropriate to describe the pace of technological change as revolutionary. Generational changes in computing have increased computational power by about a factor of ten every five to seven years, producing a total gain for the entire information technology revolution of roughly 100,000 over the past three decades.[1] It is clear that, in certain key respects, changes anticipated five or six years ago are now well on the way to fruition. The world is increasingly a vast electronic entrepôt, where broadband communications and optical technology hold the key to economic growth, trade and development. The convergence between the enabling technologies has progressed to such effect that even for purposes of exposition, it is difficult to separate out one technology from another.

COMPUTER HARDWARE

Dramatic advances in hardware have been responsible for the continued expansion of computers into our daily lives and for making many of the software advances practical. Even more exciting prospects beckon with the development of new hardware architectures and networking concepts like RISC (Reduced Instruction Set Computing), parallel processors and neural computers, and image processing.

Microprocessor technology

The microchip remains central to progress in the information and communication technologies. Silicon continues to provide the main raw material for both logic chips and memory chips, known today as Dynamic Random Access Chips (DRAMS). The cost-performance ratio which gained such astonishing momentum during the 1960s, has continued in a positive direction, delivering prodigious increases in the amount of computing power available at greatly reduced cost. Very advanced chips would feature several processors, some of reduced instruction set (RISC) design, and would have processing speeds in excess of 100 million instructions per second (MIPS).

There are two major categories of microprocessor technology: the traditional CISC (Complex Instruction Set Computing) and the more recent microprocessors based on RISC (Reduced Instruction Set Computing). The more instructions contained in a central processing unit (CPU) instruction set and the more complicated those instructions, the more clock cycles the CPU needs to complete an instruction search. Traditional CISC technology has complex sets of between 150 and 300 instructions and processes only one instruction search at a time. The higher-performance RISC chips, on the other hand, contain perhaps 70 to 80 of only the most frequently used instructions. and are capable of processing a new instruction on each clock cycle.[2]

RISC uses *smart compiler* technology, which not only translates commands from software language to machine language and sends them to the CPU, but does so in the form of *strings* of the most frequently used instructions, broken down into *pieces* for storing in a reserve memory cache. It also employs *pipelining* and multiple parallel processing, to avoid internal bottlenecks and to speed up processing.[3]

There are already signs of RISC being under threat from developments in very long word instruction (VLWI) technology, from machines which by greatly extending word length could more fully exploit the potential of parallel computing. As for the chips themselves, gallium arsenide retains its potential for speeds of up to five or six times those of silicon chips, while optical computing is no longer a science fiction fantasy. In optical computers, photons – the basic unit of light beams – replace the electrons of conventional computing, hence the field is sometimes referred to as optoelectronics or photonics. Optical computers work by manipulating laser-generated beams of light and using optical switches in place of electronic switches. Their advantages are speed, the fact that they can process information in parallel, and that, because of the elimination of electrical resistance, they are not subject to overheating.[1]

So far as silicon is concerned, new products are anticipated that will be some 8 to 16 times as powerful as the latest version of the Intel Pentium chip. Moreover, the data on CPUs will be in highly compressed form, possibly based on specialized digital signal processors (DSPs) using data-specific forms of compression, one for video, one for audio and so on. DSPs are fast, single function co-processor chips that relieve the CPU of many of the load requirements that accompany audio and video computing. They also eliminate one of the problems involved in putting advanced functionality in hardware, because they can be reprogrammed as standards change and features grow. This technology has been used in Texas Instruments' multimedia video processor (MVP), which contains four 64-bit DSPs and delivers two billion operations per second, includes a 32-bit RISC chip complete with floating point unit and contains about one-third more logic circuits than the Pentium.[4]

Parallel processing

Such has been the pace of advance in the field that traditional computer architectures are already operating as *bottlenecks* on progress. These include physical limits on operating speeds, which cannot exceed about two-thirds the speed of light, structural limits to do with sequential sequencing of processing and control operations, and limits on the knowledge representation process. The way forward in response to these problems is seen as via massively parallel architectures with a high level of connectivity between processing elements and through neural networking.[5]

For present purposes, four elements in the design of parallel digital architectures can be regarded as critical, namely, granularity, topology, *35* synchrony and control. Granularity has to do with the size and number of basic processors in a system. Those with tens to hundreds of relatively powerful processors are called coarse-grained, while those with tens of thousands to millions of simple processors are fine-grained. Physical topologies of the communication network between processors and between processors and memory are numerous, and as well as so-called static or hard-wired topologies, there are dynamic topologies in which a switching network allows data to be dynamically routed to the appropriate processors. Control and synchronization of these processors can range from totally synchronous mode to totally asynchronous modes, generally classified as single-instruction, multiple data mode (SIMD) and multiple instruction, multiple data mode (MIMD). The former execute a single instruction across many data items in parallel; the latter can execute different instructions against many data items in parallel.[5]

Neural networks computing

For some time now researchers have turned to the human brain as a model for architectures which display intelligence. However, there have been disappointments over the results obtained from the traditional symbolic digital approach. In particular, it is claimed, such pattern recognition activities as vision, speech understanding and machine learning, which are intrinsically analogue in nature, may be better suited to analogue, artificial neural network solutions.[5] In the human brain, millions of interconnected neurons exchange input and output signals and as a result, learning takes place. Neural network computing substitutes layers or arrays of processing elements and connections for the neurons and synapses in the brain. These arrays can be taught to recognize patterns and, by changing their response to change over time, can *learn*. Neural networks learn by adaptation, rather than being programmed to respond in a certain fashion.[3]

Conventional computers are fast, accurate, process only digital data and are poor at recognizing patterns. Neural computers, on the other hand, are slow, not always accurate and can handle analogue information. They have the ability to learn, to make associative recall and make decisions based on incomplete data. They learn, not by following rules, but by remembering examples and, as such, pose a serious alternative to traditional work in expert and knowledge-based systems.[1]

Neural networks can be implemented in software or hardware or in a combination of both. However, as with traditional symbol-oriented computing there are problems. Neural networks are difficult to program and it has been difficult to design effective learning algorithms that would extend beyond initial small-scale successes to a larger, real world environment. Moreover, for many applications (for example, expert systems) symbol-based knowledge is superior to circuit-based knowledge. This has prompted suggestions that the capabilities of digital circuits and neural networks could be embodied in some hybrid form combining low-level, circuit-based pattern recognition modules, with high-level circuit-based control and inference engines.[5]

Client/server

The client/server process has been described as clients and servers co-operating to do a job. At its simplest, client/server entails splitting processing operations between different hardware platforms in such a way that the effectiveness of each platform is maximized. The result can be flexibility, increased speed and ease of operation and cost savings.[6] In essence, the server is a piece of hardware which physically contains the data. The client is a piece of hardware, typically an intelligent workstation, which presents information to the user. Between the client and the server is the network, an area comprising hardware and software that is often referred to as *middleware* – that is, operating systems, gateways and systems that handle communications between different client/server processes.[6]

The interaction of two separate pieces of hardware does not necessarily imply the need for two separate computer systems on a network, one acting as client and the other as server. In fact, client/server architecture can be developed adequately within a single system which is partitioned into modules where commands and responses pass between modules such that one module acts as a request agent, the *client*, and another acts as a service provider, the *server*. It is possible for a server to also act as a client by requesting services of another client.[7]

Separation of the two key data processing components: presentation of information on the client, and manipulation of data on the server, facilitates the management of an increasingly complex data processing environment. The architecture allows software designers and developers to tune components of the architecture in isolation from each other. Different paradigms, tools and languages have evolved for specific layers of the client/server architecture.[8]

The distribution of computer power in this way can lead to significant benefits from reduced network traffic and communications costs, while expensive central computers are left free to concentrate on administrative functions such as data integrity, security and systems

37

management. The lower cost and technological flexibility of client/ server opens the way for innovative applications such as image processing, multimedia and voice mail, which might be prohibitively expensive in a traditional centralized computing environment. In such a situation, client/server provides the enabling mechanisms for these applications, defining both the framework and the components specifications to let users build flexible systems.[9]

The biggest advantage of client/server processing is probably its flexibility. These systems are much easier to change than most others and can be deployed swiftly in response to urgent business problems. Also important is scalability, the ability to enhance the power of a system through planned expansion. Client/server has been described as a direction that can apply leverage to a number of existing technologies, and as a move towards a peer-to-peer processing model where all processors, all applications and data run seamlessly on a single large network.[6]

TYPES OF COMPUTER

Among the most notable trends in computer hardware in the last decade has been that towards *downsizing*, with smaller more powerful machines being substituted for larger ones, for example minicomputers and in some cases microcomputers, for mainframe computers. Although there has been considerable development of workstations, with 32-bit microcomputers emerging with impressive processing power, vast memory, networking and graphics capabilities, mainframes remain popular for tasks requiring large scale processing. However, mainframes today are much more compact than their predecessors, thanks to advances in very large scale integration (VLSI) and emitter controlled logic (ECL) and to denser chip packing. Mainframes are expected to play a continuing role as applications servers, although in the new client/server architectures the manner in which these applications are used will be different.[10]

This trend towards downsizing is moreover, very noticeable in the area of desktop computing, with microcomputers facing a stern challenge not only from portable machines but palmtop and notebook computers. Portables range from those machines weighing anywhere between 15 to 18 pounds, which offer occasional mobility, to laptops which weigh from 8 to 14 pounds and which lend themselves to use in any number of locations from trains to planes to armchairs. Almost one in five personal computers sold in 1992 was a portable, while one forecast is that by 1997 portables and personal digital assistants are likely to account for 45 per cent of unit sales.[11] Palmtop and notebook computers, which can literally fit into the human hand, are growing fast in popularity, with almost every serious personal computer manufacturer supplying at least one range of notebook computer. The current range of machines incorporates 486 chips, high resolution colour displays, communications cards, Windows software and hard disk storage capacities of the order of 120 megabytes.

Some observers are already anticipating the possible replacement of desktop personal computers by small portables, for all but intensive scientific computing. Presently, however, the two tend to complement each other, frequently with the use of *docking stations* which enable the portable to be attached to the desktop where, using the same software, it can exploit the benefits of full size screens and keyboards and connect to the facilities available on an office network. Whatever the eventual outcome, there is a clear trend towards an increasing personalization of computing equipment, with the development of agents or Personal Digital Assistants, such as the Apple Newton MessagePad. These machines will be capable of simple data communications as well as voice and fax and will be self-learning and capable of translating inputted handwriting into machine-readable output and storage.

However, the real potential of personalization will be exploited when sufficient applications for the use of handheld computers can be developed for the public at large, rather than just for business users. Work at IBM and AT&T on so-called *personality modules* promises to do just this, with the delivery of entertainment or educational services and, quite conceivably, access to virtual shopping malls being available via credit card sized modules slotted into machines the size of cellular telephones. If successful, such ventures could transform both the scale and the social composition of the market for handheld computers. Indeed, it may well be that, as some predict, the computer of the future will in fact be a telephone.[12]

SECONDARY STORAGE

Secondary storage has to be addressed through a data channel. This process takes time, particularly in the case of data stored in sequence on magnetic tape. Much of the attention in storage today focuses upon optical technology. However, despite the fact that they can hold more data at a lower cost than hard disks, optical discs still tend to complement rather than replace hard disks. Optical storage is almost exclusively a secondary means of storing large amounts of online or near-line information. Even document imaging systems, which typically archive their data on an optical disc, usually keep the most frequently used information on a magnetic disk for fast access before storing it on the optical disc.[13] The different kinds of optical disc – CD-ROM, write-once, rewritable and multifunction – all store more than 120 megabits of data per side, and each uses slightly different technologies and serves different information storage and distribution needs.

CD-ROMs

CD-ROM is used for the distribution of information to micro-computers rather than for storing information. With these systems, the CD-ROM disc is placed in a drive unit and read by means of a laser beam and light detector which interpret the information etched into the surface of the disc. One CD-ROM holds about 635 Mbytes, of which a total of about 553 Mbytes are usable for storage. The remainder is used for a variety of functions, such as error detection.[13]

In 1987, the High Sierra standard for the arrangement of data on CD-ROMs was established by the major players in the field. This allows different retrieval programs to read data from the disc in the same way, regardless of the host computer or operating system. However, as a read-only medium that is expensive to master and duplicate, CD-ROM is suitable only for publishing. The cost of the drive and host microcomputer also add to the expense of these systems, while most CD-ROM systems are as much as 20 times slower than high capacity magnetic drives or write-once or rewritable drives.[13] Nevertheless, CD-ROM has been chosen by the Multimedia Product Council as the distribution medium for the Multimedia Personal Computer (MPC), while IBM has endorsed CD-ROM XA, a multimedia version of the CD-ROM.

Write-once

Unlike CD-ROM drives, write-once drives can both write and read. Data is placed on the disc using a write laser and a variety of possible methods, for example, the so-called ablative technique where the laser melts pits less than one micron in diameter on the surface of the disc. The data are read using a lower intensity read laser. Ablative media last for about 10 years and are expensive to produce. Sony have developed a bimetallic alloy system which it is claimed will last for 100 years. Other methods include bubble-forming, dye polymer and phase-change.[13]

There is as yet no single standard for write-once discs, with users free to choose between the ANSI XB311 standard and its ISO counterpart. Write-once discs hold enormous quantities of data, are transportable and extremely durable. Nevertheless, despite access times of about six milliseconds on the fastest drives, write-once discs are still much slower than high capacity magnetic hard disk drives. Moreover, both the drives and the discs are expensive.[13]

Write-once CDs are expected to decrease in price in coming years. In the data distribution market, they could eventually provide an economic alternative to magnetic tape for the distribution of large amounts of information. Companies that needed to circulate large databases to a network of branch offices, for example, could write them to a disc, which could then be read by CD-ROM players, instead of distributing them on tape reels or cartridges.[13]

Rewritable

Magneto-optical discs are like write-once discs with one major difference, the same track on a disc can be written over one million times. The read-write head shines an intense laser beam which heats the area being written while exposing it to a magnetic field. Depending on the polarity of the field, the magnetic surface of the disc becomes more or less reflective, the pattern of reflective and non-reflective patches reflecting the binary code of ones and noughts. To read the data, a weaker laser is shone on the patches and the light sensitive circuitry detects the patterns.

The main problems with rewritable drives are slow access speed and high cost. The fastest systems have an average access time of 47 milliseconds, compared to under 10 milliseconds for high capacity magnetic disk drives. At a minimum cost of $2,000, they are an expensive item.[13]

Multifunction

Multifunction drives take both write-once and rewritable discs. In the matter of standards, both multifunction and rewritable systems are faced with a range of alternatives, based respectively on systems led by Hewlett Packard, Pioneer and LMS and Matsushita. In terms of the amount of data they can store, the cost per megabyte is lower for rewritable discs than for magnetic media.

Multifunction drives have the advantage that they also accept write-once media, so they are good for use both as temporary storage and as archival storage. Eventually, the multifunction drives may cost less than write-once or rewritable drives, since manufacturers can reach a larger market with a single product. The main problems with multifunction drives are those of speed, cost and the incompatibility of different

41

models.[13]

Despite the impressive storage capacities of CD-ROM, there is a fair amount of dissatisfaction in the industry with the limits of current systems. The present generation of infrared lasers will be replaced by a range of red, blue and green lasers which will multiply disc capacity by a factor of four. IBM is working on a method of layering discs which will increase storage capacity another tenfold. However, the prospects for recordable data compact discs are much less rosy. Although a read-and-write format would have considerable attractions to the user, content publishers are reluctant to see such technology come on the market, fearing that this could lead to illegal copying on a massive scale.[14]

Current voice and image systems are extremely heavy users of storage, hence the importance of continuing advances in magnetic storage media. Further breakthroughs lie ahead with the first commercial versions of holographic storage, with data stored as a hologram on a plastic disc. One version, produced by Tamarack Storage Devices in the United States, reads 64,000 bits at a time, compared with 1 or 2 bits for magnetic media. The same system is expected to pack 50 gigabytes of data onto a single optical disc.[4]

COMPUTER SOFTWARE

In the software field there have been exciting developments in operating systems, in expert and knowledge-based systems, in database and group software, in personal software and in multimedia programs. In the field of personal computers, developers have been under pressure to build software which is flexible, adaptable and portable. This has resulted in a new wave of software that has moved away from the provision of standardized applications towards enabling users to build their own applications using a form of general purpose tool-box. Nevertheless, the crisis in software development continues, with the power and speed of hardware outstripping the productivity of a hard-pressed and numerically insufficient software community. As a result, software engineering techniques are increasingly being applied to the development and maintenance of all kinds of software.

UNIX

The UNIX system developed on the simple philosophy that programs, and indeed entire development domains, could be built up on the basis of individual, ready to use components and libraries of packaged subroutines. Large applications could thus be built on the basis of a few
simple commands and, just as important, the dream of reusable

software could be realized. UNIX continues to be an extremely attractive computing environment offering power, flexibility and ease-of-use. Perhaps the major reason for its popularity is its portability to all types of, and between, different releases of UNIX itself. By defining its standard development environments for system software – Applications Programming Interface (API) – and for the machines that use the system – Applications Binary Interface (ABI) – UNIX has ensured that the system will evolve in predictable ways, which of course is a critical issue for all systems developers.[15]

UNIX is a time-sharing, multitasking environment equally effective for the individual user, for those who wish to perform several tasks at the same time, and for those working in a multi-user situation. Steps to increase its level of compliance with the POSIX international standard for operating systems seem as likely to enhance the position of UNIX as to improve the prospects for greater connectivity.

Windows NT

Windows NT (New Technology) is a general purpose, multi-tasking operating system for Intel (iAXP86, Pentium), MIPS (R4000 and R4400) and DEC Alpha RISC platforms. It is aimed at three different user communities: desktop, workgroup and departmental/enterprise, although claims that the system will be equally applicable to desktop systems and servers encountered considerable scepticism in the user community from the outset. The system's critics emphasize its potential weaknesses in networking situations, its slowness of operation and the vast amount of hard disk space it occupies, but others point to the attractions of its multi-tasking, scalability and portability features.[16]

Whereas earlier versions of the Windows operating software were undeniably successful, with sales in North America alone estimated at $1.93 billion compared with those of $990 million for the Macintosh system, the experience with Windows NT has been distinctly different. Perhaps it is still a little early in the day for the market to give its verdict on Windows NT, but after about 12 months on the market, sales have not been impressive. By the end of 1993, for example, only an estimated 270,000 copies of Windows NT had been shipped, while sales of the rival IBM OS/2 system were posing a serious threat. Industry predictions are that while Microsoft can expect to sell perhaps around 1.5 million copies of Windows NT in 1994, sales of OS/2 could be in the range of 5 million for the same period.[17]

In any event, Microsoft has responded with two new versions of Windows, neither of which has as yet appeared on the market. The

Daytona version is claimed to be around 60 per cent faster than Windows NT and to use less memory. However, most of the excitement centres on the proposed release of Windows version 4.0, known as Chicago or more recently Windows 95. Although subject to delays in coming to market, Chicago forms part of a radical two-pronged strategy on the part of Microsoft. By the end of 1994, all existing users of Windows systems will be required to migrate to two totally new operating systems: Chicago, the new 32-bit version of desktop Windows and Cairo, an object-oriented version of Windows NT. In future, Microsoft will bundle Chicago in all personal computers using its operating software, as a replacement for its DOS operating system. The company claims that there will be no difficulty for users having to upgrade to the new systems, and that Chicago and Cairo will run on all existing applications for MS-DOS and Windows.[18]

Computer-Assisted Software Engineering (CASE)

The urgent need for improved software development and maintenance in less time and at reduced cost, has fuelled the demand for the development of CASE tools. CASE embraces a wide range of automated systems and software engineering tools and ranges from the production of plans and specifications to the delivery of a completed executable system. Specific benefits to be derived from CASE include reusable applications software modules and configuration management for large and complex systems. Central to the CASE approach is use of the system life cycle concept.[19]

The life cycle concept divides the entire life span of a system into generalized phases and links each phase to formal milestones, reviews and one or more deliverable products. Although, in practice, these phases have tended to be described as either *front end* or upper CASE tasks, for instance planning, requirements specification or prototyping, or *back end* or lower CASE tasks, for example, coding, implementation, testing and maintenance, it is increasingly acknowledged that this represents an oversimplification of what happens in a real world environment.[19]

CASE tools have been criticized for being both error-prone and too general in nature, and this has led to calls for the provision of application development environments (ADEs) in which developers can engineer software. Nevertheless, the use of automated techniques has brought speed and saved time and has led to real improvements in design, testing, implementation and maintenance costs. There is also the fact of major innovations in the life cycle concept, structured development techniques, rapid prototyping and object-oriented technology. CASE is, in fact, meta-software – it is software for the production of software.[19]

Reusable software

This is a concept related closely to CASE and to automated programming. Some problems arise on a regular basis and, in dealing with them, it makes sense not to have to run the full routines every time. For software to be reusable, it must be possible to link subroutines for sharing across multiple programs. This can be effected by a variety of means including, macros, command languages or shell procedures, templates and objected-oriented programming. All these techniques can be combined to form *standard* user interface libraries of reusable subroutines. Templates can be maintained for user interface constructs, command interpreters, menus, prompts and graphic objects.[3]

Object-Oriented Programming Systems (OOPS)

Object-oriented technology is having a major impact on both CASE and systems engineering. It appeals to systems users and developers both because it saves time and because it promises to improve the tasks of modelling the organization and building the business processes that support it. Moreover, by permitting the use of business terminology in the description of system requirements, OOPS enables managers and other business-oriented people to participate more actively in the system design.[20]

The basic objective of object-oriented technology is code sharing and reusability. In object-oriented programming, the approach is more flexible than that of the rigid procedures followed during conventional programming, focusing instead on a series of objects or modules which are defined according to their internal states and their relations with other objects. OOPS focuses both on the interaction of behaviours among system objects, rather than on scheduled events, and on the conditions and responses of the entire system. The central principle of object-oriented programming is that systems, rather than being *lists* of things for a computer to do, are descriptions of the objects that compose them and of the relationships among those objects. Most object-oriented systems contain a large number of standard predefined objects. Programming in the system largely consists of choosing the right set of objects, modifying them as needed, and defining the way in which they should interact.[20]

A set of inbuilt procedures defines the attributes and behaviour of these objects, providing a level of artificial intelligence not present in conventional programs. Thus the entire program does not have to be restructured to allow minor alterations to be made. Programs thus developed can be extended more easily, since new objects can be added which attract the same characteristics – data and procedures – that other objects within the same class already have.[20]

Despite such attractions, it is well to remember that object technology has been around for 25 years and has yet to attain its full potential. Ironically, by permitting selections to be made from sets of predefined objects, object programming has resulted in a great diversity of applications which at best share only the principles of object-oriented technology. There is an urgent need for standardization, for some kind of common object model. This model may emerge soon and with it a real market for object-oriented components.[21]

Open systems

The concept of open systems involves a move away from proprietary systems and single-vendor computing solutions. Open systems means different things to different people. Some would see it as meaning adoption of the UNIX system, while others would assume some association with the Open Systems Interconnection (OSI) architecture for computer networking.[22] There are, moreover, several degrees of *openness* in open systems. Pure open systems are public domain, including such popular products as Carnegie-Mellon's Mach operating system and software from the Free Software Foundation. Many commercial products adhering to standards are also considered open, but not as purely open as public domain products. Standards still allow for slight differences between commercial products.

In any open systems environment the following characteristics should be present:

– multivendor software and hardware support; consistent user interface;
– flexibility to support the rapid implementation of emerging technology;
– access to existing hardware and software; and
– facilities for managing the entire system as a single resource.[22]

It is necessary to have both Open Systems Interconnection (OSI) and Open Computer Systems (OCS) to obtain the full benefits of open systems. If only OSI is implemented, disparate computers can communicate and interoperate, but user environment, data and software portability will suffer. If OCS is implemented within a proprietary network environment, much of the interoperability benefits will be unavailable. An open system must demonstrate the following features:

- *compatibility*: applications running on the system will be able to run on future versions of the same system;
- *portability*: applications running on the operating system on a given hardware platform will run on any other vendor's computer which utilizes that operating system;
- *scalability*: applications written for the system will run on the full range of computer architectures and sizes from microcomputers to mainframes;
- *interoperability*: applications running on the system will be able to communicate with any other computer system using the same networking protocols.[22]

Open Systems Interconnection (OSI)

The concept of open systems is widely accepted in Europe, North America and elsewhere. Taken together these seven layers provide a framework or model for slotting in individual communications facilities and services provided by a computer, a communications node (which itself may be a form of computer), or by a private network. This model is vendor-independent, enabling even two proprietary and otherwise incompatible computers to at least communicate with each other. It can do even more when these computers are themselves both open systems as defined above.[22] Today, developments in open systems have expanded to include TCP/IP as used on the Internet, and other formats. These are considered in a later chapter.

End-user languages

These help reduce the cost and time of software development by allowing the end users to do their own design and programming. In this context, end users are perceived to be people who do not program for a living. In practice, however, these tools seem to be much more the province of sophisticated and experienced professionals than the ordinary end user.

Much more encouraging are developments in what are known as PC Toolkits, features found in programs such as Paradox and Lotus Notes. Combined with libraries of reusable software, with nonprocedural problem specification languages, artificial intelligence logic interfacers and advanced graphical user interfaces, these could make a reality of claims for genuine do-it-yourself end-user programming. The promise of such systems lies in the ability of users simply to specify what they want, rather than how it is to be done, and in their visual orientation, where the user just points and clicks to perform an operation.[3]

ARTIFICIAL INTELLIGENCE

Artificial intelligence (AI) is concerned with designing and programming machines to accomplish tasks that when performed by humans are considered to represent intelligent behaviour. These differ from conventional programs in that while the outcomes are specified, neither the means to achieve them nor the problems to be solved have been preordained. Intelligent programs employ complex sets of rules and databases to process data and arrive at the desired solution to the problem.[23] They are said to be concerned with the manipulation of knowledge rather than mere data. They pervade the entire spectrum of information and communication technologies, most obviously in such fields as expert systems, speech and vision, problem solving, knowledge engineering and robotics.[23]

AI is in wide use in a range of applications in industry, business and defence. One of the most active AI research areas is that of understanding how to program computers for learning and discovery. This work promises to help overcome bottlenecks in the critical and laborious process of extracting and encoding areas of expertise. Among the more popular learning approaches in use are those of inductive learning, generic algorithms and neural networks.[23] Nevertheless, there is still a considerable amount of controversy attached to the subject, with some labelling artificial intelligence a costly failure and others predicting that it will come to change the way in which we view the workings of the human mind.[1]

EXPERT SYSTEMS

Expert systems have been described as the most significant practical project to emerge from 30 years of AI research. These systems stand or fall on the quality of the knowledge which they incorporate – knowledge gleaned from the mind of human experts. This knowledge is of two types – facts and heuristics. The facts comprise information that is widely shared and acknowledged by experts in the field. Heuristics are rules of thumb or any other devices that limit the range of search solutions for problems and indicate which among several courses of action is to be preferred. Expert systems attempt to mimic the problem-solving activities and performance of an expert. Typically they are used for problems dealing with complex diagnosis, scheduling, forecasting, monitoring and control or data analysis and interpretation.[24]

The thousands of expert systems now in existence share certain characteristics in common:

- they perform at a level equivalent to that of a human expert;
- they are highly domain specific;
- they can explain their reasoning; and
- they can provide a range of alternative solutions in conditions of uncertainty.

Expert systems typically have four components:

- a knowledge base, which contains explicit knowledge in the form of facts, rules and objects;
- an inference engine, which stores the procedural knowledge or control strategy;
- a knowledge acquisition module; and
- a human computer interface, which also enables the user to seek explanation from the system.[24]

Expert system shells

Designing and building an expert system can be a costly basis, and can require access to more than simply financial resources. Expert system shells have been created to help non-specialist users, and those who lack significant financial or technological resources, to develop their own expert systems. Typically, they consist of a collection of expert system building tools, such as rule editors and rule searching logic, designed to minimize the amount of specialized knowledge and engineering and programming skills required to build a system. Most shells have a user-friendly interface that, in the building mode, accepts knowledge in the form of English-like rules, frames or object-oriented structures. Most offer an integrated environment with the popular databases, spreadsheets and graphics packages; for example, ART interfaces with Lotus and Oracle.[23]

The popularity of these systems in banking and financial services, in manufacturing and in medical, health and scientific circles is testimony to their importance. Some forecasters predict that, on the basis of current developments in expert systems, within a decade or so almost all routine tasks could be automated, including the teaching of standardized subjects such as English and mathematics, staff training and the literature-searching role of reference librarians. As many as 3,000 such expert systems may be in operation already, solving routine technical problems, with their numbers growing at a rate of 50 per cent a year.[25]

SPEECH RECOGNITION AND SYNTHESIS

Speech recognition

Although it might seem surprising to the lay observer, progress towards teaching computers to understand spoken communication remains very limited. However, the complexity of the problem is such that success depends very much on the level of understanding required and on the size of the domain. Current devices range from those which recognize only isolated words, and as a result impose unnatural patterns of speech upon the user, to those which permit continuous conversational-style speech where words may run together.[26] The size of the vocabulary of words, sounds and phrases that can be recognized depend on the system in use, but those which are genuinely independent of the speaker whose voice is to be recognized can generally support vocabularies of the order of 100 words. Indeed, it has been estimated that it would take an effort akin to that of a small Apollo project to produce a system capable of understanding the 1,000 word Basic English System which has been proposed as an international language.[26] Hence, the facility for automatic or general recognition of speech by computers is not available, and seems likely to remain so for the foreseeable future.

Current speech recognition systems are generally to be found in one of the following categories.

Speaker dependent systems

These systems recognize only the voices of trained users, operating from a database containing templates of user voices. These systems offer very high reliability and are used in applications where accuracy of recognition is essential.

Speaker independent recognition systems

These systems will understand specific words, regardless of the identity of the speaker. Their capabilities vary with the size of the vocabulary available and on the level of recognition required – say, isolated or continuous.

Speaker adaptive systems

These systems operate not on the basis of stored templates of the voice patterns of trained users, but rather they build up their databases as users interact with the system. Speaker adaptive systems employ artificial intelligence techniques and are advantageous where a large vocabulary is involved.

Although voice input continues to be viewed very much as a technology for the future, some not inconsiderable progress is being made. One example would be the Shakespeare Speechwriter, which is a word processor and document handler which can be controlled wholly or partially through voice commands. The user, most likely a middle or senior level manager, would dictate documents into a personal computer, which almost instantaneously would display the spoken words on the screen. Software converts these words into digitized data which is then stored on the computer's hard disk until needed.[27] There are also software packages available, both for Apple's System 7 operating system and for Microsoft Windows 3.1, which enable users with a suitably equipped personal computer to record short messages. Compaq likewise will include business audio as a standard feature in its middle and top end Deskpro products, and it is expected that as the momentum of multimedia computing accelerates, so too will the provision of voice technology facilities.[4]

Speech synthesis

Systems which operate on the basis of synthetically constructed speech offer much less challenge to researchers and are already in widespread use for such functions as credit card verification calls and luggage handling. The software is the key component of such systems, with programs written for the recognition of individual words or sounds or for continuous speech recognition. The quality of the speech generated depends on the coding scheme employed, which involves a tradeoff between output rate and memory requirements.

Voice technology is already widely used for telephone-based services such as voice messaging. Retailers, railway stations and other public services can replace human telephone operators with a voice messaging system which accepts messages from customers who key in relevant numbers on tone dialling telephones. New digital telephone exchanges and voice-data networks are making these facilities available to both domestic and business customers.

DATABASES

Where not so long ago, databases were automated or manual stores of records, the trend today is towards a multiplicity of content – data, text, image, graphics and voice. This trend is accompanied by the exploitation of artifical intelligence techniques to the development and operation of these databases. A recent survey of database technology revealed the following broad areas of development.

Proactive, intelligent databases

These *smart* databases would combine database management and artificial intelligence capabilities, and would be able to act on the knowledge contained within the system. This would include the ability to understand the uses to which information would be put and to alert users to trends and relationships not immediately apparent from the data.[3] A number of database products which incorporate this so-called *data mining* feature are already available on the market. One such system is Netmap, a database visualization and analysis tool which is designed to identify critical information concealed in database systems. A generic tool designed to sit on top of virtually any database, Netmap searches information sourced from one or more databases for common relationships. Entities and relationships are then presented as a graphical representation of all connected data items and all possible connections, which can be used to discover new knowledge, coincidences and opportunities.[28] Netmap also has the facility of being fully interactive, enabling the user to be part of the discovery process.

Developed in Australia, it has been used since the late 1980s by large corporations such as British Petroleum, Rover and Texaco to analyse their organizations. However, a major breakthrough came in 1992, when the software was rewritten for operation on the kind of relatively low-cost workstations that are found in manufacturing industry, financial institutions and research and development centres. It has since been employed in a number of prominent cases, including the work of the Serious Fraud Office in London on the problem over so-called *names* involved in the Lloyd's of London debt scandal, and in helping to track down the notorious *backpacker* murderer in New South Wales, Australia.[29]

Text-based management systems

Unlike traditional DBMS, which deal only with structured information, text based management systems (TBMS) are able to manage free-form text. This is effected in a variety of ways, depending on the system, but it can include such features as key word searching, the inclusion of image as well as text, and *browsing* by means of AI techniques. One commercial example of a TBMS is Lotus Agenda, which allows the importation of a variety of text data formats and uses AI techniques for organizing and retrieving text files.[3]

Hypertext

Hypertext applies a combination of both document and database systems to the management of information by means of connections and semantic associations. This system provides true multimedia capability through the integration of text, pictures, sounds, data and knowledge. The technology consists of CD-ROMs, videodiscs and hard disks, combined with sophisticated information retrieval software that allows exploration of the knowledge base through associative links. Originally designed for use by individuals on a workstation, Hypertext can now be used on a personal computer. Its current applications include online help, workgroup collaboration, interactive publication and problem resolution. As a technology it is still developing but it holds great promise as a highly sophisticated, user-friendly knowledge base.[3]

In reviewing such developments, however, it is well to remember that in database technology, as with others, commercial applications have tended to lag behind what is technically feasible. Hence, while distributed database technology connected to client/server applications is widely available in the marketplace today, significant production applications are few in number.[30] A fundamental distinction remains, therefore, between those database applications models that are centralized and those which are distributed. In the traditional centralized model, all users access data from a central source and all data definitions and enforcement procedures are held in one database repository. In the distributed model, which is still regarded as a development for the future rather than the present, applications will be installed on multiple subsystems and servers while appearing to users as a single database.[30]

Groupware

Groupware is a combination of computer hardware and software that enables a number of individuals to work as a team using a network of personal computers. This means that in addition to basic network management and communications software, there will be a need for *53* special applications software that will manage the interactions between the various members of the group. Groupware models the organization by having the system build up its own files and maintain a directory of users, plus the databases for the applications it manages. Communications management is central to the concept which both regulates work content and controls workflow between individuals, work groups, divisions and even countries.[3]

In order to use groupware, all users must use the same syntax and the same uniform system structures. Groupware is a relatively new and unproven concept and there is as yet no accepted standard, although Lotus is seeking to establish its Notes as the technical standard for groupware.[31] Moreover, the different systems in existence tend to have different perspectives; for example, some are oriented towards data and forms, others towards work centres.[3] Lotus Notes is a good example of a groupware product, an applications environment which enables people to work together more intelligently and increase productivity. One essential feature of Notes, it is claimed, is its non-sequential processes, which allow more than one person to work at a task simultaneously, while escaping from the constraints of paper-based sequential systems. Already, the software has 750,000 users, with the major accounting firm Peat Marwick alone having 15,000 staff linked up to the system.[32]

Not that Notes is perfect or the chosen solution for everyone. A Notes environment requires a substantial investment in software and dedicated servers and, not least, in staff training. It was also built around a proprietary database model, which can mean difficulties for companies with the need for systems interoperability. This particular problem has been addressed in alternative approaches to the fostering of workgroup synergy, through, for example, the development of suites and frameworks. *Suites* are integrated collections of previously unconnected applications, while *frameworks* are external environments that layer messaging, workflow and other workgroup functions on top of existing applications. Although neither of these provides a dedicated groupware package such as Notes, they can add to workgroup synergy.[27]

Several leading software producers are working on the development of suites, most notably perhaps Borland with its new *Object Exchange* (Obex) technology. Despite improvements in the workgroup functions of suites, however, they are still limited by the need for custom configuration and, more important, the managerial difficulties inherent in the need to persuade everybody involved to use the same programs. This is why some firms are opting for the use of frameworks that would put all the hardware, operating systems, transports, databases and applications under one umbrella, something that Notes cannot as yet achieve. One product which can do this is Digital Equipment Corporation's Linkworks, which provides complete transparency in workgroup activities. Moreover, while suites are moving towards end-user controlled access schemes, Linkworks offers a central control function for workflow, while allowing end users some ability to manage processes for themselves. However, it also requires the use of an additional relational database, which can add substantially to the cost.[27]

It is difficult to exaggerate the importance of this trend towards the use of groupware, which enables people in different locations to work together in *real time*, simultaneously editing a shared document, viewing presentations or engaging in discussions. Indeed, such is its perceived importance to the future of high end personal computing, that Intel is promoting its own groupware program, ProShare Personal Conferencing Software. This kind of program will ultimately merge with software and hardware for videoconferencing.[32]

Personalized software

Personalized software is designed to help individuals improve the way in which they organize their own computing. One emerging technology is that of so-called *electronic agents*, autonomous and adaptive computer programs capable of handling routine tasks for their owners. Typical tasks could include filtering electronic mail, scheduling appointments, locating information and making travel arrangements.[33] One of the more obvious uses for electronic agents is to assist users in finding the answer to questions when faced with a potentially overwhelming mass of possible sources. The range of search engines currently on the market includes systems such as AppleSearch, which enables the creation of personal search agents called *Reporters* to search and retrieve relevant information from incoming electronic information flows, and Power News, which will download news items according to user profiles.[33]

Among more advanced examples of electronic agents are what are sometimes referred to as *Knowbots*, agents that search a variety of information sources in order to find the answer to a query. Also at the development stage are what are known as *Softbots*, where the user tells the Softbot what to do and the system itself works out how to perform the task. Although in their infancy, these intelligent agents could turn out to be extremely helpful to hard-pressed managers and professionals faced with onerous workloads and incipient information overload.

VIRTUAL REALITY (VR)

Much of the conceptual groundwork was laid by the work of Ivan Sutherland with interactive computing and head-mounted displays at Harvard and MIT in the 1960s. However, it was only in the 1980s, with the availability of affordable computer power and sophisticated human computer interfaces, that there was a realistic prospect of commercially viable systems.[20] The technology takes a variety of forms, the best known of which employs a small television screen in a helmet, a glove, or alternatively a joystick, wand or six-dimensional mouse. Another form entails the use of video cameras to place and track the image of the user, or users, in a virtual graphic world, in which they interact with virtual objects. A third form involves the use of three-dimensional modelling, which is either viewed through 3-D glasses, or on a flat screen like a CAD package, or on a large curved or angled screen in order to obtain what are known as immersion effects.

Virtual reality provides a way of interacting with real or imagined environments. Whereas a computer normally relies on the user's sight, and occasionally hearing, to make interaction possible, a virtual reality system gives the user the feeling of being in the environment, like a fighter pilot in a flight simulator system. This is done by stimulating more than one sense at a time, by using natural movement as input and locking out external stimuli.[34] Virtual reality allows the user to become part of a three dimensional graphic universe and to affect what happens in it. It has three main components: it is inclusive, it is interactive and it all happens in real time.

The wrap-around view is crucial to obtaining the sense of immersion that is demanded by VR. As with human vision the system displays most of the picture in low resolution, using higher resolution for what is directly in the centre of the user's field of vision. Those systems that support sound need a highly responsive 3-D sound; if this is not adequate the illusion is lost. However, if vision and sound are difficult to replicate, touch is a particular challenge to the designers of virtual environments. The problem is twofold: reproducing the sense of feel that comes when mechano-receptors or nerves in the human skin respond to contact; and, proprioception, or feedback from the muscles. The former is so difficult to build in to virtual reality systems, that most designers do not even attempt it. With proprioception, on the other hand, a good deal of progress has been made, with robots responding to proprioceptive feedback for decades.[20]

Virtual reality is making inroads into significant areas with, for example, a growing number of applications in medical education, in space research and manufacturing industry. In the entertainment field, more than three million virtual reality games were in use in the United States by April 1993, and the market seems poised for major growth. Also in the United States, Vice President Al Gore has linked his information superhighways concept to virtual reality, with the possibility of children using the technology not just for games but for educational purposes. As in the case of current technologies such as television and video, it is easy to see such developments having negative as well as positive implications, with, for example, children, and indeed adults, retreating into their own virtual worlds at the expense of everyday social and community contact.[34] Nevertheless, the technology can be of great benefit and it remains to be seen if this potential for good is fully exploited.

MULTIMEDIA COMPUTING

The use of computer graphics is a powerful aid to making data elements more intelligible and enhancing the user-friendliness of computers. This has led to the development of a range of programs from integrated graphics packages to computer-aided instruction (CAI) and hypermedia. The trend is moving inexorably towards multimedia computing. This combines animated, high-resolution graphics and video, hi-fi sound, computer data, communications and, most important of all, interaction between the system and the user. The basic multimedia system consists of a desktop computer, a high-quality display subsystem, a CD-ROM drive and an audio storage system, usually CD-ROM and played back through a viewer software program on a desktop computer.

There are two families of multimedia program: authoring packages, which allow architects, marketing executives, advertising directors and many others to prepare sales presentations and brochures, edit videotapes, create animations and prepare colour advertisements; and reference, in which huge numbers of words, pictures and sounds are stored on a compact disc.[35]

Clearly these interactive systems have considerable potential as the vanguard of a new wave of consumer electronics products and services. However, these same interactive characteristics are already proving to be a major attraction to business, notably in such fields as training and point-of-sale. In the United Kingdom, Lloyds Bank has installed around 100 multimedia training packages to complement its existing distance learning activities; while in Germany, the Deutsche Bundespost Postdienst has installed over 2,000 PC-based multimedia learning stations on which more than 100,000 staff have already undergone training. In the United Kingdom also, a burgeoning market for *edutainment* has led to the emergence of a range of multimedia products aimed at the classroom, with a reported expenditure of more than £10 million by government on this technology between 1989 and 1993.[36]

The use of multimedia systems at point-of-sale outlets in airports, shopping malls and cultural and entertainment venues is now a worldwide activity, although apparently with somewhat mixed results. Companies frequently underestimate the complexity and hence the cost of such systems, but success stories include those at Zanussi in the United Kingdom, which claims to have boosted sales by some 30 per cent over a three year period. In the United States, Sears Roebuck plan to use interactive multimedia ordering kiosks and point-of-sale systems to reduce staffing by some 7,000 people, with anticipated annual savings of US$ 50 million.[36]

Another key characteristic of multimedia lies in its contribution to the convergence of media, communications and computer technologies, a development which is only now beginning to reveal its full potential, for example, in such areas as co-operative working and desktop videoconferencing. A recent estimate has put the growth of multimedia communications in the United States and Europe at around US$ 1.6 billion from a base of zero in 1991 to 1997.[37]

Cost remains a key area in the development of these systems, but with the amount of global development underway and co-operation between companies such as Microsoft and Intel, Siemens Nixdorf and Ericcson involved, this ought not to be a deciding factor. There is a problem of compatibility, however, with, as a rule, several standards for multimedia at virtually every level of activity. There are also technical problems to do with the amount of processing power that is required for multimedia applications, and even the rapid fall in storage costs is unlikely to compensate for increases in demand. Hence, while personal computers typically have standard hard disks of 80 to 120 megabytes capacity and standard CD-ROMs provide 500 megabytes, processing the image of a newpaper alone could account for 100 megabytes daily.[38]

Perhaps the major obstacle to the expected explosion of multimedia in both the home and business markets is that relating to the cost of creating the products. The sheer range of media typically incorporated into multimedia packages is likely to involve major sourcing costs to the various copyright holders, all amounting to potentially crippling levels of overhead production costs. The pace of development has also been retarded by legal disputes over copyright and patents rights, indeed to such an extent that a group of US companies including Apple, IBM, Digital, Microsoft and Lotus Development have formed the

Software Patent Institute and are building a database of software inventions which can be used by the Government Patent Office to help avert disputes over ownership.[39]

INPUT–OUTPUT DEVICES

Compared to the speed at which computers process data internally, getting data into and out of a computer is a very slow process. Input occurs through a range of familiar systems including keyboards, mice, trackballs, bar coders, touch screen devices and scanners. One of the most important developments in human computer interaction of the past decade has been the launch of the user-friendly Apple Macintosh. The use of a mouse to control a desktop has since spread to IBM-compatible computers through the medium of the Microsoft Windows operating system. Another current breakthrough in computer input involves the use of pens with Notebook computers. With this system, the user has no keyboard but instead writes on the screen in normal handwriting, which the program then translates into computer text.[40]

The availability of scanners has greatly increased the range and quality of information that can be inputted to a computer. Scanners allow the user to *photocopy* images onto the computer's hard disk where they are stored for easy access and editing. Although they vary widely in both price and size, all scanners are based on a high resolution sampling device, which yields high resolution scanned images, and a controller which co-ordinates the scanner and interprets its signals.[41] Scanners are currently variable in quality and occupy large amounts of disk storage space but, in the light of other developments covered in this chapter, this should only be a temporary situation.

Optical character recognition (OCR) is necessary for turning scanned documents into editable form. OCR scanners interpret the characters being scanned on a page and, instead of representing characters in terms of dots per inch, attempt to recognize the shape of the letter and transmit to the computer the number of bits that are the code for the letter. The choice of OCR software today ranges from products that are bundled with cheap handheld scanners to those which are incorporated into expensive OCR-dedicated workstations.[42] Colour and portability have also entered the scanner market, where already there is a range of good quality colour handheld systems.

Imaging involves the capture of visual images in digital form for storage and subsequent retrieval. Laser scanners capture text, graphics and data for editing and processing at workstations. The enormous amounts of data involved require mass optical storage facilities. For serious commercial operations it may also be essential to invest in high

59

speed scanning systems, systems for faxing documents directly into the computer, colour photograph image capturing technologies, high resolution displays with colour printers, and powerful compression techniques. Output devices are also required for converting images back to paper form when necessary.[40]

Computer output still tends to be from printers and a range of graphics devices that turn computer displays into presentation output, for example, plotters which draw text and figures onto paper or transparencies for presentation. As for printers, high quality, non-impact systems using laser and inkjet print engines now dominate the market. Allied to the use of sophisticated page description languages and with the additional advantage of colour, this has given a mass of users the chance to produce near-commercial standard work from their desktop computers. A great deal of time and effort has gone into the search for improvements in the human computer interface, much of it based on human reactions to, and preferences for, modes of interface, and including psychological, physiological and ergonomic approaches. Ultimately, the answers reside in people themselves and in the way they work and interrelate both within organizations and as individuals.[43]

The current front runner in human computer interfaces is the Graphical User Interface (GUI). These operating system shells enable users to manipulate codes and commands in an attractive and much less intimidating manner. Graphical user interfaces provide a graphical representation of programs and the features of a system through the use of icons, pull-down menus and scroll bars. GUIs provide a range of advanced services such as multi-tasking, memory management and device drivers, and give the entire system a common structure and appearance.[44]

GUIs have led to breakthroughs not only in common standards for user access but also have helped standardization at increasingly high levels of software. Although different environments are involved, an application built for the Apple Macintosh can be transported relatively easily to a Windows environment owing to the fact that both use a common set of functions to draw screens, control the mouse and access data.[43]

GUIs are redefining the human/computer interface in terms of the user, rather than the database. They are designed to help users specify what they want rather than how this should be done. There is still considerable room for improvement and, as it is, conflicts arise between interface and database components of the client/server architecture. However, from the user perspective such developments represent a truly radical change and it seems likely that the graphical user interface will become a standard feature of computer systems.

Current developments also suggest that the next generation of workstations will be fully multimedia in nature, combining sound, video, graphics, animation, text and data; they will have access to vast amounts of CD-ROM storage and will incorporate such intelligent features as proactive prompting and the ability to learn and adapt to the style and skill level of its user.

REFERENCES

1. Tom Forester (1993) Japan's move up the technology 'food chain'. *Prometheus*, **11**, (1), June, pp. 73–94.

2. Michelle D. Morris (1991) RISC vs CISC. In: *Managing Information Technology*. Delran, N.J.: Datapro, 1215, pp. 1–5.

3. Daniel Schutzer (1991) The latest technological trends. In: *Managing Information Technology*. Delran, NJ: Datapro, 1272, pp. 1–19.

4. Larry Stevens (1994) Are you ready for the desktop of the future? *Datamation*, **40**, (11), 1st June, pp. 60–63.

5. Morris W. Firebaugh (1988) *Artificial intelligence: a knowledge-based approach*. Boston: PWS-Kent Publishing Company, Chapter 18, pp. 615–73.

6. Graeme Philipson (1993) In search of client/server. *Informatics*, **1**, (6), August, pp. 23–28.

7. Les Laurence (1994) Client/server security. *Australian Communications*, May, pp. 127–35.

8. Casey Kiernan (1993) Faces users can relate to. *Informatics*, **1**,(7), September, pp. 75–79.

9. Philip Manchester (1993) Doorway for innovative applications–for client/server. *Financial Times*, 20th April, p. v.

10. An overview of mainframes (1991) In: *Managing Information Technology*. Delran, N.J.: Datapro, 7220, pp. 1–8.

11. Paul Taylor (1993) Small is beautiful. *Financial Times*, 26th October, p. vii.

12. John Lettice (1993) IBM poised to compete–Personal Digital Assistants. *Financial Times*, 19th February, p. x.

13. Kenny Weilerstein (1992) Optical storage: overview. In: *Managing Information Technology*. Delran, NJ: Datapro, 7265, pp. 1–7.

14. Stephanie Losee (1994) Watch out for the CD-ROM hype. *Fortune*, **130**, (6), 19th September, pp. 89–94.

15. Stephen Coffin (1991) UNIX: history, philosophy, future. In: *Managing Information Technology*. Delran, NJ: Datapro, 1217, pp. 1–10.

16. Gary G. Flood (1993) Cutting through NT mania. *Informatics*, **1**, (6), August, pp. 29–32.

17. J. William Semich (1994) Surprise. OS/2 is taking off. *Datamation*, **40**, (8), 15th April, p. 43.

18. CAIRO (1994) *Datamation*, **40**, (6), 1st March, pp. 30–33.

19. Giovanni Perone (1992) Closeup on CASE. In: *Managing Information Technology*, Delran, NJ: Datapro, 7615, pp. 1–11.

20. Alan Hald and Benn R. Konsynski (1993) Seven technologies to watch in globalization. In: *Globalization, technology and competition: the fusion of computers and telecommunications in the1990s*. Ed. Stephen P. Bradley, Jerry A. Hausman and Richard L. Nolan. Boston: Harvard Business School Press, pp. 335–58

21. Development futures (1993) *Informatics*, **1**,(7), September, pp. 33–34, 67.

22. Mary I. Hubley (1993) Moving to UNIX and Open Systems. In: *Managing Information Technology.*, Delran, N.J.: Datapro, 4237, pp. 1–7.

23. Fundamentals of artificial intelligence and expert systems.(1991) In: *Managing Information Technology*, Delran, NJ: Datapro, 7620, pp. 1–8.

24. Firebaugh (1988) *op.cit.*, Chapter 11, 335–67.

25. William E. Halal (1993), The information technology revolution: computer hardware, software and services into the 21st century. *Technological Forecasting and Social Change*, **44**, pp. 69–86.

26. Judith Massey (1993) Still at the stage of baby talk – Voice Technology. *Financial Times*, 20th April, p. xx.

27. Wendy Pickering (1994) Computer: take a memo. *Datamation*, **40**, (1), 7th January, pp. 51–52.

28. Netmap: Database visualisation and analysis. (1994) 12 pp. Commercial presentation.

29. Claire Gooding (1993) Detectives of the database. *Financial Times*, 26th August, p. 12.

30. Jack Olson (1994) Defining a new state of databases. *Informatics*, **2**, (3), pp. 41–45.

31. Alan Cane (1993) Teamwork via a PC network – for groupware. *Financial Times*, 20th April, p. viii.

32. Alan Deutschman and Rick Tertzeli (1994) Your DES in the year 1996. *Fortune*, 11th July, **130**, (1), pp. 46–51.

33. Marina Koesler and Donald T. Hawkins (1994) Intelligent agents: software servants for an electronic information world and more, *Online*, **18**, (4), July, pp. 19–32.

34. Ralph Schroeder (1993) Virtual reality in the real world: history, applications and projections. *Futures*, **25**, (9), November, pp. 963–73.

35. Daniel Green (1993) Minding your own business: software that shifts the furniture. *Financial Times*, 24th July, p. vii.

36. Jonathan Taylor (1993) A kick start for multimedia – technologically speaking. *Financial Times*, 7th September, p. 15.

37. Philip Manchester (1993), A new breed of communications – Multimedia. *Financial Times*, 18th October, p. vi.

38. George Black (1993) Testing the limits of silicon chips: multi-media, one more milestone. *Financial Times*, 26th May, p. vi.

39. Tom Foremski and Louise Kehoe (1993) Strong feelings on patent dispute. *Financial Times*, 2nd December, p. 20.

40. Tony Quinn(1993) Myth of the panacea interface: Human Machine Interaction. *Financial Times*, 26th May, p. v.

41. Mimi S. Meley (1992) Scanners: Overview. In: *Managing Information Technology*. Delran, NJ, Datapro, 7260, pp. 1–9.

42. Sue Bushell (1994) The story in pictures. *Informatics*, **2**, (2), March, pp. 37–39.

43. Wayne Yacco (1992) GUIs: a general perspective. In: *Managing Information Technology*, Delran, NJ: Datapro, 7658, pp. 1–3.

44. Philip Manchester (1993) A general purpose toolbox: applications software. *Financial Times*, 19th February, p. viii.

4 Developments in Telecommunications

In the relatively brief period since the last edition of this book, advances in telecommunications have continued apace. The influence of converging technologies continues to be evident both in the increasingly *intelligent* character of terminals, switches and networks and in the emergence of new or updated forms of telecommunications service. Falling costs for fibre optic cables and for connection equipment mean that narrowband ISDN (Integrated Services Digital Network), already a reality in many parts of the world, faces the prospect of competition from broadband transmission with, for example, voice, data and high definition television available through the same cable. The question of whether the local loop, the connection to the home or office, is copper cable or glass fibre remains unresolved. However, the logic of existing national and international networks combining to form global superhighways looks set to become reality in the foreseeable future, while the continued deregulation of telecommunications is opening up possibilities for new value added telecommunications services. Perhaps above all what is happening is the increasing personalization of telecommunications activities, be this through forms of digital assistant, pagers or mobile cell-based telephony.

DIGITIZATION

The integration of voice and data communications continues unabated with digitally coded data being exchanged on the basis of established protocols and standards. The impact of computerization is evident both in the codecs which convert analog to digital information and in the digital signal processors, which enable everything from modem signal processing, to voice and video compression and TV enhancement. Routinely today, multifunction, program-controlled communications processors are employed for front-end processing, intelligent switching and concentration. Taking the field of international telecommunications as an example, the range of digital systems now available extends from X-25 packet switched and X-400 electronic mail networks through ANSI standard frame relay technology to ISDN 2B+D channels.

Software is central to the successful operation of telecommunications and is basically of two types, telemanagement software and communications software. Telemanagement software is used for monitoring and optimizing the use of networks, and specifically in such areas as call accounting and management, cost allocation and management, asset management and process management. Communications software is used for the management and control of data communications including links between various devices and between end users and remote software applications.

TRANSMISSION

Transmission facilities in use continue to embrace a spectrum that includes copper and fibre optic cables, communications satellites and microwave radio beams.

Cable

Copper continues in use as does coaxial cable for local environments where high-speed data traffic, including television signals, is required. However, as fibre optic cable and its related equipment have fallen in price, this has been installed into a large proportion of new networks. Digitization now extends to undersea cables running between Europe and the United States, and between Japan, Australia and the United States. These state-of-the-art digital cables provide very reliable circuits that are as good as any terrestrial links and without any of the delays associated with satellite.[1]

Indeed, the latest transatlantic cable linking Greenhill, Rhode Island in the United States with Lands End in the United Kingdom, and due for installation in 1995, will consist of twin pairs of optic fibre, each with the capacity for around 600,000 simultaneous telephone calls. Known as TAT-12, and ordered by a consortium including British Telecom, France Telecom, AT&T and STC Submarine Systems, the new cable will provide 28 times the capacity of its predecessor TAT-11.[1] TAT-12 will employ an optical amplifying mechanism that dispenses with the need for the high-speed, sea bed electronic repeaters hitherto required to regenerate long-distance signals. In the new system, erbium coated amplifiers are inserted at intervals along the fibre and illuminated by high-powered lasers to boost the telecommunications signals.[1]

Broadband cable networks have the potential to carry a wide range of services normally available only from a variety of different sources. This includes information services, such as videotex, and advertising services; transactions services for such activities as teleshopping and home banking; and common carrier voice and data services.

Satellite

Communications satellites in geostationary orbit 37,000 kilometres above the equator communicate by receiving radio signals at one earth station and transmitting them back at a different frequency to another earth station. A different frequency is needed because signals sent simultaneously at the same frequency would interfere with each other. Transponders and antennae on the satellites amplify the end-user transmissions received from sending earth stations before retransmitting them to receiving earth stations. The signal at the transmitter is much stronger than the signal at the receiver.[2] Earth station antennae have very narrow beams, both to increase their gain and to avoid interference with adjacent satellites. By contrast, the antennae on communication satellites usually have broad beams so as to reach large areas, such as a country or an entire hemisphere. Some satellites have narrow spot beams for providing specialized services to limited areas or *footprints*.[2] Earth stations are of different types and complexities and may include groups of very large antennae for simultaneous communication with several satellites, uplink and downlink communication equipment, precision systems for tracking satellites and telemetry, tracking and control systems for monitoring satellite performance and maintaining them in the correct attitude to their orbital slots.[3]

Satellites transmit on three frequency bands, C-band, Ku-band and, for radio and television programmes, DBS (direct broadcast satellite). C-band downlink transmissions are in the 4 GHz region of the spectrum, which is shared with terrestrial microwave services. Ku-band downlinks operate in the 12 GHz region, while DBS operates in the 12.5 GHz region. International regulatory bodies and national organizations designate specific locations for communications satellites in the geosynchronous orbit. These *orbital slots* are in great demand and must be spaced so as to avoid interference from adjacent transmissions.[3]

Since 1964, the ownership and operation of international satellite services has been vested in the International Telecommunications Satellite Consortium (Intelsat). Established by international treaty, Intelsat provides telecommunications capacity to national telecommunications authorities, which in turn use it to provide telephone services to their customers. Intelsat leases satellite capacity to telecommunications authorities in half circuits, or the amount of capacity required to provide one end of a two-way telephony circuit which, when matched with a half circuit at the other end, provides a full circuit between two earth stations. Capacity is allocated on the basis of *units of utilization*, which are defined as the measure of entitlement, as determined by the allotment of space segment capacity, for the establishment of one end of a two-way 4-KHz telephone circuit, providing an appropriate quality of service by means of access to a satellite in the multichannel mode and an Intelsat approved earth station.[3]

Intelsat is by no means the only international satellite organization, although it was the first. Inmarsat, the International Maritime Satellite Organization began operations in 1976 providing telegraphy, telephony, telex and distress services to member countries, not just in the maritime field but also in aviation and land-based mobile communications. Eutelsat, the European Telecommunications Satellite Organization operates on similar lines to Intelsat and provides telephony, television, DBS and business services to over 400 million users in the European Union.[4]

In 1983, Intelsat introduced the International Business Satellite (IBS) service as an alternative to the public switched network for international communications. The IBS service is provided to large corporations and communication carriers as dedicated point-to-point circuits. Switched services are also available from communications carriers using their IBS circuits. The types of applications available range from services such as electronic mail, facsimile, digital voice and data and electronic funds transfer, to video and audio conferencing, computer-aided design and the remote printing of newspapers. Eutelsat's Satellite Multi Service (SMS) is the European equivalent and is compatible with IBS.[4]

In addition to such developments there is now a growing market in the provision of satellite communication on an international basis by private companies. This process began in the United States with companies such as the Orion Satellite Corporation and Panamsat, both of which established alliances with European companies (respectively British Aerospace and Arianspace) to provide international satellite communications in competition with Intelsat. This kind of operation is clearly designed to exploit the perceived opportunities available from serving large business customers, particularly on lucrative high density, long-distance transoceanic routes. However, the economics of satellite transmission make it difficult for new and especially smaller entrants, while the legal and institutional obstacles remain formidable.[15]

Telecommunications satellites, originally intended for telephony and data communication, are of course heavily used for broadcasting. The use of satellite for television broadcasting was originally for point-to-point distribution of material, but improvements in both satellite technology and the efficiency of receiving equipment has led to the development of direct to home TV broadcasting. The current range of broadcast technology is such that there are low power satellites transmitting at 10 to 20 watts per channel to cable systems, medium powered satellites of 50 watts per channel transmitting both to cable and DBS systems, and high powered satellites transmitting at 100 to 120 watts to small individual receiving antennae for direct broadcast satellite (DBS). Much higher bandwidths are available from satellite transponders with bandwidths of 36 and 73 MHz and capable of carrying either analog or digital signals.[5]

Direct Broadcast Satellite (DBS)

Direct broadcast satellite (DBS) involves the provision, direct to the homes of subscribers, of high powered satellite signals for reception by small TVRO (television receive only) antennae affordable to a mass market. Its point-multipoint distribution architecture gives DBS advantages in serving sparsely populated areas and in the economic delivery of pay-per-view television. However, it suffers serious disadvantages as a competitor to cable, notably the fact that cable can offer many more services and that it is more feasible economically to offer interactive services on cable than on DBS.[6]

Satellite Master Antenna Television (SMATV)

This involves the provision of programming signals from satellites linked to TVRO earth stations, with the signals being amplified locally before transmission to individual television receivers. The viability of these systems has increased both with the decline in the costs of TVRO earth stations and with the increased availability of high powered satellites.[6] VSAT provision has benefited from a decline in the cost of TVRO earth stations and the availability of high powered satellites. On the other hand, its programming costs are in effect being increased by

69

the need for cable TV programmes to be *scrambled* in order to prevent unauthorized access by non-subscribers. Moreover, in direct competition with cable, SMATV suffers from a slightly higher price and a smaller number of available channels.[6]

VSAT services

There has been a significant growth of these systems in Europe during the 1990s, especially in central and eastern Europe. They involve the use of small dish aerials located on customer premises for the provision of specialized communications services. There are basically two kinds of VSAT system: one-way or broadcast systems, based on a central hub station and receive-only remote terminals; and two-way or interactive systems, using remote terminals capable of both transmitting and receiving. In Europe, there is considerable use of one-way systems for access to a video service covering horse and greyhound meetings and operated by Satellite Information Systems at a chain of betting shops.[6] Although VSAT systems usually operate in the Ku-band and are intended primarily for data communications, satisfactory results can be obtained for teleconferencing applications using compressed digital signalling at a 54 or 64 Kbs rate.[7]

Microwave

Microwave communications involves point-to-point radio transmission between *line of sight* towers. Radio waves are transmitted between transmitters and receivers, each mounted on a tower to avoid interference from high buildings and similar objects. Transmission is in the 1 GHz to 30 GHz range of the electromagnetic spectrum.

CONVERGENCE

Perhaps the most exciting current development in the communications field is the convergence of telecommunications and audio-visual services, notably broadcasting and entertainment media.

Currently the advantage in provision of such services lies with broadband cable, whose interactive characteristics offer considerable potential for such services as teleshopping and telebanking, although there is no overwhelming evidence of market demand for these services. The much-vaunted Warner QUBE interactive television network in Columbus, Ohio closed down after only two years of operation. Prodigy , a joint venture of IBM and Sears Roebuck may be a more promising development. Prodigy offers its clients a wide variety of information and services such as news, financial data, weather, airline schedules and fares, games and entertainment, and banking. Indeed, Prodigy has been described as more of a shopping service than an information service because it derives so much of its revenue from advertising.[8] By using a special menu, Prodigy users can access an electronic shopping mall and order merchandise from online catalogues. Prodigy is also involved in alliances with magazine and newspaper publishers, television networks, software suppliers and telephone companies, with, for example, a deal with Nynex permitting customers to access online Yellow Pages via their personal computers. A similar electronic mall, whose total sales are now of the order of $100 million annually, is accessible on CompuServe.[8]

Nevertheless, the future for convergence may well lie in the provision of common carrier services on cable, with both telephone and cable companies being able to offer broadband video and related services. In the United States, where broadcasters face potential competition from both cable companies and telephone companies, there are significant regulatory and legal barriers to convergence.

One of the major obstacles is the terms of the modified Final Judgement which broke up AT&T and prohibits the Regional Bell Operating Companies (RBOCs) from providing information services except under specific licences, a ruling which has been interpreted as covering the provision of both cable television and video programming. It also prohibits them from providing interexchange telephone services, which the United States Department of Justice has until now interpreted as prohibiting their ownership of satellite receiving equipment for purposes of receiving interstate signals for distribution over a cable TV system.[9] In the United Kingdom, for example, where cable companies are allowed to provide telephony in their own franchise area or can apply to Oftel, the telecommunications industry regulator, to link to an adjoining area, cable companies are already providing a range of telephony services, increasingly through alliances with North American firms, including RBOCs.

Current indications based on the European experience would suggest that three main factors will apply in the convergence of communications in advanced countries: technology, regulation and market forces. The infrastructure for convergence is emerging in an increasingly flexible use of satellite, as for example, in DBS for domestic television services and VSAT for the provision of business services, and in the spread of broadband cable and mobile communications systems.[9] In the European audio-visual industry, where the cinema continues to be in crisis and the video market is growing rapidly, the most influential developments are in the television industry. Deregulation has led to the

71

emergence of new players and, with the decline in the role of state broadcasting systems, is witnessing a gradual replacement of the doctrine of general interest by one based on the power of market forces.[9]

Television

One television-based technology which offers considerable potential for service convergence is the Multiplexed Analog Component (MAC) standard. MAC standards incorporate digital packet data communication which is used for the carriage of the sound signals associated with the television programme and for authorization data to control subscription television. Every satellite channel which uses the D-MAC signalling format has a spare capacity of around one Mbps or nearly four times that of PAL and SECAM. This capacity can be used to broadcast commercial data, for example, financial information or data for retail organizations with multiple outlets.[9] In 1986, the European Commission attempted to impose the MAC standard in an attempt to supersede the existing PAL and SECAM standards. The aim was to strengthen the position of Europe in competition with the United States and the Far East, especially in the field of higher definition television (HDTV). However, the attempt failed and today, the various satellites broadcast in four non-compatible transmission standards and five encryption systems.[9]

However, the television technology that has generated the greatest expectations is high definition television (HDTV), a range of systems that will produce a television picture with 35mm clarity on a larger than normal screen. Existing proposals for HDTV call for 1,050, 1,125 or 1,250 scanning lines, in contrast with the current 525 lines of Japanese and American television and the 625 on European systems. The width to height ratio of 16:9 is comparable to that of a cinema screen. HDTV also uses state-of-the-art electronics to incorporate a wide range of additional features and functions, including the ability to store, edit, swap pictures and make adjustments using controls displayed on the screen. It also uses low-cost workstations and very intelligent terminals to link the home to external databases and entertainment services by such broad bandwidth media as fibre optic cables or direct satellite broadcasting.[10]

In this latter regard at least, HDTV can be seen as promoting the use of broadband as opposed to narrowband transmission facilities. It may also promote demand for such services as video on demand, thus stimulating the demand for more channels and for greater interactivity. However, it is an extremely expensive option, and there are serious doubts as to whether the cost can be justified in the context of current television programming.[9] Some commmentators suggest that the role of television could increasingly become that of a kind of domestic *supercomputer* delivering a range of interactive video and graphic services for entertainment, communication and education via optic fibre. Indeed, if the full potential of multimedia personal computers is realized, these could provide all the visual features of television with superior interactive capabilities.[9]

Whether and when the network signal process and digital switching technologies will emerge to make this technological option attractive on a cost basis to consumers is open to question, as is whether consumer demand will be significant for the range of video and related services that could potentially be provided.[9] It is worth noting that the PC is also receiving a major transfusion of video technology. It could well become a 'multimedia' tool in which laser discs and imaginative software combine to provide all the visual capacity offered by TV with superior interactive capabilities. To be sure, tough technical problems must be solved before the multimedia PC becomes a widely-demanded item. However, depending on whether such PCs are used as stand alone items or as networking tools, this technological development could have major implications for the demand for public switched video distribution systems.[9]

ASYMMETRICAL DIGITAL SUBSCRIBER LINE (ADSL)

This technology offers considerable potential for the delivery of video-on-demand to the home. Operating on the basis of existing telephone wires, it would not require the costly installation of coaxial cable from the video server to the home, and it does not interfere with the basic telephone service. ADSL promises to deliver up to 6 Mbps *downstream* to the home, while delivering between 64 and 640 Kbps *upstream* from the home to the exchange. This upstream channel could be used not just to order video-on-demand but also for a range of new, interactive communications activities.[11]

Much will depend on the extent to which people are prepared to pay for such services, and for the immediate future there are cheaper alternatives, including the use of digital compression technologies. For example, the standard for compressed digital video developed by the Motion Picture Experts Group (MPEG-2) can offer a 10-fold increase in the number of TV channels over current UHF broadcast channels, while the super high frequency (SHF) spectrum radio band with vast available capacity could be used to link interactive television sets back to base stations.[11]

BANDWIDTH

As the range of new computer applications increases so the demand for increased bandwidth will continue. This is particularly the case with image processing, multimedia computing and those applications which necessitate the transmission of large amounts of information. Expressed in hertz, bandwidth is defined as the difference between the two limiting frequencies of a band. More simply, it is a measure of how much data can be transmitted from one place to another in a given time.[12]

The bandwidth in a communications network can be increased in two basic ways, by increasing the size of the *pipe* which carries the data, and by reducing or compressing the size of the data, so that more of it can be carried in the same pipe. The first objective has been achieved by changing from analog to digital transmission. The second is being tackled by a range of proprietary solutions, such as plans to build the Microsoft Realtime Compression Interface (MRCI) into all future versions of MS-DOS, thereby providing software developers with a general purpose data compressor for personal computer systems. Another American company, Software Publishing Corporation (SPC) has devised a compressing system for image data which has reduced the requirements for a full screen, 24-bit colour image from about one million bits to as little as 10,000 by using a technique called *fractal transform*.[12]

NETWORKS

Networks have been described as the *circulatory system* which provides the mechanisms for moving data and messages from one computer to another. Until recently, digital networks would have been a practical proposition only for those organizations able to afford the high cost of private leased lines and with the volume of data transmission necessary to make this worthwhile. The breakthrough has come with the availability of dial-up ISDN services, a development which has made large digital bandwidth much more cost effective.[12] Not that companies can afford to ignore the need for investment in data communications. The trend is inexorably towards the growth of Enterprise Wide Networks which must be capable of delivering integrated voice and data solutions. This is reflected in market research data, which predict a rise in value for fast packet switching systems from a level of US$ 74 million in 1992 to more than US$ 2 billion by the end of 1997.[12]

Current developments in networking technology can be summed up as follows.

Integrated Services Digital Network (ISDN)

A set of protocols defined and described in Telecommunications Standards Sector (TSS) regulations, ISDN aims to support a wide range of voice and non-voice applications in the same network. Built on top of standard twisted pair telephone wires, ISDN is an end-to-end digital network that integrates enhanced voice and image features with high speed data and text transfer.

ISDN provides two rates of service, basic and primary, over B and D channels. The B channel provides transparent digital channels for voice or high-speed data transmission at 64 Kbps. The D channel provides a non-transparent channel for signalling, telemetry and low speed packet switching at 16 Kbps or 64 Kbps. A basic rate service provides two 64 Kbps B channels and one 16 Kbps D channel. A primary rate service provides thirty 64 Kbps channels and one D channel in Europe, and twenty-three 64 Kbps B channels and one 64 Kbps D channel in North America.[13]

ISDN benefits

ISDN combines the benefits of digital communications with a multitude of services, over a greater geographical area and at lower cost. Technical benefits relate to signal quality and speed. With digital transmission, repeater stations replace amplifying stations – which also amplified noise – and completely regenerate digital signals during the repeat process. They also detect and correct errors caused by noise, ensuring complete and accurate delivery of the signals regardless of how many digital links or networks the signals have to traverse. These technical advantages allow digital networks to provide higher communication rates than analog networks, while maintaining higher quality transmissions at the same time. Furthermore, with ISDN the bandwidth can be varied according to the nature of the transmission. Several different ISDN services are available, the basic version offering two lines and more advanced ones offering as many as 30 lines. It is important to understand that these are not physical lines, but rather logical lines controlled by the network software. This means that many different messages can be carried simultaneously using a single physical wire or optical fibre. Where, however, additional capacity is required, several lines can be allocated to the task.[13]

Economic benefits relate to the lower cost of constructing, operating and maintaining digital networks, as well as the throughput advantages of digital communications, where economies of scale can be realized by combining voice, data and other communications through the same network. Geographical advantages derive from the global nature of ISDN and its standardization on a worldwide basis. Long-standing incompatibilities between analog devices have been eliminated, with ISDN users being able to communicate with any other ISDN-compatible machines at rates of at least 64,000 kilobits per second. Although it is expected that the data throughput limitations of ISDN will eventually render its design obsolete, it offers tremendous improvements over typical networks available today.[13]

ASYNCHRONOUS TRANSFER MODE (ATM)

ATM has been described as '..the definitive technology for high-speed digital networks, the springboard to the next great leap forward in telecommunications'.[14] Regarded as an improvement on ISDN for widespread applications, ATM is a set of international standards that define a new method for sending large quantities of voice, data and video information simultaneously over networks. It provides a common transport mechanism for digital communications traffic, regardless of whether it takes place between computers on a local area network (LAN) or across a public telephone network.[14] Information is broken up into *packets* or *cells* each labelled with an address to which it must be delivered. However, these are fixed size packets each containing only 53 bytes of data, including five bytes used for addressing and directing data through the network. An important advantage is that the cells can be handled by hardware, which significantly increases the speed of transmission. ATM starts at speeds of 155 megabits per second and has the potential to handle rates of up to 2.4 gigabits.[14]

This development is being hailed in some quarters as leading to a paradigm shift from LANs and WANs (wide area networks) to super-fast cell-based networks capable of carrying 500 channels of digital television over fibres to the home and to personal computers. Its major advantages include: integrated broadband services – for data, voice and video; almost instantaneous and flexible call establishment; and simplified network infrastructure.[15]

ATM will use existing fibre networks and the switching will be cheap and easy to install and maintain because it uses standardized components. However, its real advantages to consumers lie in its packet-switched nature and the fact that it provides, for the first time, a universally applicable integrated service. ATM can initially exist in parallel with all present networks and gradually take over all their functions, so its introduction will be evolutionary rather than revolutionary. Moroever, as ATM networks will offer all the advantages currently entailed in private networks, they will certainly call into question the continued need for such networks.[15]

Frame Relay

Frame Relay is another technology of which great things are expected. Based on Open Systems Interconnection (OSI) standards, Frame Relay allows WAN managers to consolidate traffic from multiple protocol environments over a single circuit. It can provide bandwidth on demand at speeds over 10 times faster than those of X-25 packet switching. Enabling different applications and protocols to be transported transparently across the network, Frame Relay offers great advantages to heavy network users. It is ideal for WAN traffic originating from LANs, but less so for those applications where time is critical, such as financial data services, and where a more appropriate solution might be found in point-to-point leased lines.[15]

Network management

The more powerful and complex that networks become, and their increasingly pervasive presence in modern societies, have brought considerable difficulties in their management and control. This includes difficulties over security of access, the integrity of shared data resources, maintenance and disaster recovery.[12] Most leading computer manufacturers have designed software to match management network configuration and performance in systems which include not just their own products but those of other companies, for example, IBM's Netview and Hewlett Packard's Open View. At the broader industry level, the Simple Network Management Protocol (SNMP) is linked closely to the UNIX open systems approach and to the popular network protocol TCP/IP. The latter provides a *language* by which systems can *talk* and SNMP sits on top of it. Hence, if a fault occurs or there is an attempt at unauthorized access to the network, the SNMP mechanisms inform the central network manager software.[12]

VALUE ADDED AND DATA SERVICES (VADS)

The integration of computer and communications technologies has been instrumental in the development of a whole range of new value added and data services (VADS). These can be defined as services delivered or accessed by means of telecommunications and involving the addition of significant value added to the basic transmission and switching functions.[16] There are three broad categories of value added services, namely:

- *Enhanced communications services*: electronic mail, messaging, managed data network services, tele- and videoconferencing;
- *Transaction services*: electronic data interchange, electronic funds transfer at point of sale, home banking, tele-shopping, ticket reservations;
- *Information services*: online databases, electronic publishing services.

This list is not intended to be complete but most of the services listed are already well-established. Among those which are expected to grow to prominence in the immediate future are electonic data interchange (EDI) and videoconferencing.

Electronic Data Interchange (EDI)

Electronic data interchange is basically computer-to-computer communication, involving the interchange of standard formatted data between the computer application systems of trading partners with minimal manual intervention.[17] With EDI, standards are required to define the contents of messages and the techniques for assembling messages, in order that they can be read by the receiving system and processed automatically. These EDI standards cover five interrelated areas: messages, segments, data elements, syntax and message design guidelines.

Many of these emerged as proprietary standards which were accepted within particular industries such as automobiles, retail, distribution and pharmaceuticals. However, this led to problems when companies needed to communicate with others outside their own industry groups. To deal with this issue, national standards such as the American National Standards Institute's ANSI X 12 and the United Kingdom's TRADACOMS were devised. The emphasis is now on general movement towards the EDIFACT (Electronic Data Interchange for Administration, Commerce and Transport) standards worked out jointly by the United Nations, European and American experts. The range of business messages covered by this system continues to grow, as does acceptance of the UN/EDIFACT standard worldwide. However, because the approval procedures can be very slow, it is expected that general migration from national to the UN standard will be a long-term process.[17] Not that interconnection difficulties have been the only reason for the slower than expected take-up of EDI. Serious questions remain over the legal status of electronic mail, whether in its use as evidence in a court of law or in an audit trail. At heart, however, is a reluctance to change rather than firm up legal restrictions on the use of electronic media in such situations.[17]

Nevertheless, EDI is expected to be a core business process by the end of the 1990s, expanding beyond existing transactions processes to cover every aspect of the trading cycle and trading partner relationships. The multistandard environment is also expected to disappear by the end of the 1990s, with an ITU EDI specific protocol for X.400 expected to lead to a single communications interface for both EDI and electronic messaging.[17]

Videoconferencing

Videoconferencing is an electronic meeting in which geographically separated groups communicate using interactive audio and video technology. Until recently, videoconferencing occurred mainly on a point-to-point basis between two sites, but demand for multipoint conferences, connecting three or more sites, is growing. This is still an expensive option, with multipoint control devices to bridge audio and to switch video costing around $100,000. However, in addition to supporting multiple sites per conference, these units have the advantage that they allow users to hold more than one conference at a time.[18]

Technological advances in codecs (coder-decoders), in cameras and in audio systems and displays, as well as reduced charges on radically improved fibre optics-based telecommunications networks have all accelerated the recent growth of videoconferencing. Codecs are the critical component of digital videoconferencing, converting analog video signals into digital form, then using coding techniques to reduce signal bandwidth to allow transmission over standard digital telephone lines. Another important development has been the adoption of the TSS H.261 (PX64) video compression standard, bringing the promise of greater choice and lower equipment costs as vendors introduce mass-produced, standard-compatible equipment. As standardization gradually extends to audio, graphics and encryption, vendors will pursue integration at the board and chip level, increasing production efficiencies and lowering costs still further.

It is now feasible to have videoconferencing based on PCs, although there is still a problem over availability of the required bandwidth of at least 112 Kbps to 128 Kbps. Whereas for the foreseeable future, this seems likely to confine most PC-based videoconferencing to that which can be conducted on a LAN, features now available include multipoint conferencing. The advent of PC-based systems has been made possible by advances in chip technology, with single chips able to handle all the necessary algorithms for images, compression and interoperability. *79*

Also important, has been agreement on the H.320 set of standards for videoconferencing, established by the ITU-T in 1990.[18]

Voice messaging systems (VMSs)

Voice messaging systems, also known as voice mail systems, are probably the most basic form of voice processing. They provide the caller with the ability to leave a message for someone who is unavailable by a digital speech recording, and for the latter to be able to retrieve that message when convenient.

Electronic messaging

Electronic messaging, by radio and wire is expected to provide the backbone for electronic data interchange and electronic funds transfer, as well as for keyboard conferencing, remote LAN access and simple database enquiry. With developments such as Code Division Multiple Access (CDMA) cellular which transmits two-way messages, and Cellular Digital Packet Data (CDPD) service which provides digital paging and two-way messages, growth in Message Handling Services (MHS) over radio networks is predicted in the near future.[14] Already, there is evidence from the United States that organizations are using messaging for critical communications functions, but there is also widespread dissatisfaction over the general lack of support tools for monitoring and managing the process.[19]

MOBILE COMMUNICATIONS

One area of major growth in recent years has been that of mobile communications. At a recent symposium, mobile data communications was defined as the ability to send or receive data from a suitable terminal without any physical connection to a network – which today means radio communications. The major types of system currently available are outlined below.

Paging These are one way radio systems for transmitting data. They are available for short-range, wide-area and nationwide applications.

Trunked private mobile radio (PMR) Private users share a network of base stations interconnected by leased lines and switches. The majority of PMR systems provide voice services, however there are mobile data services which can communicate and display short text messages coded in character form.

Digital cordless telephone (CT2) This is a European standard for digital mobile telephony, which has applications in the home, telepoint and the cordless PBX.

DECT A European standard for communications between a portable telecommunications device and a base station. Its primary application is the cordless PBX, mainly due to its ability to handle large volumes of calls; however, residential, local area network and telepoint applications are also envisaged.

Analog cellular radio (AMPS) A two-way mobile telephone system which provides contiguous coverage through the use of overlapping radio cells. The available frequency band is divided up into cells which form a repeat pattern and the band is reused as many times as the pattern is repeated across the country. Communication to the mobiles in a cell is through base stations connected by fixed links to mobile switching centres.

AMPS is expected to continue in use well into the next century, especially with the development of a new range of dual mode AMPS/CDMA handsets. Its biggest disadvantage is a lack of an efficient way to handle data, and this is on the way by means of CDPD (Cellular Digital Packet Data), which will support the provision of digital messaging and two-way paging over existing cellular networks.

Cellular Digital Packet Data (CDPD) CDPD exploits the unused bandwidth that is available on all cellular channels and makes it available for data messaging without disrupting existing AMPS or CDMA services. Vacant channels are also available for most of the day since cellular systems are engineered to handle peak-load conditions. CDPD uses this free radio space to send almost real time data and messages, and the system can later be upgraded to use 'silent' channels. In any conversation, only one person is ever talking at any one time, so half the radio channels are silent, even when in use. With intelligent CDPD switching this bandwidth becomes available for rapid data bursts.[14]

There is tremendous potential to this system, which can send two average messages every second of free channel space at data transmission rates of 19.2 Kbs. This means that even the existing cellular bandwidth should be enough to support two-way radio messaging for a large part of the population, and CDPD can supply this service without the need to build and equip any new base stations – they just need to add intelligent switches.[14]

Code Division Multiple Access (CDMA) This is a cellular radio technology which uses a shared wide bandwidth and provides a good level of security without the need for a range of different encryption systems. CDMA will carry both voice and data from the start and, operating at very low power levels, it can provide low, medium or high bandwidth on demand, just like ATM. It can offer 4 Kbps voice connections and 144 Kbps channels for video and data simultaneously in the same wide radio band, and the user pays only for what is used.[14]

GSM GSM is the pan-European digital cellular system. The structure of the fixed network for GSM is similar in concept to that of analog cellular systems, with base station controllers, mobile switching centres and location registers. The radio transmission method is a narrow-band TDMA structure, with eight mobiles sharing a 200 KHz radio channel.

Digital short range radio (DSRR) DSRR is a standard for private digital short range radio. It is intended for direct communication between handsets and is designed for use at sporting events or in factories.

Personal Communication Networks (PCNs) are based on the standards and design work carried out for GSM, except they will use different frequencies and employ micro cells ranging in size from 100 metres to 1 kilometre radius.[14]

Three market segments – fixed point-of-sale, people on the move, and PC–wireless LAN connectivity – appear poised for large growth rates. With a projected worldwide 27 million users of wireless data by the end of the decade, electronic mail, fax, file transfer, EDI and other electronic messaging applications are positioned to be big beneficiaries. These emerging mobile data services can link into corporate networks at a relatively modest cost. Typical architectures include a base station, with which the mobile communicates by radio at much lower speeds than wireless LANs and over much greater distances. Here too, Cellular Digital Packet Data (CDPD) is expected to prove beneficial, with its effective bit rate of 19.2 Kbs expected to entice many more subscribers to cheaper channels.[20]

Technology market analysts are predicting that wireless communications will be the largest telecommunications growth area of the 1990s. With increasing digitization of wireless communications, broadcasters as well as telecommunications operators are invading the data transmission market, creating a projected $8 billion industry by the year 2000.[20] Wireless is already beginning to enter the market for delivery of the estimated 16 billion E-mail messages which were exchanged worldwide in 1992. Wireless credit card authorizations today take less than half the time of dedicated wire lines. There are presently an estimated 15 million users of cellular telephones in 30 countries. Estimates are that wireless data transmission will capture over 30 per cent of the US cellular market in the very near future.[20]

Nevertheless, for the foreseeable future, it is unlikely that cellular and other wireless telephony will replace communications carried on fixed wires. Fixed wire communications are cheaper and can provide much greater capacity, and the indications are that fibre is inevitably set to become part of the local network. Rather, the relationship will be a complementary one, with fixed and wireless technologies each retaining their own markets.[21]

Personal communications devices

Personal Digital Assistants (PDAs) are already in use as a communications device. With the ability to recognize handwriting and help users by making seemingly intelligent decisions on the selection of stored data and commands, these devices can be configured as personal organizers, as pagers and even as two-way radio transmitters. One example is Apple's Newton MessagePad, a small, text-handling device which is built into the computer's operating system in order to learn the user's handwriting and help them use the machine by making seemingly intelligent decisions on the selection of stored data and commands. These devices can be configured as personal organizers, as one-way alpha-numeric pagers or as two-way radio message transmitters.[14] In a few years' time, many new PDAs will be attached to fixed-wire telephones and integrated into desktop PCs. When the writing recognition problem is solved, they will provide instant messaging services to people who would never use a computer.[14] As we increasingly depend on fast ATM-type networks for accessing data, and probably for the use of special application processing, the desktop terminal will probably become little more than a highly intelligent input–output device, and this is where digital assistants or agents will play an increasing role.

Over the next few years, consumers can expect a flood of devices and services that will integrate wireless, data, fax and compressed video images, and deliver them worldwide to office PCs and mobile palmtop computers. New systems already combine notebook computers with radio modems or cellular telephone adapters. Worldwide access will also be provided by *low earth orbiting satellites* (LEOs) offering instant person-to-person communications which incorporate positioning technology that can pinpoint a receiver anywhere on the globe.[20] The infrastructure for information-based

83

societies is already well on the way to completion.

REFERENCES

1. Andrew Adonis (1993) 6,000 km under the sea: a transatlantic breakthrough for fibre optic cables. *Financial Times*, 17th August, p. 11.

2. Richard Coleman (1992) *International communications: constraints and issues*. Delran, NJ: Datapro, 1238, pp. 1–9.

3. Andrew F. Inglis (1991) *Satellite technology: an introduction*. Boston: Focal P., pp. 1–15.

4. David W. E. Rees (1990) *Satellite communications: the first quarter century of service*. New York: Wiley, pp. 29–70.

5. Rees, *op.cit.* (1990) pp. 105–30.

6. OECD (1992) *Convergence between communications technologies: case studies from North America and Western Europe*. Paris: OECD, pp. 43–51.

7. Inglis, *op.cit.* (1990), p. 25.

8. Donald T. Hawkins (1994) Electronic advertising on online information systems. *Online*, **18**, (3), March, pp. 26–39.

9. OECD (1992) *op.cit*, pp. 39–118.

10. Daniel Schutzer (1992) The latest technological advances. In: *Managing Information Technology*. Delran, NJ: Datapro, 1272, pp. 1–19.

11. Robin Whittle (1994) ADSL: bridging the Superhighway gap? *Australian Communications*, May, pp. 81–90.

12. Philip Manchester (1993) Survey of A–Z of computing (3): A measure of how data is transmitted – for bandwidth. *Financial Times*, 20th April.

13. Larry Jordan (1991) Integrated Services Digital Network (ISDN). In: *Managing Information Technology* DP, Delran, NJ: Datapro, 1270, pp. 1–15.

14. Stewart Fist (1994) Why ATM is the mode of the 90s. *Informatics*, **2**, (1), February, pp. 37–41.

15. Julie Harnett (1993) Survey of information and communications technology (14): Faster and cheaper data links – Wide Area

Networks. *Financial Times*, 23rd March, p. vi.

16. Michael Quayle (1990) Value Added Services: applications, acceptability and politics, the case of teleconferencing. *Prometheus*, **8**, (2), December, pp. 273–87.

17. Electronic Data Interchange (EDI). In: *Managing Information Technology*. Delran, NJ: Datapro, 1256, pp. 1–7.

18. Audrey Womack (1992) Videoconferencing services: overview. In: *Managing Information Technology*. Delran, NJ: Datapro, 1219, pp. 1–5.

19. Lynda Radosevich (1994) Users want better messaging tools. *Computerworld*, **16**, (38), April, p. 3.

20. Craig Johnson (1992) Wireless data: High growth in the 1990s. *TDR*, **125**, (4), pp. 7–8.

21. Andrew Adonis and Nikki Tait (1993) Mobiles break into the big times: can cellular communications replace traditional networks? *Financial Times*, 19th August, p. 15.

5   The Economics of Information

Perhaps the most memorable comment on the subject of information economics was that of George Stigler who in 1961 described it as ' ... occupying a slum dwelling in the town of economics'.[1] Whereas the problems which caused Stigler to make this remark have by no means all been solved, things have improved today, with much greater awareness of the subtleties and complexity of this sub-discipline and its central concept, information. Today, the subject is concerned not only with the production, distribution and use of information, but also with matters of organizational change, of communication and the wider political economy of information.

EVOLUTION OF A SUB-DISCIPLINE

Stigler's reference to 'slum dwellings' had to do with the fact that neoclassical economics had in truth paid scant attention to information. Economics appears to have been much better at modelling information in the abstract than at understanding the structures within which it is used. The purely competitive model assumes that in the free market all economic agents experience conditions of perfect knowledge, while the price system automatically generates sufficient information to ensure economic efficiency.[2] However, while it had been apparent to such analysts as Ronald Coase in the 1930s that firms regularly sought to bypass or suppress the price mechanism, it was not until the 1960s and 1970s that the implications of imperfect knowledge in markets where information was theoretically *costless* began to bear theoretical fruit.[3]

Don Lamberton has ascribed the emergence of information economics to a combination of circumstances including recognition of the unrealistic assumptions of neoclassical theory, a reaction to the failures of government and business policies and the potential contribution of intelligent electronics to enhanced communication, computation and control.[4] Lamberton has singled out the complementary contributions of Jacob Marshak and Fritz Machlup, as pointing the way for much that was to follow. Marshak focused on expectations and the notion of optimality, where the value of information was seen as dependent on the benefits that would flow from its use. This resulted in the start of an unbundling process, which separated out the component activities of enquiring, communicating and deciding, as well as limitations on the transmission of information. As Lamberton observed, henceforth information had to be regarded as costly.[4] Machlup studied separate components of the economic system, such as markets, the education system and policy, the linkages between them and the role of information. In so doing he developed the notion of an information industry, a phenomenon so pervasive as to resist analysis within the framework of conventional national accounting. His pioneering work on the production and distribution of knowledge in the United States in 1962 was followed by research into the nature and economic significance of information and knowledge. This inspired a considerable volume of comparative studies all over the world.

Gradually, therefore, the assumptions of Walrasian equilibrium gave way to the study of rational expectations, to patterns of behaviour under conditions of uncertainty in information searching, and to questions of co-ordination and control and the linkages between information and organization. However, in a world where information asymmetries were very much the order of the day, the economist's need to quantify things and incorporate them into complex statistical models continued to encounter serious difficulties. Faced with the perennial difficulty of devising a means for measuring information, Marc Porat adopted the device of counting value added and employment in markets. Others, such as Stigler, Arrow and Jonscher, defined information as a *reduction in uncertainty*, arguing that without uncertainty there would be no need for information. However, this still fell far short of a means by which information could be quantified, something which in turn affected further proposals for the incorporation of information into the neoclassical model, not simply as a residual, but as a commodity.[2] Indeed, the continued predilection of leading information economists to treat information as a commodity is the subject of some controversy in economics circles.

INFORMATION AS A COMMODITY

Premised as it is on the ubiquity of commodity exchange, it is scarcely surprising that mainstream economics treats information as a commodity, as both an intermediate and a consumption good. Lamberton has attempted to soften this position by pointing out that while information can be a commodity, it is so only to a limited extent. Other information economists have been more pointed in their criticism, claiming that information neither fulfils the definitional or conceptual requirements for a commodity, nor can it be reduced to the level of physical inputs to production functions. Information and knowledge, it is claimed, are enabling resources that inform and shape and catalyse other resources.[2] In order for information to behave as a commodity it must be capable of adding value and producing a return on investment, and moreover, this investment must be protectable in terms of legally enforceable ownership rights. Without exclusivity, information may have a value but it cannot command a price. However, information can be difficult to appropriate, as it can often be reproduced at minimal cost, while the cost of transmission can frequently be very low. Nevertheless, a capacity for appropriation is one of the conditions for commoditization.[2]

Another problem for the ascribed commodity status of information is its *public goods* nature. Information is a *public good* in the sense that many can *possess* the same information at the same time, and yet possession by one does not detract from the ability of others to be apprised. In fact, says Babe, it is not clear that ownership would be desirable in any event. To restrict access to those able and willing to pay is *inefficient* , since there is no additional cost entailed in allowing greater access for information already produced. While some argue that markets for information are needed to induce production, the economic case for intellectual or symbolic artifacts is certainly not clear cut.[2]

Finally, there is the fundamental problem of a lack of any standard by which information can be measured. Although there has been considerable commoditization of symbolic artifacts or *containers* of information such as, for example, compact discs, television programmes or books, and whereas the use of such information can be costed by the call, per bit or per view, none of the measures involved, whether for pricing or analytical purposes, touch directly upon the informational content from which these containers derive their value.[2] This has led to serious weaknesses in mainstream economic analyses of information industries, and to calls for the abandonment of attempts to treat information as a commodity.

INFORMATION AND ORGANIZATIONS

Another area considered ripe for change involves the study of organizations. The economic study of organizations has been concerned mainly with the costs of co-ordination, with institutions being analysed in an essentially static fashion, in terms of the efficiency of their channels of communication. In a perspective concerned mainly with the need for adjustments to bring marginal variables into equilibrium, the economy has been viewed as constrained by limits to finding and processing resources, but not to those of co-ordination and control. The operation of the price system ensures an optimal allocation of resources. More recent approaches recognize both the limits to co-ordination and control and the fact that as markets grow more complex, the need for co-ordination grows and search costs inevitably rise.[4]

Lamberton has observed that by linking the factors of knowledge and organization as new variables in a revised neoclassical theory, economists could begin to focus on a more effective model of the economic system. Others have pointed out that while necessary, such attempts threaten the symmetry of the neoclassical approach because in the real world of organizations, goals are multifaceted and often conflicting, involving much more than simply the maximization of profit.[5] Attempts to broaden the neoclassical perspective in this respect include the study of structural and behavioural change within organizations, with the advent of new, less-hierarchical entities within an information-rich environment, the so-called *flatter, leaner structures*. They also extend to the development of learning in organizations, both at the individual and at the institutional level. To this end, *cognitive economics* addresses the production of behaviourally-relevant information within organizations by means of various information–communications enhancement mechanisms, the reduction of noise and cognitive dissonance and improvements in pattern extraction. This work is complemented by developments in *evolutionary economics* founded on the fact that individuals rarely reach their goals in isolation, but as groups in communication with organizations.[6]

COST, PRICE AND VALUE IN INFORMATION ECONOMICS

Value is an extremely overloaded word, and is a concept that has attracted controversy for centuries. The crucial dichotomy between value in use and value in exchange devised centuries ago by Aristotle, is still current. However, even this apparently clear cut distinction conceals a semantic ambiguity which combines a sense of relativity, where value is defined in terms of relative scarcity and a calculus of what something might be exchanged for, and an ethical sense of value as intrinsic worth. In mainstream economics, nothing has intrinsic value. Nothing has the right to exist simply because it is. Value in exchange derives solely from human preferences and from the scarcity of items to satisfy human desires. Quite simply, value derives from the subjective and measurable calculus of individuals, where prices are the expression of utilities and revealed preferences.[7]

This question of value becomes even more complex when it is considered in relation to information. Economics is founded on the concept of scarcity. Value relates relative scarcity to utilities, yet information is almost never scarce in this sense. Moreover, traditional views which perceive information and communication as being somehow separate from the world of commodity production and exchange still retain a good deal of force. This essential *difference* of information in an economic sense is very evident in the context of production functions, where the inputs of labour, capital and raw material which combine to make up any good or service are subdivided into constituent elements, each of which can be mapped along continuous cost curves. So far as information is concerned, there are few stable production functions and no easy subdivisions.[7]

Another important example is that of the problems which have arisen in attempts to relate labour theories of value to the development of information and knowledge-based economies. While clearly nothing of economic value can be produced without intellectual or manual labour, it has proved extremely difficult to devise a theory sufficiently robust to accommodate both the web of connections linking past and present labour and the very different kinds of labour embodied in complex products. In the case of information for example, products such as computer software can be almost infinitely reproduced at very little cost. The relationship between labour input and the value of the final product dissolves. Likewise, there can be no minimum socially necessary labour needed to invent say a new superconducting material or to write a novel.[7]

These problems carry significant implications for the value in use of information in economics. Where communication takes place, for instance, it depends on common languages and protocols, and value is determined by considerations of scarcity related to the information transfer structure of communication channels.[7] Information only becomes meaningful when it is located in a specific place and time in relation to real needs and powers, and control is easier when its parameters are predictable. Furthermore, the phenomenon of half lives comes into play – that is, the time it takes for a piece of information to halve in value.[7] Moreover it is also necessary to recognize the existence of certain information asymmetries, both in the nature of the information itself and in the ability to acquire and to use such information. Lamberton links the importance of correcting such asymmetries with problems of co-ordination and control, and the need for learning processes within organizations.[4]

There is a also a cost dimension to the concept of value in information economics with, for example, Baumol's phenomenon of *cost disease* detectable in such sectors as television production and computer software, both of which depend on a mix of advanced hardware and skilled labour, and where costs tend to match those in the more labour-intensive sectors where productivity is stagnant. Despite advances in, for example, software engineering and electronic newsgathering, dependence on human labour in such creative areas shows few signs of diminishing. Moreover, the more that complex networks interconnect, the greater is the dependence on problem-solving abilities in systems design and integration.[8]

Information is increasingly linked to improvements in productivity through its contribution to individual value chains for goods and services. Nevertheless, there is evidence that the contribution of information and communication technologies to productivity at both the firm and the sectoral levels is by no means a matter of automatic progression. Rather, the tendency has been for increased modernization to bring its own costs in terms of increased levels of skill, the need for staff training and frequently, for organizational and structural change.[9]

If information and knowledge are to be exploited as sources of value, the business environment has to exhibit a complex mix of access and creativity on the one hand and the tight appropriation of economic benefits on the other. For all commodities, moreover, there is a cultural dimension; they exist within spaces of interconnected social differences and distinction, where individual utility and identity are inseparable from those of other individuals. Ths situation is typified in the packaging that surrounds the characteristic modern commodity, which can be bundled into packages which are sold not as a single dimension of utility and price but rather as elements within clusters of consumption, as lifestyles within which the goods become meaningful.[10]

The question of pricing information has long been problematic for business and government alike. In broadcasting, for instance, the public goods nature of the product has traditionally resulted in sale at zero financial cost, with the service financed through licensing systems which took no account of levels of use. Similarly, with

telecommunication services, where once the fixed costs of the network have been incurred, those of using the network are relatively zero. Finally, value in the final analysis is a highly personal judgement; what is valuable to one person will often be worthless to another.

THE INFORMATION ECONOMY

One of the most popular theoretical frameworks devised to take account of social and economic change since the 1960s has been that of the information economy. Fritz Machlup's research into the production and distribution of knowledge in the United States led not just to recognition of the concept of knowledge industries, but also to the use of national accounting data to study structural relationships and the growth process. Machlup's pioneering study provided the first of two basic measures of information activity in the economy, namely the *primary information sector* which includes the contribution to gross domestic product of those information goods and services traded on the market. The second key concept, that of the *secondary information sector* was identified in 1977 by Marc Porat and Michael Rubin. Intended to complement the primary information sector, this accounted for those inhouse and nonmarket, value added activities involved in the production of non-information goods and services, for example, employee compensation of information workers and capital consumption allowances for information equipment.[4]

Subsequent research based on the work of Machlup and Porat has resulted in fresh perspectives on the role of information in both developed and developing economies. Alongside and overlapping with the contributions of sociologists and futurists, the concept of a new information sector or sectors has issued a considerable challenge to mainstream economics. In essence, this is presented in terms of a transition within advanced economies from their original basis in agriculture to one founded on industry, moving then towards becoming service and, ultimately, information economies. Not only has this helped to consolidate the position of those who would argue for the development of information-based economies, but also it has led to the depiction of just about every aspect of economic life, every component of the economy in information-related terms. Indeed, such terms as information industry, information market and information worker have now entered into the wider language of the everyday world.

There have been varying explanations offered for the development of the information economy. To the OECD the explanation lay in increased employment in the service sector, with a concomitant decrease of employment in the primary and secondary sectors of industrialized countries. There were also changes in the structure of employment in the tertiary sector, with increased employment in the fields of personal and business services, in education and health, communication and financial services. According to Charles Jonscher, the major factor in informatization was the growth of bureaucracy and a supportive nonproducing labour force, a reflection of the tendency of technical progress to increase the complexity of the economic system, emphasizing specialization and hence the need for information workers. Baumol and Wolf, on the other hand, attributed the growth of the information portion of the US labour force from 1960 to 1980 to the substitution of non-information workers by information workers, plus the relative variations in productivity within the various industries.[11] Whatever its origin, however, considerable controversy continues to surround the information economy concept, not least because of the definitions and typologies upon which it is based.

Information typologies

Typically, researchers employ an *industrial typology* to define their primary information sector and an *occupational typology* to define their secondary information sector. Basically, those goods and services included within the primary sector must intrinsically convey information or be directly useful in producing, processing or distributing information. Moreover, industry typologies tend to focus upon knowledge production and inventive industries, information distribution and communication industries, risk management industries, search and co-ordination industries, information processing and transmission services (electronic and nonelectronic) and the manufacture of information goods required for these services. In some instances, such as those of Porat and the OECD, typologies include certain industries whose output, while not necessarily informational, is necessary for the production of information products, for example, printing and publishing machinery or office equipment. In other cases, such as those of Baumol and Wolf, only information services are included in the typology, with the production of information goods being excluded.[12]

The OECD typology in 1986 included as *information occupations* – those primarily concerned with the creation and handling of information *per se*. There has, however, been a tendency to broaden this approach to include all occupations generally involved in producing, processing or distributing information, in planning and control, and often in the production of information equipment and machinery. In the latter case, these occupations are usually viewed as part of the information infrastructure. The information occupations covered by these typologies range from the professions and management, through sales and office personnel to certain groups of manual workers. The designation information occupation is not, therefore, entirely synonymous with that of white collar worker, although typologies have been compiled which restrict inclusion to those with university or equivalent-level educations.[11]

Definitional and typological difficulties

Since Machlup first attempted to rearrange the United States national accounting data, there has been criticism of the over-inclusive nature of the categories he employed, with, for example, a category like transport and communications lumping together all forms of transport, telecommunications, postal services, media and publishing. Criticism has also extended to subsequent definitions of information occupations which, as described by the OECD in 1986, were those primarily concerned with the creation and handling of information *per se*. Babe has pointed out that there are huge disparities in *labour intensity* in Porat's typology, where some activities such as live theatre or authorship are highly labour-intensive, while others such as global telecommunications are highly capital intensive, with much of the information generated and transmitted being processed and analysed by machines rather than people.[2] The OECD typology has been similarly criticized for the inclusion of, for example, computer specialists along with such a diverse collection of occupations as those of secretaries, photographers, managers, shipping and receiving clerks, judges and lawyers, members of the clergy, sports trainers and instructors; informational status of some of the occupations included was considered to be ambiguous, as for example in respect of medical doctors and registered nurses, ticket collectors and engine drivers.[11]

General critique of the information economy thesis

Although the broad implication of the Machlup–Porat approach is for the separate treatment of information activities within the economy, there are problems to do with the heterogeneous nature of information and the difficulties of collapsing it into a single sector. Porat in fact, argued that the production, processing and distribution of information goods and services should be thought of as an activity. Likewise, while the clear implication is that information activities can and should be studied in monetary terms and treated as subsets of broader processes of economic-commodity exchanges, there is a problem, referred to above, of the limitations attaching to the commodity status of   95 information, not least the impossibility of measurement.

In the context of measurement, Lamberton has raised the different issue of what he terms *recorded diversity* in primary information sector accounting. He asks questions about the composition of official figures which suggest that, for example, Australia is twice as information-intensive as Sweden, while Malaysia and Sweden are at about the same level of informatization. He is also uneasy about the practice of allocating activities to primary and secondary information sectors without much apparent regard to productivity patterns.[4] It is also important to bear in mind that it is not so much the size of these information sectors that matters, as their actual contribution to national productivity. Comparing Japan and the United States in the two periods 1980 to 1985 and 1985 to 1989 respectively, Dordick and Wang discovered that whereas in the first period high levels of productivity in manufacturing went hand in hand with growth of the information sector, the picture changed markedly in the second period. In the Japanese case, with an information sector which grew only marginally in the second period, there were dramatic increases in manufacturing productivity. However, in the United States, where in this second period, the information workforce grew to become over 50 per cent of the total labour force, the level of growth in manufacturing productivity levelled off.[13]

Another important question in any assessment of the information economy concerns the relative status of information in modern economies. On the one hand, it can be argued that there is nothing particularly special about the role of information in modern societies. Information has been important in every society, and in advanced societies such as the United States, once new technologies such as steam, the automobile and the telephone have all appeared they have been absorbed into the economic system. Hence, in America today, the information economy can be regarded as simply a case of the old manufacturing economy using the power and speed of newer information and communications technologies to its advantage.[14] Nevertheless, the extent to which information has been commodified and the crucial role played by trade in information goods and services today, suggests that change of a truly qualitative nature has occurred. Today, it is not simply a matter of the importance of information as a source of value added and a major contributor to employment and to Gross Domestic Product; information and its associated technologies are major contributors to the production of other, non-information goods and services, and play an infrastructural role in the economy as a whole. New technology underpins the $16 trillion-a-year global derivatives trading business and is transforming industries from distribution to retail. A key trend, however, is that whereby *digitization* is leading to new synergies between all manner of activities – as for example in the kinds of cross-fertilization of ideas that already exist between the manufacturing and entertainment industries, where the same types of advanced computer graphics and workstations have been employed in making special effects for Hollywood films and in the design and manufacture of automobiles.[14] As evidence for the increasingly pervasive nature of such developments is the fact that, in the period of roughly 1990 to 1994, industry in the United States spent more on computers and communications equipment than on all other capital equipment combined – more than on all the machinery needed for services, manufacturing, mining, agriculture, construction or whatever.[14]

One of the most controversial elements in the information economy thesis remains the so-called *march through the sectors*, the transition in advanced societies from agricultural to industrial and then to information-based economies. The evidence for such a transformation is at best inconclusive. During the period 1950–1980, in Great Britain and the USA, the economy in fact followed the sequence of development put forward by the information economy approach; an increase in the information component of the labour force was associated with a significant decline in industrial employment. But during the same period for Australia, West Germany and Canada, industrial employment fell by only 5 per cent or less, while it actually increased in Japan.[11]

A further criticism of the information economy approach is a tendency to focus almost exclusively on sectoral contributions to the labour force and employment. Attention should also be paid to industrial and sectoral contributions to national production. Hence, while figures for the United States in 1980 showed that 45 per cent of the labour force was employed in the information sector and less than 25 per cent in manufacturing, this increase in information employment and decrease in industrial employment were accommodated not by a substantial increase in the service sector's share in overall production, but by a slight decline. On the contrary, the secondary sector's share of national production increased due to major gains in productivity, with fewer workers being required to produce the same quantity of goods.[11]

A related flaw in the information economy approach has been a tendency to separate manufacturing from services activities. Lamberton ascribes this practice to difficulties of definition, a lack of good statistics and a preoccupation with real assets as opposed to intangibles like patents and business intelligence. Manufacturing continues to be important, but it has to be understood that its productivity, trade performance and profitability revolve around the *97* management and exploitation of information. Arguably the much talked about deindustrialization process was in fact more of a shift of producer, that is information, services out of recorded manufacturing activity than a real decline.[4] This point has also been made by Ian Miles and Jay Gershuny, who have argued that not enough attention has been paid to the extent to which the tertiary services sector grew *because* of growth in manufacturing, and thus the extent to which services would not simply soak up surplus labour displaced from manufacturing. They also disputed claims for a separate *information sector* on the grounds that the processing, storage and transmission of information in modern economies is pervasive and that in fact, all sectors were becoming more *information intensive.*[15]

Such reservations notwithstanding, there have been difficulties in attempting to fit emerging forms of economic activity into existing industrial and occupational classifications. In this regard, new ways of looking at the labour force are helpful, for example, as in the work of Robert Reich, who has suggested reclassification into three groups: the residual production sector, consumer services and the manipulation of symbols.[16] There is also evidence for a shift towards an informational mode of production whose fundamental inputs are knowledge rather than material-based. This global phenomenon has risen from the convergence of new developments in organizational structure and in information and communication technologies. It carries profound implications for three sectors: the informational-manufacturing sector; the information-using, or symbol-manipulating producer services sector; and the consumer services sector, itself increasingly concerned with the manipulation of information.[17]

The *information-manufacturing sector* has emerged in both traditional industrial areas and in greenfield sites specially designed for high technology manufacturing. It is heavily reliant upon an infrastructure which includes business and organizational structures, research and development, and excellent transport and telecommunications links. This shift to the informational mode in manufacturing has had different effects in different countries and regions. In some cases it has led to the kind of situation described above, where the higher productivity of a declining workforce has resulted in increased production. In others, it has produced gains in high technology manufacturing employment.[17]

The *producer-services sector* is closely linked to developments in high technology manufacturing, and includes such activities as: research and development, technical and business consultancy services, data processing and other information services. The role of producer services is also closely connected with the increasing scale and complexity of modern corporate organizations, with serious implications for the conduct and location of activities. The fast-growing field and information-intensive field of *consumer services* includes such categories as educational and health services and travel and tourism.[17] It is also expanding to include the delivery of home-based services in retail sales, banking and financial services and entertainment.

Clearly, therefore, any serious analysis of the sequence of economic development as portrayed in the information economy thesis, must take account of a wide range of factors including the degree of industrialization of the economy, the level of industrial competitiveness, capitalization of industrial production and, particularly for developing nations, the country's economic and political conditions and its position within the international trade order.[11]

THE ECONOMICS OF TELECOMMUNICATIONS NETWORKS

One of the key messages emerging from research into the information economy is that of the capacity of information to add value to economic activity through dissemination within and between organizations, and within and between regions and countries. Information exchange by means of interpersonal networks facilitates the general flow of information in the most evident of high technology industries, which are particularly information intensive and dependent on the rapid exploitation of huge quantities of new information.[18]

Advances in information and communication technologies have, in effect, multiplied the inherent characteristics of the information resource with, for example, ISDN and, increasingly, broadband networks impacting upon the efficiency and internal structure of firms and on their relationships with customers and suppliers, as well as with competitors. At the regional and national level, such developments can be seen as double-edged, given the power of multinational corporations to influence development by decisions of location or expansion, and by virtue of their ability to bypass local telecommunications networks and communicate directly with their customers. By the same token, entire regions, and especially cities can lose out as the spatial geography of the information economy results in the shift of resources and business along the newly emerging information highways to lower cost centres in a different country or continent.[19] Hence, the advent of telecommunications-based networking has led to calls for the development, not of telecommunications policy, but of information policy to deal with, the complexity of the issues involved.[18]

Indeed, telecommunications networks are now the basic infrastructure of the modern economic system, a structural pre-condition for economic systems to grow into the information economy. *99*

The increased availability and capacity of communication networks stresses the basic characteristics of interdependence, inappropriability and externality of information as a commodity. At the same time it makes information an ever-growing strategic input in decision making, in production and in consumption, with access to information a central issue for all economic agents.[20]

The economics of information networks is now emerging within a broader economic theory of information production and use, including such components as:

- the economics of the generation of technological innovations;
- the economics of diffusion of technological innovations;
- the economics of market competition;
- regional economics;
- the theory of industrial organization;
- the theory of the firm.[20]

Something of the contribution of these developments can be gauged in terms of their impact upon firms, regions and markets. One aspect is the tendency for *externalities* or forms of direct interdependence among the members of an economic system that do not operate through the market mechanism or that are not fully mediated by prices. Externalities are thought to arise when growth investments and technological change in an industry cause capacity expansion and decline of product prices and factor costs. These externalities affect the behaviour of firms supplying those productive factors and using those products. Often *clusters* of industries emerge around the externalities spilling from core technologies and make it possible to increase the levels of productivity and competitiveness of all the firms which interact in the flows of exchanges of goods, services and information. Moreover, the increased availability of skilled manpower and the opportunities for training and learning benefit the other firms within the economic system.[20]

Another outcome can be the emergence of network firms to take advantage of externalities and increase the level of appropriability of the benefits of technological innovation and reduce the public goods character of knowledge. Network firms are characterized by interlocking directorates, long term contracts, joint-ventures, cross-licensing, technology clubs and swapping of minority stakes. They can also serve as structures which enable organizations to learn from the selective integration of localized learning opportunities on the network. Co-operation among such firms is selective and revolves around certain well-defined tasks and objectives, with safeguards built into the system to prevent abuse.[20]

CONCLUSION

With modern economies now heavily dependent upon intellectual capital, and with digital technologies transforming not just the pace and structure, but also the very nature of organizations and industries, the role of information economics becomes more important than ever. It seems clear, moreover, that more than mere quantification is involved here, and that some acknowledgement will be needed of the cultural and political, as well as the exchange values of information flows. In a global economy, this carries major implications for the development of policies to tackle the social and informational aspects of such matters as network economics and transborder dataflows.[21]

To observers such as Lamberton, the acknowledged deficiencies of neoclassical economics can be remedied through adjustment, with the inclusion of organizational and learning theories and with some modification of the position of the market and competition. To others, what is required is nothing less than abandonment of the Pareto-optimal world of neoclassical economics, and its replacement by a more caring and relevant set of theories that take into account the communicative, social, political and cultural imperatives present in national and international economies in an information-intensive world. Hence, observes Vincent Mosco, it is time for a return to a broader concept of political economy, in which social relations and cultural values are given equal weight with exchange values.[22] Although the times seem scarcely propitious for such a transformation, nothing in this world can ever be ruled out of consideration, not least in the inherently cyclical realm of economics. It is to be hoped that whatever the outcome, economists will continue to pay increased attention to the role and significance of the information factor.

REFERENCES

1. G.J. Stigler (1961) The economics of information, a perspective. *Economic Journal Supplement*, **75**, pp. 21–41.

2. Robert E. Babe (1994) The place of information in economics. In: *Information and communication in economics*, Robert E. Babe (ed.). Boston: Kluwer Academic Publishers, pp. 41–68.

3. Geoff Mulgan (1991) *Communication and control: networks and the new economies of communications*. Cambridge, England: Polity Press, 302 pp.

4. Donald McL. Lamberton (1994) The information economy revisited. In: Babe, *op.cit.*, pp.1–33.

5. Mulgann (1991) *op. cit.*, p. 165

6. Gilles Paquet (1994) From the information economy to evolutionary cognitive economics. In: Babe, *op.cit.*, pp. 34–40.

7. Mulgann, (1991) *op cit.*, pp. 170–72.

8. Mulgann (1991), *op. cit.*, p. 176.

9. Herbert S. Dordick and Georgette Wang (1993), *The information society: a retrospective view*. Newbury Park, California: Sage, p. 101.

10. Mulgann (1991), *op. cit.*, p. 177.

11. Rene Poirier (1990) The information economy approach: characteristics, limitations and future prospects. *The Information Society*, **7**, pp. 245–85.

12. Organization for Economic Cooperation and Development (1986) *Trends in the information economy*. Paris: OECD, 42 pp. (ICCP Series, no.11).

13. Dordick and Wang (1993) *op.cit.*, p. 92.

14. John Huey (1994) Waking up to the new economy. *Fortune*, **129**, (13), 27th June, pp. 22–28.

15. Jay Gershuny and Ian Miles (1983) *The new service economy*. London: Frances Pinter.

16. Robert Reich (1991) *The work of nations*. New York: Alfred A. Knopf, 531 pp.

17. Peter Hall (1992) Cities in the informational economy. *Urban Futures*, **2**, (1), February, (Special Issue, 5), pp. 1–12

18. Stuart MacDonald (1992) Information networks and information exchange. In: *The economics of information networks*, C. Antonelli (ed.). Amsterdam: North Holland, pp. 51–69.

19. Mark Hepworth (1994) The information economy in a spatial context: city-states in a global village. In: Babe, *op.cit.*, pp. 211–29.

20. Cristiano Antonelli (1982) The economic theory of information networks. In: *The economics of information networks*, C. Antonelli (ed.). Amsterdam: North Holland, pp. 5–27.

21. Sandra Braman (1994), Commodities as sign systems: Commentary. In: Babe, *op.cit.*, pp. 92–103.

22. Vincent Mosco (1994) The political economy of communication: lessons from the founders. In: Babe, *op.cit.*, pp. 105–24.

6 The Social Impact of Information and Communications Technologies

Of central concern to the study of information societies are those questions arising from the social impact and implications of the information and communication technologies. Taken to extremes this could embrace life in its entirety, the study of which could well reach encyclopaedic proportions. In this single chapter all that is attempted is an assessment of impact in such important information-related spheres as data security and protection, computer crime, privacy, intellectual property, censorship and freedom of expression, computer-mediated work and the networking of society.

SECURITY OF INFORMATION

Information stored on computer systems is often far more valuable to an organization than the computer hardware itself. Whether the basis of day to day operational efficiency or a source of competitive advantage, it must be protected against loss, damage, improper use or unauthorized access. All computer systems are vulnerable to accidental data loss through the operation of natural phenomena such as fires and floods and from hardware and software errors, telecommunications failures, electrical outages and power fluctuations. In fact, with a reported 60 per cent to 70 per cent of disasters caused by power failure, many organizations have installed uninterruptible power supply (UPS) systems and backup diesel generators to secure their information.[1] It is obvious that as it becomes increasingly underpinned by information and communications technologies, society itself is vulnerable to such phenomena. Unfortunately, a much more serious threat to the security of information and communications systems emanates from a burgeoning criminal fraternity drawn to the lure of lucrative, and at times relatively easy, profits in an information intensive society.

COMPUTER CRIME

Computer crime can be broadly defined as a criminal act either aimed at a computer or carried out with its assistance. This includes the unauthorized use of, or access to, information systems, or the modification of programs either for profit or for malicious intent. The most common form of computer crime involves theft. Computer theft can involve the theft of money, for example the illegal transfer of funds from one bank account to another; the theft of information, for example by tapping into data transmission lines or databases without payment; or the theft of goods by diverting them to the wrong destination.[2]

Criminal techniques

The most public manifestation of computer crime is the practice known as *hacking*, which basically entails use of the telephone system to gain unauthorized access to computer systems and their data. Hacking is defined as a search for access codes. This search can be random or can use highly sophisticated techniques to avoid detection. *Manual hacking*, using only a telephone, is also known as finger hacking and is the technique of trying number after number until a valid access code is detected. *Computer hacking* uses computers programmed to dial target numbers and to search for access codes either sequentially, randomly or algorithmically.[3] In Australia in 1986, in response to the growing threat of hacking in major companies, the state government set up a special team within the Victorian Police Bureau of Criminal Intelligence (BCI). The investigation, codenamed 'Operation Manna', found that the amount of criminal hacking activities was far greater than was initially believed to be the case and, indeed, that the problem was being deliberately understated by banks and other corporate institutions for fear that public confidence would be undermined.[4]

A related form of electronic crime and one that also involves hacking is the unauthorized entry into PBX and voice mail systems. In this case, the hackers manipulate the system to negate its security measures and obtain access codes, passwords and telephone numbers for sale to the highest bidder.[5] In the United Kingdom, British Telecom has its own internal 'detective agency' with the task of finding and prosecuting those who are abusing the telephone network. Many modern PBX systems are set up so that salespeople can call the office and dial a four-digit number that gives them access to the company switchboard in order to make business calls. Hackers exploit this practice by creating computer programs that trawl 0800 numbers to find the four-digit codes that will grant them access to free calls. Not only can the hackers use this facility to call anywhere in the world, but also as they are using a company switchboard and not their own telephones, they are virtually impossible to trace. Even where the hackers are caught, there is the problem of convicting them. If say, a hacker dials an 0800 number in London, routes himself to New York and then dials out to Holland, which of the three countries' telephone companies has actually been defrauded? Indeed, only the 0800 number will have been logged, so without evidence from an itemized bill can any offence be proven at all?[6]

The people who engage in such practices, the hackers, range from the bright and inquisitive student to those with criminal intent; they can be motivated by curiosity, ego, greed or a sense of grievance against the owners of the system. In the case of computer crime, however, criminals have devised a variety of means of gaining illegal entry, sometimes from the same site and frequently from a remote location. Prominent among methods employed for remote intrusion into systems are *viruses*, *worms* and *trojan horses*.

Viruses

Computer viruses are programs that modify other programs and reproduce endlessly, infecting other programs. Much as happens in the case of biological viruses, the virus invades the computer system by means of an *infected* program, which then replicates by instructing the host program to insert fragments of code into other programs. The *infected* programs proceed to pass on the virus until the point is reached at which with the infection sufficiently spread, the viruses become active and destroy all software on the system.

Worms

A worm is a program that replicates itself and spreads from one computer to another. A worm is a stand alone program. It is suited to 'sneaking' from one computer site to another computer site. Once the work has sneaked into the target computer system, it may leak information to the outside world, destroy the system, or simply become a nuisance and slow the computer down to a sluggish pace. A worm is the most technically sophisticated form of attack on a system. It is the least likely to be detected and is superb at leaking sensitive information.

Trojan horses

A trojan horse is a set of program procedures that will sometimes perform unauthorized functions but will usually allow the program to perform its intended purpose. For example, someone who wants to destroy a database might send its owners a file which, when run, can be silently destroying the database.[5]

Two well-known methods for attacking computers onsite are what are known as *salami techniques* and *logic bombs*. Salami techniques typically would involve a bank employee writing a program which would round the numbers on all accounts down to the nearest cent, and deposit the residue to his or her own account. Eventually these *slices* will add up to a large salami, with the crime likely to remain undetected until the criminal decides to make off with the proceeds.[5]

A logic bomb is a program written by an employee, designed to perform destructive or fraudulent actions. A programmer might put onto the system a program which periodically checks to see if his name is present on the electronic payroll. If the name is not present, then the program would destroy critical information. That way, if the employee were dismissed, the company's computer system would be destroyed in revenge for the dismissal.[5]

The scale of the threat to computer security was encapsulated a couple of years ago as the seven Es: Error, Embezzlement, Ego, Eavesdropping, Espionage, Emnity and Extortion. It is estimated that at least $2 billion in direct costs are lost annually through computer crime in the United States, and that even this is the tip of the iceberg.[7]

Improving computer security

Computer security covers a broad range of responsibilities from the denial of unauthorized physical access to computer facilities to the protection of networks and their data. It is a constant task and one whose success can never be entirely guaranteed. In the process a range of security methods is used to protect data and equipment, including:

- *Physical access controls*: where access is restricted to authorized users only, by means of security badges, magnetic card readers and biological detection methods.
- *Procedural controls*: including the use of security guards and sign-in logs.
- *Technical controls*: including the use of passwords, locking devices

and closed circuit television surveillance.[8]

Computer security can be improved greatly by the simple expedient of password control. There is now special access control software that identifies users and their levels of authorization and restricts them to these authorized functions. Unfortunately, such software will not protect an organization against frauds committed by employees in the course of their duties.[2]

Measures in place to prevent misuse of systems by outside callers, include *dial back* systems which disconnect external users, calling them back once their password has been verified, and *smart cards* similar to those used in automatic teller machines, with a chip inside the remote terminal programmed to verify that the caller is an authorized user. Also in use are scrambling technique devices and encryption devices, such as digital signal processors, which render telecommunications or computer signals meaningless to any unauthorized user. These are expensive systems and even the best encryption codes are vulnerable to being broken and hence must be changed frequently.[2] It is also possible to employ software programs which monitor and indentify operators and the times at which they accessed the system. These packages can also highlight an abnormal number of correction entries, which often indicates the trial and error approach of the computer criminal.[8]

At the leading edge of technology are a number of *biometric security techniques*, practical only for use in high security and defence organizations. Designed to measure those physical traits which make each person unique, these systems currently include:

- *Electronic fingerprinting*: where scanners read the fingerprints of users every time they press a button with their thumb, and the results are then compared against digital files of authorized user fingerprint records.
- *Retina scanning*: where a scanner reads the pattern of blood vessels contained on the back of the human eyeball.
- *Signature dynamics*: which focus not on the appearance of handwriting, which can be forged, but instead on subtle changes in motion and pressure, which cannot. Once again, the results are compared with records of the authorized signature.
- *Keystroke dynamics*: which applies the same technique as used in signature dynamics to use of the keyboard.
- *Hand geometry*: where the length of the fingers, the thickness of the palm and the shape of the hand are all measured and the results stored digitally for later comparison.

109

- *Voice recognition*: where the technology has developed to the point where it measures not merely the sound of human voices, but which tracks the actual physiology that produces speech.
- *Neural network identification*: where very advanced records are compiled, based on patterns of nerves in the human face.
- *DNA fingerprinting*: where the genetic portrait of the DNA fingerprint is stored and compared with those of people seeking to access the facility.[9]

Quite apart from the cost and benefit dimension to such attempts at improvement in computer security, in the final analysis this has to be a management rather than a technical problem. People are the source of the problem of computer crime and in their management and control lies the best chance of tackling the problem.

LEGAL REDRESS AGAINST CRIMINAL BEHAVIOUR

In November 1991, a Cornell graduate student, Robert Tappan Morris, released a worm program into the Internet. This, the greatest computer security violation of all time, caused thousands of computers to fail at universities, government laboratories and corporations all over the world. Morris was eventually caught and convicted, receiving a $10,000 fine and 400 hours of community service. In view of the seriousness of this attack on the world computing community, many will feel that the punishment for this particular crime was unduly lenient.[5]

Indeed, given the sheer scale of intrusion, damage and fraud involved in attacks upon computer systems, it is hard to understand why so many people are intent on some form of decriminalization of this inherently anti-social behaviour. Although intrusion into a database may not necessarily meet the traditional legal definition of theft, to wit, *depriving the owners or authorized users of its use*, theft is theft and unauthorized use is unacceptable. Furthermore, to attempt to justify such actions with talk of so-called victimless crime, where the targets are not individuals but giant corporations, is dangerous and irresponsible. Moreover, where in the past it could often be difficult for organizations to prove that criminal conduct had occurred, because unlawful entry into databases did not entail actual physical intrusion, laws now exist which recognize electronic theft as being similar to physical theft.[1]

A law enacted to deal with hacking in the United Kingdom in 1991 makes unauthorized entry punishable as a misdemeanour, and entry with malicious intent a felony. In the United States, several states have passed special legislation to expand their computer crime laws to cover the insertion of viruses and other rogue programs into software or network systems.[1] In the Australian state of Victoria, the Crimes (Computers) Act, 1988 carries fines of up to $84,000 or 10 years in jail.[10]

In attempting to tackle the question of information security at a multinational level, the Organization for Economic Co-operation and Development (OECD) adopted its own *Guidelines for the Security of Information Systems* in November 1992. Noting the growing importance of information systems in all aspects of national and international life, the OECD drew particular attention to the vulnerability of electronic information to unauthorized access, use, misappropriation, alteration and destruction. Its *Guidelines* apply to both the public and private sectors, to all kinds of information systems, and are capable of being suplemented by additional measures and procedures for the security of information systems.[10]

PRIVACY

Quite apart from the cost of computer systems, their development raises the question of balance between the need for security and the importance of preventing the abuse of records and hence, encroaching on the personal privacy of the data subjects concerned. *Privacy* (informational or data privacy) is a broad term referring to the utilization, sometimes even exploitation of information about people for various purposes. It is an information-use issue, although the word is sometimes used loosely as a synonym for confidentiality or even secrecy.[11] In the near future, privacy will have to be considered in the larger networked sense. For example, a 'user' of personal information or of a system must be understood to mean not only an individual, but also a process acting across the network on behalf of a human user, or on behalf of another system or an organization.[12]

As more computer networks come online, transaction generated information about individual citizens can be mixed and matched with census data, postal codes and other publicly available information. People are becoming apprehensive about the nature and scale of such data collection and yet, digital data are almost totally unregulated because they do not fit into any of the legal boxes developed in the past. Traditionally, the established laws governing communications apply specifically to mail, newspaper, cable television and radio broadcasting. Signals in a digital environment do not differentiate among voice, video and data.[11]

Given the vast amount of personal information that is held in modern information systems, the potential for improper use of information is very high. Threats to information privacy can arise as the unintended consequences of government or administrative decisions or as the result of direct commercial transactions. In the United States, for example, concern has been expressed over the widespread use of Social Security numbers by tax authorities, by vehicle licensing departments and by welfare agencies in pursuit of parents evading payment orders. There is always the possibility of this information being appropriated for misuse. A prime example of such misuse is its acquisition for sale by credit reporting agencies who operate in a largely unregulated market.[11]

If personal information is to be used for appropriate purposes and a proper balance maintained between record keepers and data subjects, and between organizations and individuals, then the necessary safeguards, administrative and legal must be established. If, for example, tax file numbers are to be used in support of other activities, such as tracking down welfare offenders, then the system must be capable not only of detecting and correcting errors but of affording full redress to those data subjects injured by either the erroneous or wrongful use of the information.[13]

Logical as such statements sound, their implementation into workable policies is not by any means straightforward. Given the sheer range and scale of data collection by central and local government alone and the seemingly limitless capacity of technology to manipulate such data, one has sympathy with the point of view that described privacy as akin in status to the pachyderm.[14] In Ireland, concern has recently been expressed at the threat posed to privacy rights from the proposed introduction of a Revenue Social Insurance (RSI) number, which can go beyond the confines of tax and social welfare to open the door to some form of national identity system.[15]

The very real dangers of insider corruption were illustrated in the investigation conducted from 1990 to 1992 in Australia by the New South Wales *Independent Commission Against Corruption* (ICAC). The focus of the enquiry was a multi-million dollar trade in confidential information from local, state and Commonwealth government records, typically involving public officials, enquiry agents and companies in banking, financial services and the law. The information traded included unlisted telephone numbers, addresses, passport particulars, bank account details, pension details, criminal histories and immigration information. A total of 155 people and organizations were found to have engaged in corrupt conduct, with a further 101 guilty of engaging in behaviour which allowed, encouraged or caused corrupt conduct.[16]

This case raised serious questions about standards of public conduct, not least those of the finance and insurance industries, which knowingly connived in the illegal acquisition of information for their own purposes. It also revealed serious policy deficiencies in regard to information collection and control, particularly the need to limit the number of access points to such information and install effective audit systems to check on the operation of these limits. More fundamentally, it raised questions about the need to collect so much personal information in the first place. Such large scale invasions of privacy as were revealed in this instance are alarming and difficult to resolve, but it is important that society comes up with a solution.[16]

In Canada, where for over a decade there has been machinery to assist citizens in exercising their privacy rights in relations with the central government, the Privacy Commissioner has issued a useful checklist of privacy related issues including:

- *Openness/transparency*: where individuals are aware of the fact that new data collection procedures are being developed and of their implications for citizens, not least their right to object.
- *Informed consent*: the need for individuals to be informed and their consent obtained for all disclosures of information publicly collected and processed.
- *Access*: individual citizens must have the right of access to and correction of, the information held about them as the result of any transaction.
- *Matching*: Systems shared by several users should be segregated internally to prevent possible matching or cross-over of personal information during a transaction.
- *Gatekeeping:* There has to be adequate security to prevent misuse or inadvertent access to information about individuals. Along with this goes the responsibility of those entering the information into the system to ensure its reliability.
- *Respect*: All participants in the data collection process must understand and adhere to the principles of privacy ethics or laws.[17]

The need for attention to such issues is apparent not only in the proliferation of personal dossiers in a multitude of public and private organizations, but also in the ability of organizations to use computers to search each other's files and match their respective data sets, for example, matching tax returns with membership lists for clubs and societies.[17] Other developments include the use of computer programs for employee monitoring and surveillance: for example, the monitoring of telephone use and of keystrokes on terminals.

Two recent developments would seem to indicate that, if anything, the threat to privacy is growing more serious, the more sophisticated that technology becomes. One is the proposal in the United States for a national citizen database, containing the names of every citizen or legal alien with a Social Security number or Green Card. The database has been proposed by the Commission for Immigration Reform as an aid to prospective employers, who could use it to verify the information supplied to them by applicants for employment. The proposal is supported by both parties in the Congress, but has caused concern in human rights circles.[18] The other is the appearance of groups of people who specialize in retrieving and exploiting information from databases, the so-called *detectives of the database*. For a fee these *detectives* will delve into databases, mine the data and provide their clients with extremely sensitive information about data subjects.[19] Perhaps most worrying is the fact that in such instances, the invasion of privacy can easily be rationalized in terms of efficiency and productivity. It is such developments that have led privacy abuses to be described as perhaps the most serious problem associated with information societies.[13]

DATA PROTECTION LEGISLATION

In the United States a number of laws have been passed in the privacy field, starting with the Privacy Act of 1974. This allowed individual citizens to examine and make corrections to records maintained by the government. Its passage raised social concern and consciousness of misuse of the personal information collected and condensed in computer systems. Congress also passed the 1984 Counterfeit Access Device and Computer Fraud and Abuse Act, making it a misdemeanour to gain unauthorized access to federal computers.[20]

In 1986, the Computer Fraud and Abuse Act, extended federal jurisdiction over interstate computer crimes in the private sector. It applies to all computers used by the federal government and federally insured institutions, making it a misdemeanour to post stolen passwords, or obtain, or look at data in any computer containing federal information. That same year, the Electronic Communications Privacy Act made it illegal for persons to intercept electronic communications, such as electronic funds transfers (EFTs) and electronic mail, without prior authorization.[20]

On October 15th 1992, the European Commission announced its amended proposal for a framework directive on the protection of the individual with regard to the processing of personal data and on the free movement of such data. The proposed directive was intended to remove obstacles to the free movement of personal data between member states, both because of the need to harmonize arrangements for the impending single European market, and to counteract incompatibilities between existing legislation in some countries and, indeed, its absence in others.[21] The Directive enshrined the principles of the Council of Europe Convention on data protection (No. 108), which had already been ratified by seven EC member states. Important changes included a focus on personal data and removal of the differences between public and private sector data. Another important dimension is that of *subsidiarity*, whereby the Directive lays down the main guidelines for legislation, leaving member states considerable discretion in implementing the common principles.[22]

Despite these changes, the revised proposal has been criticized for the breadth of its definition of processing and the amount of information it is required to provide to subjects, both of which carry cost implications. Ironically, also, it is claimed that rather than protecting the rights of individuals, the Directive might infringe them. Specifically, Articles 7, 8, 26 and 27 are said to endanger the right of free communication. Likewise, service industries such as banking, insurance, aviation and the travel trade are likely to be subjected to costly procedures for which there is no real justification.[23] Criticism also extends to treatment of transborder dataflows, where it is argued the Directive should have aimed for equivalent treatment of data transferred to a third party in another country, rather than simply requiring an adequate level of protection. Where lower standards apply in these third countries, the purpose of the EC data protection legislation will be frustrated.[22] It seems likely that further changes to this Directive are going to be necessary. It has even been argued that the best approach would be for European Union member states simply to set a date by which they would implement the existing Council of Europe Convention, Number 108.[22]

INTELLECTUAL PROPERTY

The ubiquitous presence and enabling characteristics of the information and communication technologies inevitably reach into the legal arena, with implications for traditional concepts of ownership and property. Their ability to redefine the boundaries of time and space, and the ease with which electronic information can be manipulated and transmitted are particularly difficult challenges to a legal regime founded on tangible documents. At its most basic this can involve confusion as to the roles and identities of authors, publishers, custodians or users of electronic information.[12]

In the United States, for example, under the 1976 revision of the Copyright Law it is assumed that any original work is protected by an unpublished copyright until it is published. The difficulty with electronic information relates to when the work is actually published and by whom, if anyone, it is copyrightable. The traditional arrangements between authors, publishers and libraries are no longer appropriate for an electronic environment in which users can access and download information at will, and frequently with little regard to either ownership rights or the need to pay royalties. Furthermore, with the growth not just of international but of global networks, copyright and intellectual property have become subject to the ultimate uncertainty and extraterritoriality of cyberspace. Cyberspace is any zone which is created by means of human imagination with the aid of electronic technology.

Put in less esoteric terms this involves such basic questions as the protection of ownership rights on networks which typically comprise a mix of commercial and noncommercial information providers. As the law of intellectual property currently stands in the United States in relation to databases, for example, only original expressions may be copyrighted, not facts or ideas. Hence, computer users can scan as much information as they like, and unless they copy the exact organization of, or presentation of, the software programs used to sort this information, no infringement of copyright occurs.[24]

The essence of the problem of threats to intellectual property comes down to the power of current technologies to reproduce and rework ideas and remove them from the control of their rightful owners. Nowhere is the problem more acute than in the field of computer software, a problem that involves not just illegal copying, but genuine difficulties of interpretation over what is original and what is not, and what is private and what is in the public domain. Indeed, it is increasingly difficult to define exactly what software is, when, in principle, any software can be frozen into hardware in the form of microchips.[12] Attempts to resolve these matters by the use of copyright have been less than a total success with, indeed, the attempt to enforce ownership rights in products such as Wordstar having been finally abandoned. Although software companies continue to resort to copyright, patent and trade secret laws in order to obtain redress against those who would infringe on their rights, a much more imaginative range of measures is now in play, including co-operation between producers and users in the form of *shareware* and software membership clubs.

In the wider sphere of control over the use of intellectual property, a useful approach may be that which addresses the matter of flows rather than stocks of information. The Dutch *Commission on Computer Crime* has proposed that control in such cases could be defined as the intention of the sender or producer of any piece of information addressed over a network. If the message is addressed or encrypted for a particular transmission, then unauthorized use constitutes theft. In all other cases use is permitted. By this means, the law begins to recognize that communication is concerned with channels rather than with things. Inevitably, however, in a networked and increasingly interconnected world, it is realistic to view any success in total control over information as at best conditional and temporary.

CENSORSHIP AND FREE SPEECH

Another area of everyday life already feeling the pressures of change in an information-conscious society concerns the exchange of information and ideas. Open societies around the globe have long established traditions of freedom of speech and expression, with reasonable legal safeguards against abuse. It is ironic that these hard won freedoms should currently be facing a threat from a quarter widely hailed as liberating and enabling, namely computer and communications networks. A disturbing example of this problem is the behaviour of users of the Internet, a vast computer network that connects more than 7 million people at 1.2 million attached hosts in 117 countries. Although there have been complaints from a variety of users of the network, allegedly upset by the political, religious or racist content of messages, the most contentious issue to date has been that of alleged pornography on the Internet.[25]

What is important in a free society is not whether or not this material is pornographic, but how network administrators and users should respond to it. At heart is a debate about the balance between free speech and censorship. This is really a new version of an old problem, one encountered for centuries in the world of the printed word, but it is none the less difficult for that. Indeed, on the Internet the issues facing administrators have been described as including those of free speech, obscenity, sexual harassment and degradation of women, the 'proper' use of limited university resources, the purpose of universities, the relation between pornography and behaviour and feminism and pornography.[25]

Underlying this list of concerns it is easy to see the operation of agendas other than those of communication over widely dispersed networks of computers. From the over 4,000 newsgroups to be found on the Internet, less than 20 were identified as offensive in a pornographic *117* sense. The urge to control such material must be seen in the context of previous and ongoing attacks on the print media, and must be resisted with equal vigour. The fact is that, in order to be exposed to such material, the offended parties must first opt to read it by giving the requisite command. This is even more the case with graphics, because pictures are transmitted in coded form and must first be downloaded and then decoded using special software. To ban all such material would be draconian and, in effect, would make it difficult to decide where to draw the line, as inevitably, the number of interest groups or offended parties seeking such redress would proliferate. The preferred approach would be to permit freedom of expression within the bounds of normal decency and indeed the rules and protocols of the electronic media, while encouraging the opponents of pornography to invoke existing and extensive sexual harassment procedures against the perpetrators.[25]

In the United Kingdom, in an attempt to address the wider problem of computer pornography, both the Criminal Justice Bill and the Obscene Publications Act were updated in 1994 to cover computer images. At the same time, police powers of search, seizure and arrest were extended to cover computer material. The main target is pornographic computer imagery which can be distributed either via compact discs or over modems to personal computers.[26] Although the authorities' intentions are clear, it is easy to see why some people are sceptical of such measures. The advent of cyberspace has presented an apparently insoluble problem to the censors simply because there is nothing to trim or to cut, so much of what happens occurs in the zone of the human imagination. With the onset of interactive multimedia technology and widespread access to personal computers and broadband transmission channels, the job of the censor becomes well-nigh impossible. Suddenly it is the *medium* that is the problem as much as the content. Control of this material would require access to every telephone line in the country and the kind of police powers of search and arrest that would simply be unacceptable in a democracy.[27]

WORK

During the 1970s and 1980s, much of the focus on the impact of new technology upon work was on whether the general effect was beneficial or detrimental. Concerns with technologically-induced unemployment continue to this day, with figures to show that between 1990 and 1994 more than 3,000 jobs for computer hardware technicians have been lost in Canada, as a result of the increased reliability of machines, with a further 2,500 predicted to disappear by 1996.[28] Nowadays, however, debate has broadened to take into account not just technological change but such significant social and political factors as gender, the control and organization of work and the social design of systems.

There is no aspect of the debate on the social impact of technology that has been more polarized between optimistic and pessimistic schools of thought than that of its impact upon employment and conditions of work. The so-called *technological utopians* present a humanistic vision of knowledge-intensive, creative and co-operative work, while to *anti-utopians* the future is one of dehumanized and repetitive employment in a working environment controlled by machines. As Kling has shown, these opposing perspectives share a common belief in the social impact of technological development, and both adhere to linear analyses of a relatively limited set of potential social changes.[29]

In an age when computerization will continue to be a pervasive presence, the impact of technological change will not yield readily to generalized interpretations of a black and white nature. Different people, different workplaces and organizations will respond in different and unpredictable fashion to the application of similar technologies and systems. Indeed, to really begin to understand the social impact of information and communications technology, it is necessary to look first at the organizational and social settings into which these technologies are to be deployed. Issues of gender, and the occupational structures into which women workers tend to be locked are, for example, critical to the control and organization of work, most notably in white collar occupations.

Other controversial dimensions relate to the use of computers for group supported work, either in the office or by means of teleworking, and for monitoring and measuring employee performance. This embraces the critical issue of the impact of new technology on the skills of employees, an aspect where both *deskilling* and *upskilling* can occur depending upon a wide variety of factors including the job, the employee, the workplace and the specific technology in use. Undoubtedly, the introduction of all such systems and particularly information systems, must be approached from the perspective of social design, which embraces the opinions and values of eventual users of the system, and which embodies recognition of the importance of the human and social infrastructure to the successful operation of any new system.[29]

One area in which there is now growing interest is that which concerns the relationship between work time and leisure time. Several forecasters are predicting that the eventual outcome of current technological change will be a reduction of employment levels in all sectors of the economy, in *white collar* as well as *blue collar* occupations.[29] The more imaginative forecasters anticipate new arrangements for work organization such that society can be organized to leave time for individual autonomous activities consequent on a reduction of the time needed to be spent on the job and a sharing of socially necessary work among the greatest number of people.[30] Exactly what such arrangements would be and how they would be funded, remains unclear. Moreover, if modern societies are to abandon or, at least, seriously modify their attitudes to the work ethic, there will need to be major social and cultural adjustments for which little precedent exists.[30]

Telework

Earlier and optimistic forecasts foresaw the widespread adoption of telework within society. Instead of people commuting to work, the opportunity would exist for them to work at home or in telecottages or other communal centres. This potential would extend across the spectrum from routine information processing tasks to advanced knowledge-intensive work. It would become possible as a result of the emergence of flexible, high-speed communications technology and increasingly cheaper computing power. These technologies could in effect place hardware and software, databases and multimedia information which hitherto had resided mainly in city centre offices into homes in the suburbs or in non-metropolitan areas.[31]

In the United States and the European Union, teleworking has been adopted in a wide range of sectors including telecommunications, computer hardware and software, banking and insurance, national and local government, printing and publishing, and the retail trade. Despite optimistic forecasts in the 1970s and 1980s, it has not become as widespread as was expected, possibly because of its failure to fit in with existing organizational hierarchies and with procedures for monitoring worker performance. Evidence from a study conducted by Xerox in the United Kingdom identified six features of work organization necesary to the successful implementation of telework. These were:

- It must be adaptive rather than rigid.
- It must have consistently lower overhead costs.
- It must enhance individual contributions.
- It must enhance creativity.
- It must be organic and involve people.
- It must motivate the production of quality work.[32]

In Australia, in February 1994, the Industrial Relations Commissioner Greg Smith ordered the immediate introduction of a 12-month industrial award to cover approved federal public servants, which would allow them to telework from home three days a week.[33] Although this led to a flood of applications from public servants wishing to work from home, it is expected to be at least a couple of years before this demand translates into any large scale incidence of teleworking. Among the reasons offered for this prediction were the need for a proper technical infrastructure to support the project, including security measures for the information, and the absence of viable applications. Moreover, while management expressed reservations about the potential productivity payoff from teleworking, there remained unresolved issues to do with health insurance, workers' compensation and working conditions.[33]

Research undertaken by Telecom Australia in mid-1993 found that people working from home were generally more productive, and were both happier and healthier, but spent more time talking on the phone to colleagues to make up for the missing social element. Worker productivity increased by about 18 per cent for participants and anxiety about deadlines and general work pressure fell by about 15 per cent. The incidence of sick leave was lower, possibly because people were able to work at their own pace and could start later in the day if they were not feeling well.[34]

Almost 10 per cent of participants in the Telecom study reported feelings of isolation from the office. The study involved 31 people with no children in the house, who were set up with home office areas. They tended to work longer hours, felt more self-reliant and generally thought they had better control of their lives. However, experts insist that human contact is still vital and could never be completely phased out of the workplace.[34]

Not that telework has to be based on the home. It can take place in neighbourhood work centres and satellite offices equipped with the necessary electronic resources. Evidence from Europe suggests that people prefer to work in groups of 10 to 12 in neighbourhood work centres, and, moreover, that such arrangements can generate new employment. Although the operation of these telework centres varies from place to place according to local needs and conditions, they typically provide support services for business and a venue for community-based activities.[32]

Nevertheless, as Tom Forester has pointed out there are still comparatively few people working from home, either on a full-time or a part-time basis, and, of these, only a minority could be counted as *telecommuters* or high-tech homeworkers, who use information technology equipment to process and/or to transmit their intellectual products.[35] With hindsight this should come as no great surprise, given that most homes and apartments are too small to accommodate office activities and that working from home seems to suit some people and not others. Whether or not there is any significant increase in the proportions of the labour force working from home rather than the office, remains to be seen. It seems likely that there will be an increase in the number of people doing some work at home, as flexible working patterns become more widespread and as the portability of computing and communications technology increases.[35]

Notwithstanding the less than overwhelming body of evidence for the take up of opportunities for teleworking, there are those who predict its expansion on an international, indeed, global scale. Thus has emerged the concept of the *electronic immigrant*, someone who remains in their own country but telecommutes over great distances, perhaps many thousands of miles.[36] Electronic immigrants are most likely to fall into one of two occupational groups, professional and technical, and clerical and secretarial. The successful use of such staff will entail major transformation in organizational structures and management practices, and in such elements as productivity, efficiency and the length of the working day. Indeed, a new holistic approach will be necessary to the working conditions and lifestyle of the employee.[36] Moreover, in view of the fact that, in the great majority of cases, the employing organizations will be large multinational corporations, there are implications here for relations between these companies and governments both at home and overseas. This includes concerns over the potential for a new kind of *electronic colonialism*, with those countries that are providing the labour being vulnerable to pressure from foreign multinationals. On the other hand, the *migrant* countries will not suffer the loss of skilled labour overseas and would benefit from capital transfers in the form of the wages paid to teleworkers.[36]

It is easy to dismiss such predictions as *utopian*, especially as they raise the possibility of greatly reduced discrimination in patterns of employment, with race, sex, age and level of physical ability much less important in a global network environment. On the other hand, there is recognition of the possibility of exploitation through limiting the work available to that which requires only minimal literacy, keyboard and communication skills. Acknowledgement is also made of the possibility of severe disruption of the global telecommunications system through the action of so-called *techno-terrorists*, and of *electronic totalitarianism* being practised by countries that might hold a monopoly on information and communication technologies. There is no disputing the fact of electronic migration nor indeed of electronic crime. However, few writers are predicting that telecommuting will become the norm, rather that it offers potential benefits both to individuals and society. For present purposes it provides an interesting additional dimension to speculation on the wider social impact of the information and communication technologies.

OTHER HOME-BASED BUSINESS ACTIVITIES

Among the explanations for the slower than expected increase in home-based activity is the failure of such key elements of so-called *home informatics* as home banking and home shopping. Home banking has apparently foundered because it is not particularly useful, notably because it cannot be used for cash transactions, and that most customers do not conduct sufficient transactions to justify the cost. Home banking experiments in both Europe and the United States have failed to develop beyond their initial beginnings, with the most successful of such ventures being that of the Verbraucher Bank in Hamburg, Germany which with a total of 50,000 customers was apparently the most successful such service in the world. Hence, observed Forester, home banking would have to be seen as a flop.[35]

Home shopping has been judged to be an even bigger failure with a combination of complicated systems, limited choice and lack of social contact seemingly too offputting to woo customers for even such ambitious and expensive ventures as Viewtron in the United States, which lost $50 million dollars in its short three-year life span.[35] It is possible that, with current developments in both imaging techniques and in virtual reality, the attractions of home shopping will be enhanced to the point that it could reach the kind of critical mass necessary to make it a success. Moreover, recent agreements between Microsoft and several financial services companies, which would enable users to access home banking facilities by means of the Microsoft Money software package on their home computers, could lead to a radical change in the status of such activities. It could indeed lead to the convergence of computing and telecommunications services for the provision of a complete package of entertainment, information, communication and educational needs.[37]

THE NETWORKING OF SOCIETY

The Internet

Although emerging for use by individual organizations such as airlines   *123* and banks or by communities of researchers in various countries, large wide area networks have an immense potential for social impact. The impetus for such developments came from the United States with Arpanet, BITNET and CSNET, all intended originally for use by widely dispersed groups of researchers. These links grew on an international basis, with, for example, BITNET linking up to EARN, its European counterpart. Later national networks such as JANET in the United Kingdom and AARNet in Australia emerged to become, in effect, nodes in a worldwide network.

These activities have culminated in the Internet, an enterprise which dates back to 1969 and a network set up by the United States Department of Defense, and which now operates under the auspices of the US National Science Foundation. The Internet is, in fact, a *network of networks* connecting over 100,000 computers and millions of users around the world. While predominantly academic and research based, the Internet has an increasing proportion of commercial and industrial users. Take up of these facilities has been phenomenal and although use is free to the great majority of people who access the Internet, it is costing national authorities considerable sums of money both in operational terms and in terms of system development and upgrades. The volume of use is also causing problems, with near saturation approaching at peak times. The inevitability of a more commercial approach to management and operation of the Internet, almost certainly on some form of fee paying basis, has significant implications for millions of users.

In many ways, the Internet is the epitome of the social use of technology in information-based societies. An obvious example is the emergence of specialist discussion groups or *netgroups* which have proliferated on the Internet as forums for the open exchange of ideas and information, ranging from the frankly trivial to the serious, from *Star Trek* to the protection of the environment. A fascinating example was the interchange of ideas and information which took place on the Internet during the Gulf War of 1990–91, when researchers in several countries discussing the Scud missile crisis, could obtain first hand information from Israeli colleagues even as the missiles were falling on Tel Aviv. Another powerful illustration of the potential impact of the Internet lies in its implications for scholarly publishing, where rather than endure the delays of the traditional system, authors can simply post their contributions on a central electronic bulletin board, which readers could access either for abstracts or the full version of the paper. Indeed, Elsevier Science publishers have launched their *University Licensing Program* a three-year project which allows some 15 universities to access and download Elsevier research journals over the

Internet. This could truly cause a revolution in the publishing industry.

Apart from the cost of developing the infrastructure necessary to manage the system, there is growing concern over data security on the Internet. This issue has been highlighted to some extent by the growing interest being shown by commercial organizations in using the Internet. Its size, diversity and dynamic nature make the Internet a difficult environment in which to solve security and privacy problems, but these are being tackled nevertheless. The more interesting challenges are those which relate to the increased involvement of commercial organizations and the structural and funding implications which this would carry.

Information superhighways

Currently the most exciting mass technology project, and the one which promises to have the most profound impact upon society as a whole, is that for the National Information Infrastructure (NII) in the United States. An alliance between the Federal Government and a broad range of industries, the concept emerged as the brainchild of United States Vice President Al Gore. It has led to similar and complementary developments throughout the world. The information superhighway describes networks of optic fibre and coaxial cable linked by sophisticated switches that can deliver voice, data, image, text and video signals all in the same digital language. That is, everything from ordinary telephone conversations and faxes to broadband services such as access to databases, video phones, interactive television and 500 to 1,000 channels of pay-TV.

In the United States it has been proclaimed as the foundation for a national transformation to an information-based society, and a key element in national efforts to sustain leadership in the world economy. Government and industry are evolving a new model of competition which will enable telecommunications, cable television, computer hardware and software companies, and entertainment corporations to work together to create and operate information superhighways. To this end, the Cross Industry Working Team (XIWT) has been formed, an alliance of 28 companies including AT&T, Apple Computer, Citicorp, BellSouth, Digital, IBM and Hewlett Packard to foster technologies that can cross traditional industry boundaries and help create the NII. This involves common technological approaches, pilot projects and technology forums.[38]

In a separate initiative, Bellcore and a number of partners in the television, telephone and manufacturing industry are engaged in a *Collaboration on Information Infrastructure* to develop and demonstrate *125* prototype technologies for the NII, particularly prototype software that will enable the general public to navigate these networks. The ultimate promise of these activities is a vast range of electronic services including electronic shopping malls, collaborative electronic education and distance learning, electronic libraries, multimedia information and multimedia messaging, and interactive multimedia entertainment.[38]

In view of the newness of the project, there is still considerable uncertainty as to what exactly the information superhighway will entail. Oracle Corporation has described the project as having five basic components: content, storage, network, applications and consumer devices:

- *content*: information as text, still images, sound, video and so on;
- *storage*: vast 'information warehouses', in fact, powerful servers;
- *network*: web of networks including everything from twisted copper pairs, to fibre, broadcast and cellular plus satellite links;
- *application*: a range of application software to address content;
- *consumer devices*: a range of interfaces including PCs, personal digital assistants, interactive and conventional television, and cellular, traditional and smart telephones.

It is envisaged that the typical home or business in the United States will have several devices capable of connection to the information superhighway.[39]

The range of services available to domestic users will include:

- *entertainment*: with viewer control over programmes for 24 hours a day;
- *healthcare*: with information sharing and even diagnosis and treatment by means of interactive video link-up;
- *news*: with consumers able to point and click to select information for personally tailored new items;
- *retail sales*: with a 24 hours a day, virtual global mall accessed by two-way video and digitized salespeople.[39]

There is a need for standards and regulations, for *rules of the road* for the information superhighway to prevent exploitation and criminal abuse. Privacy will be an obvious problem area, given that every transaction will be recorded somewhere. So who is to access and manipulate these records and what kinds of use are they to make of them? This in turn raises fundamental questions as to who should draw up such rules and, critically, who will pay the start-up costs of the system. The Federal Government in the United States has opted for a system in which private enterprise builds and pays for the superhighway, with government ensuring that conditions are right for investment, largely through the deregulation of all forms of telecommunications. At the same time, Vice President Al Gore has declared that there will be no relaxation of existing restrictions without strong commitments and safeguards for a public right of way on the information highway.[39]

Not everybody is enamoured of the superhighway initiative and there are clearly going to be potential social costs in addition to the massive financial outlays required. In Australia, for example, potential inequities have been identified in the likelihood that carriers, seeking to recover the cost of installing modern networks from their customers, are likely to favour high-income and heavily populated areas to the detriment of poor and rural areas. This brings into sharp focus the central question of universal service in an information-intensive society.[40] At the moment, most people would simply have a telephone, but this is changing. Some residents in remote areas, where the postal service is irregular, would regard facsimile as an indispensable service, whereas hearing and speech-impaired people might prefer to use electronic mail. Moreover, personal computers are now essential for many tertiary and secondary level education courses and are important for linking to online libraries.[40]

In Australia consumer groups are already urging that the statutory definition of universal service be expanded from one that includes provision of a standard phone service on a reasonably accessible and equitable basis, to embrace universal affordability, universal technological standards and universal telecoms and participation in society.[40] However, the quest for universal access must also take into account the difficulties of encouraging commercial companies to provide this service, as well as those of finding ways of compensating firms for losses incurred in the attempt.[39] Although the Clinton Administration has vowed to tackle the potential social inequities that could accompany superhighway developments, promising to reduce regulation in return for free access to schools, libraries and hospitals, there continue to be those who doubt the effectiveness of such policies. Indeed, fears that the measures necessary to ensure this new vision of universal service could lead to a requirement to provide free video-on-demand and entertainment services to the poor and, in effect, would mean increased regulation, have led to calls for sweeping deregulation up to and including the repeal of the 1992 Cable Act in the United States.[41]

A wide range of interests must be accommodated. The owners of entertainment and information want new ways to deliver it. The owners of delivery conduits want to build bigger *pipes* and want to be free to send all kinds of content down them. Manufacturers and software developers want to put a new box in every living room and new kinds of software to run it. The US government wants to clear away the obstacles to all this and grow a vast new postindustrial industry on existing US commercial strengths in new technologies and entertainment media. However, while it is fine to seek to open up new markets by breaking down the legal impediments to competition, this does not address very serious issues of electronic era democracy and accountability.[42]

Some would see the information superhighway as the ultimate example of technological determinism and little more than a marketing effort on the part of those companies who will benefit from sales of equipment and services. Others fear for an essentially anti-communal impact, which all the time moves people away from direct face-to-face interaction, and erodes the concept of *public* and replaces it with the very different concept of a mass of people.[39] Among the more pointed criticisms of the Clinton Administration's approach to these problems, are those which would view the whole thrust towards competition in telecommunications as anathema to the public good in a mature democratic society. Such perceptions see the passage of information superhighway legislation as indicative of the worst elements of marketplace morality and tantamount to a massive transfer of wealth from the middle class to corporate centres of wealth, and a takeover of the information services industry by so-called Bell Operating Company monopolists.[43]

It is not necessary to accept this argument in its entirety to be concerned about a whole package of information highway related legislation currently moving through the Congress, and the wider implications for universal service and access to information. If, for example, the long distance telecommunications carriers are permitted to deliver services direct to large corporate users on private networks, thereby bypassing the local exchange network, universal service, which is funded largely on the basis of network access payments from long distance carriers to local network operators, would be in jeopardy. Likewise, the entry of the *Baby Bells* into such fields as information services and electronic publishing could have the undesirable effect of producing anticompetitive conglomerates which combine both the content and conduit dimensions.[43] Clearly there is much more to proposals for information superhighways than the potential provision of instant electronic access to a fortunate citizenry. It is still far too early to anticipate the outcome of such developments, but clearly the stage is being set for what is likely to be a long running drama.

THE SOCIAL IMPACT OF INFORMATION AND COMMUNICATION TECHNOLOGIES

Although it may on occasions have promised more than it has apparently been able to deliver, the promise of information and communications technology has by no means failed to materialize. If anything, it is in the social sphere and with regard to the impact of these technologies on the way of life, that the discrepancies between potential and performance have been most noticeable. Although considerable care must be taken with social forecasting, the excesses of which are in no small measure the root cause of current disillusionment with the contribution of technology to society, much can be gained from a study of current trends. Hence, the degree to which computers have penetrated daily life can truly be depicted as ubiquitous, and promising to mark a real turning point in the way we live, work and play.[44]

There is still no easy answer to the question of whether information and communication technologies will fit into existing social patterns or whether social behaviour will be modified to fit the technology. Allowing for differences between and within countries, it is forecast that the overall effect of this revolutionary technology will be to send a great wave of innovation flowing through modern societies during the early part of the 21st century. This is only a forecast, but if it is valid, then the eventual outcome should be not only a dramatic shift in the technological base of modern societies, but a dramatic social revolution as well.[44]

Certainly the promoters and supporters of the information superhighway are in no doubt as to its revolutionary potential for social change. United States Vice President Al Gore believes that the project will educate, promote democracy and save lives. The founder and Chief Executive Officer of Oracle Corporation, Larry Ellison, claims that it will alter life as we know it. According to Ellison, we will not just talk or shop on the information highway, but we will live in it.[39]

Those who would dismiss such comments out of hand would do well to ponder the implications of some of the activities of games groups on the Internet. The extent to which those involved in these pursuits appear to confuse, or at least interleave, reality and fantasy is perplexing in the least. One well-known case was that which occurred in the context of a game called LamdaMOO, in a magic-infested mansion that existed only in the form of words on the screen, but which to many of the players involved, appears to have become a real community. In this Multi-user Dimension or MUD over 1,500 players would assemble in the mansion, creating their own characters moving from room to room and interacting with each other acording to well-defined rules. The erstwhile peace of this imaginary environment was shattered last year when one of the residents of the house raped another. The subsequent outcry among the players, and demands for retribution from the victim, quickly reached the point where those involved seem to have had difficulty in separating the imaginary incident from the appalling real life crime that it reproduced in cyberspace.[45]

Julian Dibbell, who originally reported this story in New York's *Village Voice*, perceived a deeper significance to the incident. To Dibbell here was further evidence of the final stages of our passage into the information age, a paradigm shift that is likely to demolish the classic liberal firewall between word and deed. The act of typing commands into a computer results in more than mere communication, and in fact makes things happen through that conflation of speech and action that is the hallmark of computer-mediated worlds.[46] Whether or not one agrees with Dibbell or regards the influence of interactive media as anything other than harmless escapism, there are clear grounds for arguing that it will be in the social and human sphere that the impact of the information and communication technologies will be most profound.

NOTES AND REFERENCES

1. Carl B. Jackson (1992) The need for security. In: *Managing Information Technology*. Delran, NJ: Datapro, 6010, pp. 1–12.

2. Tom Forester and Perry Morrison (1990) Computer crime: new problem for the information society. *Prometheus*, **8**, (2), December, pp. 257–72.

3. Ira Hertzoff (1992) Voice network fraud. In: *Managing Information Technology*. Delran, NJ: Datapro, 1434, pp. 1–9.

4. Hugo Kelly (1988) Law aims to hunt computer hackers. *The Age*, Melbourne, 7th December.

5. John G. Burch (1992) Systems analysis, design and implementation. Boston: Boyd & Fraser, pp. 451–53.

6. Robert Schrifeen (1993) Freefone lines set off spate of 'data rape'. *Sunday Times*, 14th November, p. 11.

7. Information security news (1993) *Information Management & Computer Security*, **1**, (1), p. 9.

8. Richard H. Baker (1991) Physical security techniques. In: *Managing*

Information Technology, Delran, NJ: Datapro, 6030, pp.1–14.

9. Andrew S. Tannenbaum (1992) *Modern operating systems*. Englewood Wood Cliffs, NJ: Prentice Hall, pp. 184–86.

10. *Transnational Data & Communication Report* (1993) January–February, p. 30.

11. Willis H. Ware (1993) The new faces of privacy. *The Information Society*, **9**, pp. 195–210.

12. Anne W. Branscomb (1991) Common law for the electronic frontier. *Scientific American*, September, pp. 112–116.

13. Jerry L. Salvaggio (1989) Is privacy possible in an Information Society? In: *The information society: economic, social and structural issues*. Hillsdale, NJ: Lawrence Erlbaum Associates Inc., pp. 115–29.

14. Data Protection (1993) *Transnational Data & Communication Report*, **16**, (2), March–April, pp. 39–42.

15. Thad Dunning (1993) *Transnational Data & Communication Report*, **16**, (5), September–October, pp. 28–32.

16. Ian Temby (1993) Australia exposes illegal data sales. *Transnational Data & Communication Report*, **16**, (1), January–February, pp. 26–29.

17. Thad Dunning (1993) Data protection. *Transnational Data & Communication Report*, **16**, (5), March–April, pp. 39–42.

18. *Information Week* (1994) 22nd August, p. 20.

19. *New York Times* (1994) 18th August, C1.

20. Jay Bloombecker (1990) US Computer crime legislation: a review. *Managing Information Technology*, Delran, NJ: Datapro, 1430, pp. 1–28.

21. EC Data Protection (1993) (Special Report) *Transnational Data & Communication Report*, **15**, (6), November–December, p. 31.

22. Jan Barkvens and Marc Schauss (1992) New EC data protection era. *Transnational Data & Communication Report*, **15**, (6), November–December, pp. 43–45.

23. Simitis sees improvement in EC data protection revision (1992) *Transnational Data & Communication Report*, **15**, (5), November–December, p. 42.

24. Mitchell Kapor (1991) Civil liberties in cyberspace. *Scientific*

American, September, pp. 116–20.

25. Richard S. Rosenberg (1993) Free speech, pornography, sexual harassment and electronic networks. *The Information Society*, **9**, pp. 285–331.

26. Michael Prescott and Howard Foster (1994) Police get new powers to fight computer porn. *Sunday Times*, July.

27. Stephen Amidon (1994) Lost in cyberspace. *Sunday Times*, *Culture*, 17th July, pp. 9–11.

28. *Toronto Financial Post* (1994) 23rd August, p. 6 (taken from the Internet).

29. Rob Kling and Charles Dunlop (1993) Controversies about computerization and the character of white collar worklife. *The Information Society*, **9**, pp. 1–29.

30. Herbert Applebaum (1992) Work and its future. *Futures*, **24**, (4), May, pp. 36–50.

31. F.W. Newton (1993) Australia's information landscapes. *Prometheus*, **11**, (1), June, pp. 3–39.

32. Penelope Schoeffel, Alison Loveridge and Carl Davidson (1993) Telework: issues for New Zealand. *Prometheus*, **11**, (1), June, pp. 49–60.

33. Philip Sim (1994) Telecommuting, still a long way off. *Computerworld*, April, p. 29.

34. Ben Mitchell (1994) Workforce of the future stays home. *The Sunday Age*, Melbourne, 20th February, p. 18.

35. Tom Forester (1991) The electronic cottage revisited: towards the flexible workstyle. *Urban Futures*, **2**, (1), (Special Issue, 5) pp. 27–33.

36. Virgil L.P. Blake and Thomas T. Suprenant (1990) Electronic immigrants in the information age: some policy considerations. *The Information Society*, **7**, pp. 233–44.

37. Geoff Wheelright (1993) Homing in on a new market: Microsoft plans for PCs in the home. *Financial Times*, 21st December, p. 8.

38. Louise Kehoe (1993) US moves one step nearer the 'information highway'. *Financial Times*, 14th December, p. 26.

39. Adam Lincoln (1994) Dawn of a new information age? *Managing Information Systems*, **3**, (3), April, pp. 70–73.

40. Ben Potter (1994) Waiting for directions on the technological superhighway. *The Age*, Melbourne, 11th February, p. 14.

41. *Wall Street Journal* (1994) 17th August, A12.

42. McKenzie Wark (1994) *The Australian*, Melbourne, 16th May, p. 26.

43. Vigdor Schreibman (1994) Closing the 'values gap': the crisis point. *Federal Information News Syndicate*, **11**, (18), 29th August (taken from the Internet).

44. Halal, William E. (1993) The information technology revolution: computer hardware, software and services into the 21st century. *Technological Forecasting and Social Change*, **44**, pp. 69–86.

45. Julian Dibbell (1994) Data rape: a tale of torture and terrorism online. *Good Weekend, the Age Magazine*, Melbourne, 9th February, pp. 26–32.

46. Stephen Amidon (1994) Lost in cyberspace. *Sunday Times, Arts & Culture*, 17th July, pp. 8–10.

7   The Information-based Industries

Of all the topics covered in this book, few present more of a challenge than the one covered in this chapter. The problem is essentially one of perception and of the role and place of these industries within the economy. In this chapter the focus will be upon a range of *information-based* goods and services activities which have a high value-added content and increasingly are taking on the characteristics of *knowledge* industries. This includes the computer hardware and software industries, telecommunications equipment and services, and a range of information content businesses spanning a spectrum from media to consultancy services. Given the scale of information-based activity and the sheer pace of change, treatment will be selective and not all of these areas are covered in the same detail. The main objective will be to place the information-based industries within the broader context of information-based economies and societies, and to provide an overview of what has been lucidly described as a mosaic of different, albeit complementary products and services.[1]

GLOBALIZATION AND CONVERGENCE

The truly global nature of business today is nowhere more apparent than in the case of these information-based industries. This not only means that companies are compelled to think in terms of economies of scope as well as of scale, but to enter into alliances at home and abroad in order to achieve these. As a result, it can be hard to determine where the activities of one company begin and those of another take over, with the phenomena of outsourcing and global reach everywhere in evidence. Where not long ago it was common to talk in terms of national champions, of for example, British or American computer companies, it is difficult to categorize global industry in this fashion. A more accurate description would be that offered by Robert Reich to explain the activities of those American corporations which, in effect, have disconnected themselves from the United States, emerging as *global webs* within which much of the value they produce comes from other places.[2]

Convergence is the outcome of a complex interplay between such factors as advances in the information and communications technologies, the liberalization and deregulation of trade and capital markets, and the development of global competition. It has led to the blurring of boundaries both within and between industries, for example between computer hardware and software industries, between computing and telecommunications and between communications and broadcasting. It has also led to a restructuring of markets and organizations and of the business strategies of the companies competing in those markets.

MAJOR DEVELOPMENTS IN THE COMPUTER INDUSTRY

Today there is a worldwide market of about $15 billion for equipment to make chips for computers. Manufacturers use this equipment to make $50 billion worth of chips, which go into $700 billion worth of computers. If one then adds vast sums spent on software for computers and the numbers of individuals who work with computers, it is clear that the computer industry is well over a trillion dollar industry.[3] Table 1 gives an indication of the state of the United States market for large scale systems at the end of 1993.

Nevertheless, in recent years the industry as a whole has experienced sluggish sales and declining employment, prices and profitability. Mainframe manufacturers in particular have experienced pressure on their margins as users have adopted open systems, workstations and networked personal computers as a low cost alternative to expensive proprietary brand mainframe computers. Hence during 1992 to 1993, IBM's mainframe revenue fell by 47 per cent, with total mainframe sales of $4.3 billion. Another major mainframe manufacturer, Amdahl, had a similar experience, with a 42 per cent fall in sales and revenue losses of $580 million. In software, changes in the multi-user segment of the computer market are affecting the market shares of the various operating systems. UNIX and Windows NT are expected to grow strongly, while other operating systems are expected either to decline or experience zero growth in market share. While the cost of manufacturing packaged

Table 1
The Top 10 in large-scale systems, 1993

(Revenue in $millions)

Rank	Company	1993	1992	Change (%)	Market share (%)
1	IBM	4,318.0	8,190.0	−47	53
2	Unisys	1,648.4	1,966.0	−16	20
3	Amdahl	857.0	1,489.6	−42	11
4	Cray	651.6	550.5	18	8
5	AT&T	145.0	142.7	2	2
6	Intel	92.2	60.0	54	1
7	Hewlett Packard	83.6	75.0	11	1
8	Digital	55.0	50.0	10.0	1
9	Control Data	37.0	108.0	−66	0
10	Pyramid	11.5	N/A	N/A	0

Source: *Datamation*, June 15th 1994.

software is low and falling with quantity, the cost of developing new software is high, as software tends to become more complex with each new edition. The economics of the software industry is similar to that of the music and publishing industries. Software developers are becoming software publishers and leaving the manufacturing, marketing and distribution of software to other firms.[4] Table 2 shows the top 10 software companies in the United States at the end of 1993.

Perhaps nothing illustrates both the volatility of the computer industry and the unforgiving nature of markets than the fate of IBM. In 1989, IBM accounted for nearly one quarter of the revenue of the top 100 computer manufacturers. It was the market leader in every country except the former Soviet Union and Japan, and was eight to ten times the size of its nearest rivals.[5] Four short years later, IBM posted a loss for the final quarter of 1992 of $5.46 billion, the highest ever in United States corporate history.

While resisting calls for the breakup of the company, the new Chairman of IBM, Lou Gerstner, saw the need for *rightsizing* IBM to restore the company to profitability. He called for a series of very tough-minded strategies that would deliver performance in the marketplace. The company's primary problem was its cost structure. It was selling about $65 billion worth of products a year, but at the end of the day it was not making a profit. In a bid to restore the company to competitiveness, Gerstner identified microelectronics and multimedia *137*

Table 2
The Top 10 in software, 1993

(Revenue in $ millions)

Rank	Company	1993	1992	Change (%)	Market share (%)
1	IBM	10,953.0	11,365.9	−4	36
2	Microsoft	3,740.0	2,960.2	26	12
3	Computer Associates	2,054.8	1,770.8	16	7
4	Oracle	1,337.5	1,033.0	29	4
5	Novell	1,033.0	933.0	11	3
6	Digital	955.0	800.0	19	3
7	Lotus	883.0	810.1	9	3
8	Unisys	779.9	712.0	10	3
9	WordPerfect	707.0	579.0	22	2
10	Hewlett Packard	499.2	413.0	21	2

Source: *Datamation*, June 15th 1994.

computing as two key areas, while confirming that IBM would not hesitate to withdraw from segments of the computer market in which it was not either a technology leader or making profits.[6] In fact, the company had already to some extent demonstrated this resolve by deciding not to promote the Power PC microprocessor as the standard for its range of products, but instead to wait and see what the market wanted. That this decision in effect entailed a change of strategy was not lost on industry watchers, who then began to speculate as to the future of the Power PC.[7]

In its struggle for competitiveness IBM has had to abandon its traditional employment practices and go for large scale redundancies. It has also had to cut expenditure on research and development and recognize that its future as a company is not necessarily tied to the manufacture of mainframe computers. Nor is it alone in this regard. With losses for the fourth year in succession in 1993, net losses which for that year alone amounted to $2.2 billion, Digital Equipment Corporation was similarly forced into major restructuring, large scale redundancies and reductions of 10 million square feet of manufacturing and office space. In May 1994, the company introduced a new strategy based on a shift towards the production of low-cost, high-volume machines rather than their traditional high end systems. The intention was to reduce unacceptably high overhead costs while halting a decline in revenues, as customers moved away to cheaper, industry standard systems.[8] The basic problem for Digital is that having started its downsizing efforts somewhat late in the day, it must perform a difficult balancing act between reducing costs while maintaining product quality.

Unlike its major rival, IBM, Apple finished 1992 on a high note, with its share price almost doubling in the second half of the year and sales of the Powerbook computer alone reaching over $1 billion. One of the factors behind this was a change of strategy, which saw Apple go from being a middle-of-the-range manufacturer of desktop computers to a company with a proliferation of brands right across the market, including Powerbook Duos – portables sold with adaptors that turn them into desktops – colour screen versions of older models and additions to a range of high-powered, high profit margin machines, the Quadras. There were however, problems of meeting demand in these new markets and even more serious, the challenge from Microsoft Windows on the software front.[9]

Apple owes much of its success to the attractions of its software. However, by 1993, profit margins on personal computer sales had declined so much that John Sculley was replaced as Chief Executive by Michael Spindler. New business thrusts were identified in *enterprise computing*, with the launch of its first servers for use in corporate networks, and in a new range of pocket computers that would help people organize their daily affairs and send messages. The company, nevertheless, had to be mindful of the over-expectations generated by John Sculley's promotion of the Apple Newton, with perhaps 100,000 machines being sold rather than the millions apparently expected, and the cancellation of a similar project by Intel and delays to others being mounted by IBM and Compaq. Apple also had to keep sight of the fact that, for the foreseeable future, its core business would remain the Macintosh.[11]

The personal computer market is now divided into high end machines, broadly defined by IBM's PS/2 range, and lower priced value for money machines from less well-known companies. It is also maturing into a commodity business, with greatly reduced margins, and product cycles reduced from two to three years in the 1980s, to six to 18 months in recent years. Some have forecast that by the mid-1990s, there will only be three dominant global players in the personal computer market.[11]

The computer industry today is faced with the growing power of users, people who have been liberated from the dominance of established proprietary brands by open systems, leading to falling hardware prices, increased software portability and systems integration. Client/server computing is another major influence for systems integration and one setting the scene for a major shift in the balance of power within the computer industry. Although IBM would be seeking to become a dominant player in these markets, it will have to fight hard to succeed. It has clearly signalled its intentions with the introduction in mid-1994 of its Openedition software which, with its UNIX-like characteristics, will enable MVS-based mainframe computers to operate as multifaceted network servers capable of working with any number of distributed platforms using the Open Software Foundations Distributed Computing Environment technologies.[12] The ultimate key to success will probably lie in the ability of companies to develop architectures that can become industry standards, in the way the MS-DOS and Windows have in the past.

Intel and Microsoft are currently well-placed to pursue this goal of market-domination. Intel is the world's largest semiconductor company and, with gross profit margins of around 60 per cent, is estimated to be doubling in size every two years. A number of personal computer makers including IBM, Compaq and Hewlett Packard have already announced products based on the latest Intel Pentium chip, the successor to the 486. Microsoft is the world's largest personal computer company. It has developed a broad range of products but most noticeably MS-DOS and Windows, the most broadly used operating system in the PC world. The latest such offering is Windows NT, an operating system designed for client/server systems, making it possible for users to work on several programs simultaneously and for several users to share the same computer.

A successor to Windows NT, known as Chicago, is on the way and clearly comes with a considerable pedigree. In the meantime, in the field of networking software for personal computers, Novell is well on the way to setting the standard, while Lotus Development Corporation is setting the pace in groupware with its Lotus Notes. Without doubt, however, the big prizes lie in multimedia and it may well be that those companies who control the design of multimedia systems will be the IBMs of tomorrow's data processing industry. In the meantime, however, it is worth remembering that IBM has slimmed down and has repositioned itself for today's client/server market. As Tables 1 to 5 illustrate, IBM is still far and away the top information technology producer in the world.

Multimedia is quite obviously a crucial element within the fast-developing computing industry, and will be considered further below. In the meantime, it is important to emphasize the diversification that is taking place within an industry which is characterized by very short product life cycles and relentless pressure for sales – an industry which for all practical purposes has been commoditized. As Beaumont and Sutherland point out, the capacity of rivals to spoil, copy, reverse engineer or clone products has forced companies to go worldwide as soon as practicable, by joint venture, licensing or serving as original equipment manufacturers to other companies who then resell the products under their own names in a process known as *rebadging*.[13]

Under the inexorable pressure of the need to increase sales and boost market shares, companies which formerly specialized in hardware or software production are diversifying into consultancy and facilities management. Unisys, for example, now regards itself as an impartial adviser to its customers, in direct competition with consultancy firms. In seeking to add value to their products by moving into consultancy, computer companies are competing in markets for systems integration and support, business process reengineering, business systems strategy formulation, recruitment and project management.[13]

With facilities management or outsourcing, specialist providers take over the management of information technology facilities, including that of older mainframe or *legacy systems,* leaving the client free to concentrate upon core business. This is a field in which the American company Electronic Data Systems has become very prominent, treating IT centres as potential profit centres and taking a proportion of savings or profits from the newly-managed operation as its payment.[14] Table 3 shows the top 10 maintenance companies in the United States at the end of 1993. This diversification is part of a major economic transformation which is seeing even closer convergence between the computer and the telecommunications industries. One major manifestation of this convergence is networking, with inter- and intra-company communication exploding on all manner of networks from LANs to the Internet. Hence, according to the Chief Executive Officer of AT&T, his company is fundamentally a networking company, bringing people, information and services together. AT&T's large customers want all their computer capacity integrated into networks so they can get real time information from their customers and then make faster, better-informed operating decisions. Here is another explanation for the rapid growth of such computer consulting giants as EDS and Andersen Computing, and for the repositioning of IBM as a solutions company.[15] Indeed, the computer services sector is expected to offer the best opportunities for two particular types of companies, large global players on the one hand, and small niche players on the other. Medium sized firms are seen to be operating at a disadvantage because the cost of providing computer services generally grows with the size of a project, and economies of scale tend to accrue only when a project becomes very large.[16] The top 10 computer services companies in the United States at the end of 1993 are shown in Table 4.

Table 3
The Top 10 maintenance, 1993

(Revenue in $millions)

Rank	Company	1993	1992	Change (%)	Market share (%)
1	IBM	7,295.0	7,610.0	−4	33
2	Digital	4,568.0	4,421.5	3	20
3	Hewlett Packard	2,932.0	2,800.0	5	13
4	AT&T	1,743.0	1,712.4	2	8
5	Unisys	1,444.0	1,686.0	−14	6
6	Bell Atlantic	634.2	620.0	2	3
7	Sun Micro-systems	539.0	470.0	15	2
8	Amdahl	474.0	N/A	N/A	2
9	Memorex Telex	356.3	394.0	−10	2
10	Tandem	303.5	310.0	−2	1

Source: *Datamation*, June 15th 1994.

Table 4
The Top 10 computer services companies, 1993

(Revenue in $millions)

Rank	Company	1993	1992	Change (%)	Market share (%)
1	IBM	9,711.0	7,352.0	32	21
2	EDS	8,507.3	8,155.2	4	18
3	Andersen Consulting	2,588.7	2,445.0	6	5
4	CSC	2,502.0	2,474.4	1	5
5	ADP	2,339.2	2,075.0	13	5
6	TRW	1,900.0	1,800.0	6	4
7	Digital	1,875.0	1,570.3	19	4
8	Unisys	1,593.1	1,336.0	19	3
9	First Data	1,500.0	1,205.0	24	3
10	AT&T	1,235.0	1,198.7	3	3

Source: *Datamation*, June 15th 1994.

MAJOR DEVELOPMENTS IN THE TELECOMMUNICATIONS INDUSTRY

Telecommunications is the fastest growing of the world's largest industries. In 1992, the market for international telecommunications traffic grew by around 13 per cent, or at about ten times the growth of global Gross Domestic Product over the same period. Along with growth, the watchwords of international telecommunications today are competition and privatization.[17] Competition and privatization go hand in hand, with something like 20 privatizations of national public telecommunications operations predicted to take place in the next two or three years. This is resulting in competition in domestic as well as in international markets, in mobile and data communications and increasingly, in voice telephony.[17] Despite the worldwide trend towards privatization and liberalization, however, the telecommunications industry is still widely subject to regulation of one kind or another.

These developments represent a radical shift from the days when telecommunications was viewed as a natural monopoly, and one that was frequently operated under state control. Advances in information and communication technologies, an enormous and continuing demand for information services in business and industry, a changing political climate around the world and the deregulation of telecommunications markets, have all combined to challenge the monopoly position. As a result, in the United States, Japan and the United Kingdom, the volume of international telecommunications traffic added by new carriers in 1992 was, for the first time, greater than the volume of traffic added by the main established carriers. In the United States, MCI added more traffic than AT&T; in the United Kingdom, Mercury added more than British Telecom; while IDC and ITK together added more traffic than KDD in Japan.[17] The disappearance of monopolies is also evident in the dismantling of traditional relationships between local equipment suppliers and the national public telecommunications administrations. This has been accompanied by wholesale rationalization of the telecommunications equipment industry, leaving only a handful of global players.[18] Table 5 shows the top 10 companies in data communications in the United States.

It is clear that no country today can sustain economic growth without a modern telecommunications infrastructure. In the developed world, where telephones are easily available and affordable, the emphasis is on competition, commercial efficiency, new networks, particularly for cellular mobile services, and the introduction of value-added products and services. In the emerging world, the emphasis is on fixed line growth and the provision of advanced services in major cities in order to retain and attract inward investors.[19] At the forefront of development are plans for networks of personal communications services (PCS), which are ultimately expected to be a multi-billion dollar business, and for multimedia, the prospect of which has been said to cause more excitement than any other subject in today's telecommunications industry.[17]

A major outcome of these and related changes has been the

143

Table 5
The Top 10 in data communications, 1993

(Revenue in $millions)					
Rank	**Company**	**1993**	**1992**	**Change (%)**	**Market share (%)**
1	AT&T	2,600.0	2,470.0	5	19
2	Northern Telecom	2,250.0	2,100.0	7	16
3	IBM	2,200.0	2,200.0	0	23
4	Cisco	928.0	473.2	96	7
5	Motorola	820.0	745.0	10	6
6	Hewlett Packard	780.0	630.0	24	6
7	SynOptics	704.5	388.8	81	5
8	3Com	696.0	502.2	39	5
9	Cabletron	539.6	363.1	49	4
10	Digital	340.0	250.0	36	2

Source: *Datamation*, June 15th 1994.

establishment of a series of alliances throughout the information-based industries, alliances between companies which were formerly competitors. This does not mean that these organizations have ceased to be rivals, rather that there are strategic opportunities for both parties in these arrangements, which in any case are clearly subject to further change in the future.

ALLIANCES IN THE COMPUTER INDUSTRY

Among significant alliances within the computer industry is that of Apple with IBM. Joint ventures include work on the Power PC microprocessor and on the Taligent software project, aiming to produce software that would be particularly effective for screen graphics. Although a certain amount of uncertainty still surrounds the future of the Power PC project following IBM's announcement that it is postponing release of its Power PC computers until the first half of 1995, the fact that Apple is expected, for the first time, to license its Macintosh software to other personal computer manufacturers is interpreted in some industry circles as further evidence of collaboration with IBM. Although at the time of writing, IBM is just one of several potential partners, others named include Fujitsu and Olivetti, this would seem a logical development given the existing co-operation between IBM and Apple, and the former's acknowledged shortage of applications software for the Power PC.[20] Meanwhile, Apple has also been co-operating with Motorola on the production of a more efficient kind of microchip using RISC technology.

In another recent ground-breaking development, Microsoft has chosen ICL to service its products and customers across Europe. This is the first pan-European deal Microsoft has signed under a new strategy of concentrating on software development, while seeking business partners to service and support large customers. Service and support includes maintenance systems, integration, consultancy and training. This looks like a good deal for both companies. For ICL, it offers a further opportunity to diversify into software and services as a defence against shrinking profit margins in the hardware market. To Microsoft, it supplies partners better equipped than themselves to support customers using their new and complex Windows NT operating software.[21]

Similarly, as they shift the focus to high value-added products, Japanese companies are increasingly looking for alliances and OEM deals with overseas companies to supply them with those products that are less profitable for them to produce, but which they still need to complement their product line-up. Hence, Fujitsu has an arrangement with Siemens Nixdorf whereby it obtains low end mainframe computer technology from Siemens in return for supplying the German company with higher end machines.[22]

An alliance which has recently run into trouble is that between Intel and Compaq, who in the past have collaborated in bringing personal computers to the marketplace. The cause of the problem is an $80 million advertising campaign mounted by Intel and aimed at promoting sales of their Pentium chip. Compaq objected on the grounds that, by acting unilaterally to promote its own brand name chips and circuit boards, Intel was threatening to undermine Compaq's business by boosting the sales of competitors' machines. Moreover, by seeking to influence customers directly, it was claimed, Intel was acting improperly for a component distributor.[23]

This case provides a useful illustration of the potential complexity of these alliances, and not least of the way in which the interests of the respective partners can diverge. Compaq was displeased because, from its perspective, an arrangement which was to have been of mutual benefit to both parties, looked set to begin to work against its own interests as a company. Intel on the other hand, was mindful of the threat to its market share posed by potential clone makers such as Advanced Micro Devices and Nextgen. To add to the confusion, Compaq was already employing AMD microprocessors in its latest machines, while Compaq had a minority stake in Nextgen. Furthermore, Nextgen and Cyrix, another smaller chip company, had contracted with IBM to make microprocessor clones which could compete with the Pentium.[23]   *145*

Intel has threatened to retaliate through the manufacture of even more powerful chips. This is a course of action which in view of the company's technical strength and market power, neither Compaq nor any other adversary could afford to take lightly. Perhaps even more pointed is the message that in order for the full benefits of multimedia computing to be realized, computers will need to incorporate the capabilities provided by the Pentium chip. For Compaq this message is reinforced by the fact that Pentium-based PCs from less well known manufacturers usually cost only about $500 more than Compaq's multimedia machines. However, this is a dispute with much wider implications than are raised by the interests of the two protagonists, because, as the technology grows more complex, such alliances are going to become increasingly necessary.[23]

ALLIANCES IN THE TELECOMMUNICATIONS INDUSTRY

To exploit emerging markets and defend market share, telecommunications alliances are being forged all over the world. Typically these global alliances involve partners from different countries and often from different continents. Among recent alliances is one involving France Telecom and Deutsche Telekom, who have joined forces to counter the efforts of rival alliances such as that between British Telecom and MCI. The core of the Franco-German alliance will be a European backbone offering enhanced telecommunications services to multinational companies, including private networks that cross borders. This could be not just a European, but a global giant, with Deutsche Telekom and France Telecom respectively, the world's second and third largest carriers of international telecoms traffic. In 1992, their combined traffic base was marginally behind that of AT&T and more than three times that of British Telecom, which ranks fourth. Although there are doubts as to the level of current demand for such services among multinational corporations, there is ample scope for market expansion as the new alliances succeed in developing and customizing advanced services over their dedicated networks.[24]

Another impressive alliance, this time on a transatlantic basis, is that which has seen British Telecom take a 20 per cent stake in MCI, the second largest telecommunications carrier in the United States. Even for a company the size of British Telecom, this was an extremely costly investment, amounting to around four years of uncommitted cash flow, or more than the total projected capital expenditure of Cable & Wireless (British Telecom's main United Kingdom competitor through its Mercury subsidiary) on all projects, at home and abroad, for the next three years.[25] Nevertheless to British Telecom, which also is targeting the outsourcing requirements of multinational corporations, some 40 per cent of which are based in the United States, the investment was justified in terms of establishing a credible presence in that country. Moreover, like its Franco-German rivals, British Telecom is faced with the threat of increased competition at home in local, long-distance and mobile markets. Faced with the prospect of falling market share at home, the company is determined to seek compensation abroad.[25]

Moreover, the actions of other leading international operators would seem to validate the notion of *global stride*. In May 1993, AT&T launched Worldsource, a partnership with five Asia–Pacific carriers, to be extended to Europe in 1994. The strategy was the same, to capture markets in global outsourcing. Moreover, in answer to the sceptics who would question the demand for such services, AT&T estimates that in addition to the 2,000 to 3,000 multinational corporations who are potential customers, there are some 35,000 smaller transnational corporations with over 150,000 subsidiaries who, having far less telecommunications expertise, could find single-supplier packages attractive.[25]

AT&T has, in fact, gone further down the road by entering into alliance not just with other telecommunications companies, but with computing and data services firms. In 1989 it bought Istel, the United Kingdom IT services company, then in 1991 it acquired NCT, then the fifth largest computing group in the United States. Attempts by British Telecom to strike a similar deal with Electronic Data Systems in the United States have so far failed to bring fruit. Nevertheless, its current American partner MCI, is recognized as having its own ambitions for further alliances in data transmission and multimedia.[25]

Indeed, in the United States, the trend is towards multimedia alliances between telecommunications operators and entertainment, cable and computing companies. In the past few months alone, there have been deals between US West and Time Warner, Bell Atlantic and TCI, and Southwestern Bell and Cox Enterprises. In the United States, 10 years after the breakup of AT&T, the regulatory regime is coming apart as the country braces itself for a new world of multimedia, interactive communications. The sector is facing a period of extremely fast change, technologically and structurally, which will produce both big winners and losers.[22]

Technological change is starting to render the barriers created by the Greene decision obsolete, for example barring the Baby Bells from the long-distance market and from equipment manufacture and the provision of information services. In particular, the ability to translate video, audio and data into digital form and then transmit it along fibre optic lines is blurring the distinction between the telecommunications, *147* computer and media businesses.[22] As a result, the local monopolies previously enjoyed by the Baby Bells are under pressure from a number of sources, including the so-called Competitive Access Providers (CAPs) which having gained the right to interconnect their networks to those of the local telephone companies, operate highly efficient fibre optic networks in metropolitan areas and cream off bulk traffic from business customers. They also face competition from long-distance companies who are now competing in the medium-distance market, and from a growing number of cellular providers who can offer an alternative to the Bell companies' wired networks.[22]

However, the regional Bell operating companies are themselves among the most important players in the cellular market, since each of them was granted one of two cellular licences in their service areas when these were handed out in the early 1980s. However, they face competition from independents, which is likely to grow stronger following AT&Ts deal with McCaw Cellular. This deal really worries the Baby Bells, as they fear it will eventually enable AT&T to bypass their lines, thus stripping them of part of their huge access fees. They complain that it represents AT&T's return to the local service market, and are themselves redoubling their long-standing efforts for access to the long-distance market.[22]

Ironically, these efforts seemed to have succeeded in mid-1994 when the United States Senate's Commerce Committee reached agreement on a draft telecommunications reform bill, which contained a timetable and conditions for entry of the Baby Bells to the long distance and cable television markets. However, the draft bill foundered owing to opposition from the Bell Operating companies, who were still dissatisfied with the provisions of the proposed legislation.[26]

Nevertheless, the Baby Bells have already managed to circumvent some of the restrictions imposed by the Greene decision. In 1991 they managed to get a relaxation of the ban which prevented them from entering the information services industry. This prepared the way for Southwestern Bell, serving Texas and neighbouring states, to make the telephone industry's first big investment in the cable television industry when, in February 1992, it bought two cable systems in Washington DC for $650 million. This was followed by a $2.5 billion investment by US West (which serves the Rocky Mountain states and Pacific Northwest) in the cable entertainment operations of Time Warner, the second largest cable operator in the US and a leading producer of filmed entertainment. Not to be outdone, the cable companies are keen to gain a share of the local telecommunications business. Many of the Competitive Access Providers are owned by cable companies, some of which are also developing plans to enter the

148

exciting field of radio-based personal communications systems (PCS), which is expected to begin operating in the US over the next two to three years.[22]

Not surprisingly in an increasingly global economy, multimedia alliances also span the globe. These include those of the Apple Corporation which has entered into alliances with the Japanese consumer electronics companies Hitachi and Sharp and with Siemens of Germany; of AT&T with Matsushita of Japan and Olivetti of Italy; and of Ericcson of Sweden with Intel and Hewlett Packard of the United States. Moreover, in response to falling sales in their domestic market, as well as tapping into the creativity of the American multimedia industry, Japanese consumer electronics are investing widely in United States companies, ranging from large film studios to small venture companies. Hence, Matsushita not only owns MCA, the entertainment group, but has a stake in a small, emerging company called 300 which is developing advanced multimedia products.[22] The attractions of such ventures have been highlighted in the Frost & Sullivan report which predicts that by the year 2000 the market will have quadrupled to a level of over $20 billion in the United States alone, driven by applications in infotainment, education and publishing.[27]

MAJOR DEVELOPMENTS IN THE ELECTRONIC INFORMATION SERVICES INDUSTRY

Although remote access to electronic databases has formed the basis of an international information services industry for several decades, the increasing globalization of the electronic domain carries major implications for those currently engaged in the industry. Hitherto, it has been largely a matter of database hosts and providers, of the increasing range and sophistication of information services available – in full text and multimedia formats, and of the likely impact of CD-ROM on online provision, or of the end user on the intermediary. Today, the source of concern is the threat of global competition not just from traditional players within the electronic information services industry, but from sources emanating from cyberspace.

Current work on intelligent filters, which can program a computer to check files for relevant keywords, and the availability of tools such as Mosaic which can directly locate material on the Internet, carry profound implications for the providers of online information services. The most obvious conclusion is that already there has been a considerable blurring of the boundaries between online information services and those available on the Internet. This message has not been lost on companies such as America Online, Prodigy and CompuServe, *149* who are not only seeking to become major points of access to the Internet, but also to develop a range of more sophisticated value-added online products.[28]

Trends in the database industry

At one level the trends in the database industry are extremely positive with growth on all fronts – numbers of databases in the world, numbers of producers and, albeit at a slower rate, the numbers of vendors. Some indication of the scale and pace of this growth can be gained from Tables 5 and 6.

The figures in Table 7 are based on estimates and refer only to the use of word-oriented databases from major United States vendors. Although the number of word-oriented databases continues to grow, and noticeably so in the case of full-text and directory-type databases, there has been considerable expansion in the production of newer database products. Hence, the number of image/video databases has quadrupled since 1990 alone, while those of audio databases increased by almost 150 per cent between 1988 and 1993. Software databases are

Table 6
World database growth: selected dates, 1979–1994

Year	Number of databases	Number of producers	Number of online services
1979	300	221	59
1980	411	269	71
1981	641	411	135
1982	919	612	189
1983	1,360	820	244
1984	1,807	1,069	327
1985			
1986	2,369	1,379	454
1987	2,823	1,568	528
1988	3,135	1,685	555
1989	3,535	1,813	610
1990	3,943	1,950	645
1991	4,332	2,120	718
1992	4,447	2,033	772
1993	5,569	2,221	824
1994	5,569	2,232	822

Source: *Gale Directory of Databases*, 1994.

Table 7
World database usage: selected dates, 1975– 1992

Year	Searches (million/year)
1975	1
1980	5
1985	15
1990	34.5
1991	14.4
1992	51.78

Source: *Gale Directory of Databases*, 1994.

also a feature, growing from a figure of five to 57 between 1988 and 1992, and falling back to 38 in 1993.[29] A key feature of industry development in recent years has been that of the growth of the *portable* sector of the database market, as illustrated in Table 8.

The advent of portable databases sparked off a debate on whether or not CD-ROM posed a serious threat to the market for online information services. Although the debate continues in certain quarters, there is an emerging consensus that some measure of *peaceful coexistence* can obtain between online and offline vendors. More significant in the long run are likely to be demands for simpler means of searching online databases and a trend away from traditional charging mechanisms based on connect time and offline printing costs. Faster telecommunications systems have reduced the time that users have to spend online and, in response to such developments, vendors are employing a variety of charging methods, including charging users more for access at higher baud rates, charging for commands issued or for computer resources used.[30]

These trends were predicted in 1990 by the Link Resources

Table 8
Growth of the *portable* database industry, 1990–1994

Year	Number of CD-ROM products	Number of diskette products	Number of magnetic products
1990	409	66	108
1991	737	418	350
1992	934	545	430
1993	1,278	659	572
1994 (current)	1,779	850	607

Source: *Gale Directory of Databases*, 1994.

Corporation in the United States. It was forecast that by 1994 the North American market for electronic information would have grown to something of the order of $8.6 billion, with the big earners being financial information, travel reservation systems, marketing and credit information. For Europe by the same date, the electronic information market was predicted to have grown to a level of $5.8 billion, of which financial services were expected to gross perhaps $4.76 million.[31] Moreover, even in 1990, the customers of electronic information services in North America were overwhelmingly end users. Whereas librarians and information specialists were powerful resource users and leaders, they purchased less than 7 per cent of information services and rarely, if ever, used the more specialized services such as consumer and business credit, legal, real estate and other services that were built for and used by industry professionals. Finally, the CD-ROM market in the United States was expected to grow from $352.1 million in 1988 to $2.881 billion in 1994.[31] The accuracy of the forecast is much less important than the continuing strength of the trends upon which they were based. This is nowhere more apparent than in the rise of multimedia.

Trends in the multimedia industry

In its current incarnation, interactive multimedia is largely comprised of CD-ROM discs that are played on personal computers with colour screens, sound cards, hard disk and CD-ROM drives. It also tends to be a term which is used extremely loosely, with the majority of currently available titles not truly interactive. However, interactive multimedia is fast becoming network-based, using global networks that link computer with computer and, thus, user with user. More importantly, these products define both the *content* and the *context* in which the user can find, manipulate and interpret informative, educational and entertaining material.[32]

CD-ROM is set to remain the dominant distribution medium for interactive multimedia content for perhaps up to ten years. Displayed to users via computer screens and graphical user interfaces, it has penetrated both the corporate networks and the consumer market. Indeed, all interactive multimedia segments are now, or are rapidly becoming *consumer-centred*. Already, suppliers whose business depends on customized interactive products for professional markets, face the threat of competition from new mass market interactive tools that are both easy to use and competitively priced. The global CD-ROM player installed base is forecast to quadruple to 45 million units over the period from 1994 to 1996.[32]

Table 9
Selected global players in CD-ROM-based multimedia, 1994

Product	Company
Software	Microsoft; IBM; Applesoft; CSC
Recorded music	Warner Chappell Music; Sony Music; EMI Music; News/Festival/Mushroom
Film and TV	The Hollywood majors
Books	Pearson/Penguin; Pearson/Longman Cheshire; Reid Heinemann; News/HarperCollins
Electronic games	Sega; Electronic Arts; Nintendo; Pearson/Software Toolworks

Source: *Commerce in Context*, 1994.

Although some would question whether or not the PC/CD-ROM installed base is the appropriate vehicle for interactive multimedia content development and publishing, it is there and it is still growing. There is another aspect to such development however, which carries significant implications not only for the electronic information industry but also for telecommunications services. This derives from the ability of personal computer users all over the world to connect to and interact with the Internet.

TRADING ON THE INTERNET

Although only in its infancy, the Internet is already emerging as a factor in the convergence battles within the information-based industries. What started out as a facility for the academic and research community is becoming increasingly commercialized. Commercial users already generate a higher volume of traffic on the Internet than do academic or non-commercial users. The demand is such that commercial electronic mail services have been forced to provide gateways to the Internet. Using such facilities and capacity leased from network providers, computer users are now beginning to go into business for themselves and compete directly with telecommunications services companies. A number of newspaper publishers in the United States are bypassing commercial online services such as CompuServe, America Online and Prodigy, who it is claimed swallow up 80 per cent or more of the connect-time revenues of online newspapers. Instead, the newspapers are offering the service themselves over the Internet, and at highly competitive prices. Similar threats could arise in the market for value-added networks where an Internet infrastructure offering major scale economies could undercut the prices of existing providers.[32]

153

Moreover, this is happening not within the confines of a formally managed and structured organization, but rather within a loosely-configured *network of networks* that is growing at bewildering speed. Changes to the structure and operation of the Internet are inevitable, otherwise it risks running into major capacity problems and, ultimately, some form of information anarchy. In a very short period of time, usage of the Internet has grown to over 20 million users worldwide and with an estimated growth rate of 15 per cent per month, it could reach several hundreds of millions in five years' time. Indeed, recent figures reported a growth of 132 per cent during 1992 and largely within the private and commercial sector.[33] This growing volume of commercial activity will force its own kinds of change, as the Internet shows clear signs of developing into an alternative value-added marketplace in direct competition with existing information-based industries. One potential source of change is the reduction in funding levels to NSFNET the (main Internet backbone) planned by the United States government for November 1994. Another, is the decision of CIX, the Commercial Internet Exchange, a cluster of some 65 commercial service providers in the United States, to introduce a $14,000 access fee to their part of the network for all non-CIX members. This is timed to coincide with the change in government funding.[33]

The type and range of services available on the Internet is maturing all the time. In addition to structured data and text, sound, graphics and images can also be transmitted, and it is not altogether unlikely that some form of videophone service could be available on the Internet well before the telecommunications companies are in a position to launch their official services (ACS). The kinds of service provided to users will depend not just on the high capacity backbones and switches of the Internet but also on the last link in the chain, the *tails* between the backbone and the users. These tails can be either broad or narrowband depending on the particular application or service. Some indication of the potential range of services that could be provided on the Internet is given in Tables 10 and 11.

THE INTERNET AND THE ONLINE INFORMATION INDUSTRY

Martha Williams has identified both threats and opportunities on the Internet for the producers of online databases. On the positive side she envisages *opportunities* for:

- *market testing*: using the Internet as a cheap and effective means of researching and test marketing products;
- *access to vendor sites*: where users could access databases

154

Table 10
Potential narrowband service on the Internet

Electronic newspapers
Electronic encyclopaedias and other reference material
Community Bulletin Boards
Security services and utility metering
Home banking
Classified advertising
Business data transfer

Source: Australian Computer Society, 1994.

Table 11
Potential broadband services on the Internet

Videoconferencing
Home shopping (including image and/or video)
Video-on-demand
High definition television
Medical services (including remote diagnostics)

Source: Australian Computer Society, 1994.

available through vendors such as Dialog, BRS, NLM, MDC or West by telenetting to the vendor through the Internet;

- *distribution and document delivery*: delivery in bitmapped form of documents and graphics whose transmission on current commercial networks would be uneconomic;
- *vending databases*: where vendors could mount their databases on their own computers in Z.39.50 format for accessing by users through the Internet;
- *creation of virtual systems*: users in specific subject fields could access different resources and widespread collections through a common intelligent interface, with the effect and appearance to users being that of access to a single collection.[34]

Among the more *negative* aspects of the Internet for database producers were:

- *copyright*: where material is available electronically it is vulnerable to misuse by means of downloading and copying; this is seen to be potentially an even greater problem where the exposure occurs not just on existing commercial networks but on *155*

the Internet;
- *exclusion/bypassing*: along with primary and secondary publishers, online vendors risk being cut out of the value chain as the creators of materials can make their products available in electronic form, thus circumventing formal industry channels.[34]

Nevertheless, the Internet or its successors are clearly here to stay and the information-based industries must move to take advantage of the business opportunities that this presents. The key to success, says Williams, will lie in finding out what kinds of information people need and want and embodying this information in products, and developing the interfaces, storage and retrieval systems and presentation methodologies for delivering results through the Internet.[34]

Whether on the Internet or not, increasing interest is being generated in the potential of online information services as vehicles for advertising. Although there is currently no advertising on such leading online services as Dialog, Dow Jones/News Retrieval or NEXIS/LEXIS, it would be a bold person who would rule out the possibility for all time. For service providers, advertising offers a new and potentially lucrative source of revenue, which could reduce their dependence on user subscriptions and other fees. For advertisers, online could provide an additional and different type of channel to normal media outlets. Almost uniquely, however, electronic advertising is linked to transactions in such a way that consumers can transmit orders immediately on seeing an advertisement, thereby greatly accelerating the fulfilment process to the benefit of everyone in the merchandising chain.[35] Nevertheless, quite apart from technological problems and those related to the relatively small size of the market, there could be major difficulties in persuading the users of online services to accept advertising as part of the package. Apart from the irritation factor, it would be unrealistic to expect users to meet the costs of this unsolicited advertising if, by being forced to see it, they were running up additional connection charges.[35]

As evidence of unfavourable user reaction to electronic advertising, there is the reported cancellation of subscriptions to the Prodigy service by users unhappy with the appearance of advertisements on their screens. Although exploitation of the Internet for such purposes is expressly forbidden by the National Science Foundation's *Acceptable Use Policy* (ACP), the policy itself appears in need of revision given that advertising is already a fact of life on the Internet. The expansion of such practices seems as inevitable as the general commercialization of the Internet. The most likely obstacles to its development would seem to be the currently limited graphics capabilities of the medium and the need for advertisements to be very carefully targeted in recognition of the peculiar social and cultural milieu of the Internet as a marketplace.[35]

NEW BUSINESSES ON THE SUPERHIGHWAY

Few such restrictions are predicted for advertising or seemingly anything else on the global superhighway, which is attracting a level of hyperbole which far exceeds that attending the information society forecasts of the 1970s and 1980s. Given the rate of growth of the Internet and the success of existing electronic consumer services as diverse as Minitel in France and Prodigy and CompuServe in the United States, such optimism is only to be expected. Although some people in information systems circles have sounded a note of caution about such heady developments as broadband multimedia-based businesses, it is the expectations and *vision* of entrepreneurs and business managers that is driving such developments at the moment. In the United States, Commercenet is working to provide its members with the same EDI capabilities on the Internet that large companies currently enjoy on private data networks. The expectation is that Commercenet users will be able to conduct business by using EDI formats and also engage in such activities as videoconferencing. Companies such as Lockheed Missiles & Space and Hewlett Packard are already considering the opportunities of using Commercenet to reach new markets.[36] In the meantime, some of the biggest names of corporate America are already using the Internet for a wide range of activities, including:

- Price Waterhouse: enabling customers to interact with value-added databases through software tools like Mosaic.
- Schlumberger: making business databases available for data mining activities, and transmitting geological-monitoring data to investors.
- Citicorp: working with a consortium of seven major banks to assemble the package of technologies necessary for *virtual banking*, enabling cheques to clear in seconds from homes, offices and other locations on the superhighway.[36]

Companies such as J.P. Morgan and Schlumberger are giving their staff Mosaic, thus enabling them to navigate the Internet, tapping into audio and video clips as well as text, without having to know where the items are stored. These services point the way to the future of electronic trading on the superhighway. They also underline the importance of service quality and security, matters which in turn are heavily dependent on standards.

THE IMPORTANCE OF STANDARDS

Standards are a key element in the internal infrastructure of the information-based industries. In the absence of viable and widely-acceptable standards, neither the industry nor its customers will be able to operate effectively and profitably. Standards are intended to facilitate interoperability between systems and equipment, to ensure that any device or software can communicate with another device or software through conformance to an interface. The standard defines this interface, but does not specify exactly how the device or software itself is written.[37] A standard is a guideline, not a physical law. Standards are often merely starting points for the development of real products, and the variations that exist within products that appear to conform to a set of standards can be extremely troublesome.[37]

Some idea of the scale of the task involved in the setting of standards can be gleaned from the sheer diversity of transmission media, computing devices and applications that have to be covered by standards. This diversity creates a broad range of communications features that a user-to-user connection employs. Hence, the requirements for supercomputers running high resolution graphics programs on local cable would be very different from those required to support electronic mail communication between users of simple terminals.[38]

Although the major promoters of standards are the information industry, government agencies and very large corporations, the vast majority of those affected are small companies and single users. Standards tend to emerge because their time has come, because all concerned can see the logic of some kind of joint development. The role of the customer is critical in this process: when customers want standards, vendors have to comply.[39]

Standards in the computer industry

In the computer industry, standards have developed in a somewhat ad hoc and at times even chaotic manner. This has resulted in waste and market inefficiencies and, most important, in unnecessary expense and inconvenience to users. Although, in the short term, this situation may have worked to the advantage of the owners of proprietary hardware and software systems, there appear to have been few real winners. One of the most important influences in the introduction of standards to the computer industry was the emergence of UNIX in the mid-1980s, as the first multivendor operating system for microcomputers. This had the effect of opening the way for the development of standard interfaces, as opposed to the proprietary single-vendor interfaces which had hitherto prevailed.[39] The possibility of being able to interconnect and communicate between different machines and to *port* or migrate from one system to the other, heralded a watershed in computing, with users and new entrants to the industry being to a considerable extent released from the stultifying grip of proprietary systems.

The move towards open systems

The move towards open systems in computing has not been altogether painless, and there have been complaints in several quarters about the cost of the changeover and its allegedly adverse effects upon system performance and security.[40] Furthermore, proprietary environments continue to survive even where different products comply to the open systems standard. An obvious case in point is that of UNIX, where although both UNIX System V and OSF/1 would claim to be *the* standard operating system for open systems, and, whereas both adhere to the same standards, they are in fact very different.[40] Problems of this nature are continually being addressed by national standards bodies, industry groupings and user forums; for example, the American National Standards Institute (ANSI), the European Information Technology Standards Institute (ETSI), X-Open, the Open Software Foundation and the Corporation for Open Systems (COS).[41]

These various standards bodies around the world work closely together in an attempt to prevent overlap or conflict in their activities. Past instances of co-operation have included delegation of the design of the POSIX interface from ANSI to the IEEE, and co-operation between ANSI and the International Standards Organization (ISO) in helping to make the C software language into an international standard.[41] The presence of standards both reduces the risk of organizations buying into systems which could become technologically obsolescent, and saves them the major expense of developing customized products.[39]

Data communications standards

The move towards open network architectures was equally welcomed in telecommunications, where a lack of standards threatened the creation and expansion of networks and, in effect, risked jeopardizing the likelihood of free trade in telecommunications products and services. In telecommunications also, standards emerge from a variety of sources, including government and intergovernmental agencies, *159* industry and trade associations. The most significant players are the International Telecommunications Union (ITU) and the International Standards Organization (ISO). Within the ITU, the Telecoms Standardization Sector (TSS), formerly CCITT, is the major body for telecommunications standards, although the International Radio Consultative Committee (CCIR) works on such relevant areas as satellite communications.[39]

Communications standards require the definition of standardized procedures or protocols for the efficient exchange of data and the interaction of communications equipment. Modern data communications protocols are defined in network architectures that interact through a *layered* approach. Each layer may support several different protocols designed for specific network operations and definite functions crucial to the communication process but independent of the other layers. Messages exchanged between peer layers are enveloped and transmitted through the other layers, picking up and shedding other layers along the way, but no communication occurs among these layers unless they are peer layers.[42]

Open systems interconnection

This concept was formalized by the International Standards Organization in the late 1970s as the OSI Basic Reference Model. OSI is not an operating system that permits the porting of application programs between computers. Rather, it is a set of standards that enables different types of remote computer to interoperate, that is to communicate and work together. Its seven layers together provide a framework or model for *slotting* in individual communications facilities and services provided by a computer, a communications node – which itself may be a form of computer – or by a private or public network. This model is vendor-independent, enabling even two proprietary and otherwise incompatible computers to at least communicate with each other. It can do even more when these computers are themselves both open systems.[42]

GOSIP

In 1979, the search for standards for interoperable data communications in the United States led to the emergence of the Government OSI Protocol or GOSIP. Since 1990, all federal agencies have had to conform to GOSIP in procuring networking products. GOSIP specifies only OSI protocols which have reached the final stages of standardization, thus minimizing the likelihood of product obsolescence in the light of subsequent changes. GOSIP was intended to accelerate the development of OSI standards and products, not only in government but in the private sector, and ultimately to take over from TCP/IP.[40]

OSI and proprietary architectures

When the ISO defined its OSI basic reference Model (ISO 7498 and 7498/ADI) in 1979, users for the first time had an alternative to IBM's proprietary Systems Network Architecture (SNA). The purpose of the OSI model – interoperability in a multivendor environment – was fundamentally different from the proprietary nature of SNA. Although both OSI and SNA are seven-layer networks, the layers do not match exactly and are incompatible. Increasingly, pressure from customers demanding open, nonproprietary platforms has forced IBM and other major companies, such as Digital and NCR, into a mainstream OSI approach. IBM now supports three major networking standards: OSI, TCP/IP and FDDI. Digital's Advantage-Networks architecture enables users to transmit data from among OSI, TCP/IP and DECnet applications, while network management is supported with Digital's Enterprise Management Architecture (EMA).[40]

OSI and TCP/IP

Transmission Control Protocol/Internet Protocol are actually two separate protocols occupying layers number four (transport) and number three (network) respectively of the OSI model. The IP layer routes data among multiple networks without monitoring the transmission, while the TCP layer ensures that the data is sent in sequence and is error free.

Developed by the United States Defense Department in 1976, TCP/IP has emerged as a serious rival to OSI, with a large customer base among users seeking a protocol that can be used for multivendor computer networks. TCP/IP is a relatively straightforward and robust system and as such is extremely popular with users. It seems set to benefit from the enormous growth of the Internet but, on the other hand, a large community of government agencies, vendors, trade associations and users are committed to the use of OSI. With a growing array of applications protocols such as X.400, X.55 and EDI, OSI continues to be perceived in many quarters as the vehicle for universal connectivity.[40] It may well be that some form of hybrid will emerge, with large scale migration to OSI, but with the added functionality of TCP/IP and running on TCP/IP infrastructure. In many commercial networking

161

applications, vendors are already blending different protocol stacks from different sources to match user needs. For instance, one vendor's network protocol might graft together different layers from OSI, TCP/IP and IBM's SNA. Moreover, an increasing number of vendors, including Unisys and Amdahl, have introduced products that support multiple protocols.[40] In any case even OSI will be no panacea. Proprietary architectures will in all likelihood continue to thrive alongside OSI-based networks, especially for closed user groups, and in the final analysis, the market will decide.[40]

POSIX

The Portable Operating System Interface for Computer Environments (POSIX), is a standard vendor-independent interface between a software and an application system. POSIX provides true portability as its interface software can run over different operating systems, irrespective of hardware. Therefore, it fills a gap in the coverage of OSI, which does not specify software portability.[40]

Applications Portability Profile (APP)

This standard addresses certain networking, database and user interface issues that were not provided for under POSIX. The APP toolbox specifies software interfaces for operating system and networking services. Using these services, developers can write software programs for porting across a number of different computing platforms. The toolbox for developing portable software applications includes: operating system; database management; data interchange; network services; user interface; and programming services.[43]

Standards for linking computer and telecommunications networks

Another area in urgent need of standardization is that involving the physical links and software which will enable computer networks to intercept and understand the very different signals emanating from telephones. Two competing sets of alliances, one between AT&T and Novell, the other involving Intel and Microsoft, are vying to come up with the solution.[43]

The AT&T/Novell approach, which is better suited for large networks, involves the building of a single high-capacity bridge that connects the corporate telephone switch and the main computer of a PC network. Everyone with a PC on the network will be able to place calls and retrieve voice mail through this central link, known as TSAPI (NetWare Telephony Services API). The Intel/Microsoft scheme, known as Windows Telephony API (TAPI), entails building individual bridges into each office, with the telephone plugging directly into the PC where the communications software resides. It is, therefore, better suited for smaller companies. Both systems offer a cheap alternative to the hitherto expensive business of linking up computer and telephone networks, for example, enabling staff to access screenfuls of data the instant a call comes in.[44]

TAPI is said to have the greater potential of the two systems in that it is part of Microsoft's WOSA, with close links to Microsoft's mail, multimedia and voice-digitizing APIs. The new Windows 4.0 (Windows 95) or Chicago software will include TAPI capabilities. Although there is no logical incompatibility between the two systems, there seems little hope of their both being supported in the one product, and the competition to set the standard goes on.[44]

The progressive advance of standardization has resulted in the opening up of markets for all manner of products from micro-processors to networks to operating software. Meanwhile, firms continue to strive for the so-called *killer applications* which promise their developers either major market share or acceptance as the industry standard. One potential candidate is the PHS (Personal Handy Phone), a Japanese cellular technology which costs about one-third that of existing systems and also offers bandwidth sufficiently wide to accommodate multimedia transmission. It is already being hailed as the coming pan-Asian standard for wireless communications.[45] Another candidate for killer application status is videotelephony, where in the light of current developments in videophone and videoconferencing technology, a major breakthrough is predicted for the year 2000.

CONCLUSION

The information-based industries remain critical to the performance of the global economy. In global terms they are characterized by rapid growth, advances in technology and in methods of information delivery and a high propensity for mergers and acquisitions between companies. While undoubtedly affected by recession, the experience of these industries has varied both in sectoral and in geographical terms. Computer and telecommunications software and services have prospered, while markets for computer hardware have become increasingly competitive, especially for mainframe systems. Despite the difficulties facing IBM and other mainframe manufacturers, the overall strength of the information-based industries in the United States *163* remains sufficient to keep it in pole position. Japan, for all its success in computer hardware and in consumer electronics, has been particularly badly hit by recession and the effects of a rising yen.

Furthermore, the trend towards the commoditization of personal computers and the demise of proprietary systems has now spread to the hitherto closed markets of Japan. In Japan, moreover, as in Europe and the United States, considerable store is being placed in the potential of mobile communications and multimedia systems as vehicles for further growth within the information-based industries. Japanese manufacturers are gearing up to provide such key technologies as liquid crystal displays, long-lasting batteries and advanced memory chips, while at the same time diversifying into software and content markets, increasingly on the basis of international alliances.

While striving to create a single market in which its information-based industries could attain critical mass, Europe has probably lost the battle for hardware and software sales to the United States and Japan. However, the situation is more complicated in the area of content services, for example in journal publishing and online information, fields in which Europe has traditionally been strong.[46] Europe continues to display its strengths in electronic information, but it remains vulnerable in all markets to United States competitors including Dialog Information Services, the National Library of Medicine, Mead Data Corporation, Orbit, BRS, Telerate, Knight-Ridder and Quotron. The United Kingdom continues to be Europe's largest electronic information market, particularly in financial information, through companies such as Reuters, Extel and Datastream. Although France with the major host Telesystemes-Questel, Italy with ESA-IRS and Germany with STN all sustain a serious presence, there are few really pan-European players and firms such as Reuters and Genios remain noticeable exceptions.[31]

Concern has been expressed about inherent weaknesses in the European information content industries, and also about competition from heavily-subsidized companies in the United States. Competition between European commercial database hosts is weakening the industry and, it is claimed, resulted in the loss of the biomedical host DataStar to Dialog. Furthermore, where Europe is unwilling to subsidize information, the American online industry can compete on world markets through publicly-funded hosts such as the National Library of Medicine, which offers cheap access to such standard files as Medline, Toxline and AGRIS. Concern has also been expressed about the threat to European publishers from electronic competition on the Internet, and the fact that certain key databases are accessible only on United States hosts.[46]

Moreover, in increasingly turbulent markets, there is now a serious possibility of competition from what would hitherto have been an unexpected source. After many years as a major importer of information, Japan is now embarked on building up its own electronic information industry, with reported annual growth rates of 30 per cent and in excess of 100 vendors, nearly half of whom are producing and selling their own databases. As elsewhere, CD-ROM is also undergoing rapid expansion in Japan, with sales predicted to increase from a level of 106.3 billion yen in 1988 to around 2.5 trillion yen in the first decade of the next century.[31]

Competition is also increasingly fierce in the media and entertainment industries, with Europe again nervous about the strength of the competition from the United States. Whether the technological potential for convergence of the broadcasting and telecommunications industries is realized in market terms, depends to a considerable extent on the outcome of ongoing attempts at deregulation. In the final analysis, however, it will be market forces in a global economy that will determine the direction of the information-based industries for the next century.

REFERENCES

1. John Beaumont and Ewan Sutherland (1992) *Information resources management: management in our knowledge-based society and economy*. Oxford: Butterworth Heineman, 309pp.

2. Robert Reich (1991) *The work of nations*. New York: Alfred A. Knopf, 331pp.

3. Henry Lucas (1991) A guide to computer systems. In: *Managing Information Technology*. Delran, NJ: Datapro, 7210, pp. 1–9.

4. *Industry ratings: computers* (1993) (21st July) Australia: Standard & Poor, 27pp.

5. Herbert S. Dordick and Georgette Wang (1993) *The information society: a retrospective view*. Newbury Park, Calif.: Sage Publications, 168pp.

6. Louise Kehoe (1993) International company news: Gerstner sees no place for a vision at IBM. *Financial Times*, 28th July, p. 24.

7. Louise Kehoe (1994) More on the vision thing. *Financial Times*, 13th May, p. 17.

8. Alan Cane (1994) Fingers crossed as Digital gets to grips. *Financial*

Times, 26th July, p. 17.

9. Daniel Green (1993) Survey of personal and portable computers (4): every variety from Apple on display. *Financial Times*, 19th February, p. iii.

10. Louise Kehoe (1993) International company news: Apple faces up to decline in PC profit margins. *Financial Times*, 22nd June, p. 30.

11. *Industry ratings: computers, op.cit.*, p. 4.

12. Mike Ricciuti (1994) The mainframe as server: is IBM totally bonkers or brilliant? *Datamation*, **40**, (10), pp. 61–64.

13. Beaumont and Sutherland (1992) *op.cit.*, p. 61.

14. Claire Gooding (1993) Survey of using computers in business (1): Big change in users expectations. *Financial Times*, 21st September, p. 1.

15. John Hoey (1994) Waking up to the new economy. *Fortune* **129**, (13), 27th June, pp. 22–28.

16. *Industry Ratings: computers, op.cit.*, p. 6.

17. Andrew Adonis (1993) Survey of international telecommunications (1): era of explosive growth. *Financial Times*, 18th October, p. 1.

18. *Industry ratings: telecommunications* (1993). Australia: Standard & Poor, 23rd June, 28pp.

19. Andrew Adonis (1993) Survey of IMF, world economy and finance (43): stuff of dreams a decade ago, *Financial Times*, 24th September, p. xxv.

20. Lousie Kehoe (1994) Apple to allow Macintosh clones. *Financial Times*, 19th September, p. 21.

21. Alan Cane (1994) Microsoft signs up ICL for servicing. *Financial Times*, 8th August, p. 15.

22. Martin Dickson (1993) Survey of international telecommunications (9) whirlwind of change; developments in the United States. *Financial Times*, 18th October, p. viii.

23. Louise Kehoe and Alan Cane (1994) Chips are down for PC partners. *Financial Times*, 20th September, p. 21.

24. Andrew Adonis (1993) A brief encounter, now line is engaged: the Franco-German telecoms pact was prompted by growing global

competition. *Financial Times*, 9th December, p. 23.

25. Andrew Adonis (1993) Global links down the line: BT's venture with MCI is a pricey but plausible strategy. *Financial Times*, 5th June, p. 11.

26. George Graham (1994) US telecoms reform bill abandoned in Senate. *Financial Times*, 24/25 September, p. 26.

27. *Datamation* (1994) 15th August, pp. 47–48

28. Alan Deutschman and Rick Tetzeli (1994) Your DES in the year 1996. *Fortune*, **130**, (1), 11th July, pp. 46–51.

29. Martha E. Williams (1994) The state of databases today. In: *Gale Directory of Databases*, Vol. 2. Detroit: Gale research Inc., p. x.

30. Sherry Quinn (1993) Australian databases and information services: summary of developments 1988 to 1992. In: *Information Online & On-Disc, Proceedings of the 7th Australasian Online & On Disc Conference*, Sydney, (19–21 January), pp. 49–69.

31. Margaret T. Fischer, Judith Feder and John Gurnsey (1990) The electronic information industry and forecast: in Europe, North America and Japan. In: *Online Information 90, Proceedings of the International Online Information Conference*, London, (11–13 December), pp. 515–24.

32. Roger Buckeridge and Terry Cutler (1994), *Commerce in context: building Australia's future in interactive multimedia markets*. Melbourne: Cutler & Company.

33. Peter Young (1994) Internet shake-out looms. *Computerworld*, (Australia), August, p. 8.

34. Martha E.Williams (1994) The Internet: implications for the information industry and database providers. *Online & CD-ROM Review*, **18**, (3), p. 149.

35. Donald T. Hawkins (1994) Electronic advertising on online information systems. *Online*, March, pp. 26–39.

36. Donald Frazier and Kris Herbst (1994) Get ready to profit from the Infobahn. *Datamation*, 15th May, pp. 50–56.

37. Doug Smith (1992) Getting involved with communications standards. In: *Managing Information Technology*, Delran, NJ: Datapro, 8405, pp. 1–4.

38. Thomas Nolle and Charles Haggerty (1992) Data communications

standards: overview. In: *Managing Information Technology*. Delran, NJ: Datapro, 8410, pp. 1–12.

39. Standards and the UNIX industry (1992) In: *Managing Information Technology*. Delran, NJ: Datapro, 8430, pp. 1–12.

40. ISO Reference Model for Open Systems Interconnection (1991) In: *Managing Information Technology*. Delran, NJ: Datapro, 8440, pp. 1–16.

41. The importance of computer industry standards (1991) In: *Managing Information Technology*. Delran, NJ: Datapro, 8010, pp. 1–12.

42. Julie Harnett (1993) Survey of information and communications technology (14): faster and cheaper data links – Wide Area Networks. *Financial Times*, 23rd March, p. vi.

43. Andrew Kupfer (1994) Augmenting your desktop with telecom: phones and PCs start to merge. *Fortune*, 11th July, pp. 54–58.

44. Paul Strauss (1994) Welcome to client-server PBX computing. *Datamation*, 1st June, pp. 49–52.

45. Robert Patton (1994) Cutting the cord. *Financial Times*, 1st September, p. 19.

46. Karel J. Leeflang (1994) Is Europe's position in the information market weakening? *Information Services & Use*, **14**, pp. 1–8.

8 Information Management

Information management is a concept that means different things to different people; it is extremely context and application specific. The setting can be the public or private sector, a non-profit organization or a commercial enterprise. The objective can be the management of communications, or of information services, or of global data flows within a multinational corporation. The common denominator in these and other information management environments is management of a corporate resource critical to the attainment of organizational aims and objectives. These aims can include short-term competitiveness, longer-term comparative advantage, increased productivity or market share and the delivery of high-quality services. Although technology platforms are important enablers of such activities, the critical factors are human resources and information content, and an appreciation of certain organizational and cultural constraints. This chapter looks at the nature and characteristics of information management as a key corporate activity in a global information-based economy and society.

THE NEED FOR INFORMATION MANAGEMENT

In its current incarnation, information management began as a response to the flood of paperwork in the United States Federal Government. Whereas initially technology might have been expected to alleviate if not actually solve this problem, if anything the reverse has been the case. Because of the proliferation of modern information technologies and of new techniques for searching, accessing and retrieving information, organizations today are even more exposed to the paradox of threatened inundation from irrelevant or unnecessary information and a dangerous paucity of that which is needed. At the heart of this paradox, says Woody Horton, is why we need information management.[1]

Another force underlying this need for information management has been that of organizational change and in particular, the effects of *downsizing*, which has helped to transform the manner in which major companies handle information. Managers everywhere are faced with a common and growing problem, that of too much information and not enough time to sift out the irrelevant and deal with the important. Where once the telling analogy for such developments was that of the *information explosion*, the current version in the United States is the so-called *infobog*, a pervasive, invasive information structure that is part of all our lives. Rather than paperwork reduction, total shipments of office paper in the United States have increased by 53 per cent since 1983. Indeed, Americans now possess 148.6 million electronic mail addresses, cellular telephones, pagers, facsimile machines and answering machines, which represents an increase of 365 per cent since 1987. What is worse, there are fewer promises of total electronic solutions to this dilemma; indeed, we are told that the information overload is here to stay.[2]

Nor is the threat of information overload the only or, indeed, the most important influence underlying the need for information management. Information is a major element in global competition, present as content and product and as enabler and facilitator in both information-based and more traditional businesses. There are both opportunities and threats in this information-intensive business environment; opportunities for the creation of new markets and the transformation of existing ones, and the threat of competition from new products and services using innovative methods of production and delivery. Increasingly, corporate success will be determined by the ability to use information effectively throughout the organization, and to manage these information resources strategically.[3]

WHAT IS INFORMATION MANAGEMENT?

With due regard for the importance of context and perception, information management can be said to be all of the following:

- a subset of the discipline of management;
- high level management of a critical organizational resource;
- a corporate activity fundamental to the health and survival of organizations;

- a spectrum of activities ranging from the management of paper, through the management of information technologies to strategic management.

Information management, therefore, is management of the information resources of an organization in pursuit of its aims and objectives. As such it requires the application of standard management processes of planning and control, while seeking to ensure the day-to-day flows of information for decision-making and the concurrence of information and business strategies within the organization.[4]

There are as many definitions of information management as there are perceptions of what is entailed. In this chapter, Burk and Horton's definition of *Information Resources Management* will be employed. It is for all practical purposes, synonymous with the term *information management* and is defined as:

> The application of traditional management processes, particularly resource management principles, to the stewardship of an organization's information resources and assets. Corporate IRM policies focus upon inventorying; defining requirements; costing, valuing and fixing accountability for safe-keeping and results.[5]

INFORMATION AS ASSET AND RESOURCE

In the same way as there has been controversy over the definition of information management, so also have there been difficulties when it comes to describing information as a *resource*. Hence, it is claimed, information cannot, in general, be accounted for in the same way as other resources, given the difficulties of appropriation and ownership. Indeed, it is argued, by concentrating upon the formal IRM approach, there is the risk that whole classes of informal but useful information will be excluded from consideration. In reading too much into the word *resource* and overly concentrating on promoting an analogy with tangible resources, there lies the danger of negating the real value of information.[6] Such objections raise the same kind of points as apply to the status of information as a commodity. While valid in themselves, however, one has to bear in mind the context and the use to which the information is put. In fact, while information may differ from other resources in some ways, in others it is really quite similar and, indeed, common objectives are at work, in that:

- We want to maximize the value of what we get out of using them.
- We want to minimize the costs involved in acquiring and using   *171*

them.
- We have to fix accountability for their use.
- We have to ensure a continuous supply of this resource.[1]

It seems clear that in the general, everyday sense, many businesses are already at the point where they regard information as a resource, particularly those which operate within information-based industries. Woody Horton who is unequivocal in his treatment of information as a resource, goes further and distinguishes conceptually between information as a resource and information as an asset. *Assets* are the content of the information, be it in a book, a databank or a CD-ROM; the asset is the value we obtain from using the information. Information *resources,* on the other hand, are all the expenses that go into establishing and operating information resource entities such as libraries, computer centres, statistical offices and so on.[1]

INFORMATION MANAGERS

There is no shortage of contenders for the title of *information manager* and the struggle for *information turf* continues both across and within disciplinary boundaries. Furthermore, this is a struggle which is occurring both at the individual and at the institutional level. Although the title of information manager is increasingly common within the traditional library and information professions, at those points in the spectrum that entail the management of information technology and/or performance of a strategic management function, the position tends to be filled by individuals from data processing and general management backgrounds. Much of course depends upon the circumstances of individual organizations and on the initiative and career development paths of particular individuals.

At the institutional level, there was considerable anticipation in the middle and late 1980s, that the rise of information management would inevitably lead to the appearance of a new star in the information firmament, the Chief Information Officer. This person would be a member of the senior management team of the organization, with a significant role in setting information strategy and responsible for all information-related expenditures, and for the integrated management of information sources and services in support of business objectives. The need for such a person arose because:

- Many businesses had recognized the need to manage information as a corporate resource.
- Increases in the power and capabilities of IT were making

organizational structures for information services in many corporations obsolete.

- The rise of end users and the power and sophistication of new technologies were making the information systems function more complex and difficult to manage.
- Senior executives were disappointed with the benefits obtained from their considerable expenditures on information systems.
- Information technology became fashionable as a route to competitive advantage.

The post of Chief Information Officer (CIO) would be different from that of traditional data processing and information systems management in two significant respects: the CIO would be a member of the top management team and would play a key role in developing company strategy.[7] Enthusiasm for the idea seems to have waxed and waned at intervals. One study conducted at the end of the 1980s, found that whereas of some 200 organizations surveyed, 70 per cent reported having someone functioning as a CIO, in most instances, the position lacked a central or co-ordinating focus.[8]

Today, the concept of a CIO seems to have grown again somewhat in popularity, even if the title is not universally applied to the individuals who function in that role, common alternative titles being vice-president or director of information systems. The day-to-day responsibilities of the job can vary significantly from company to company, depending on differences in corporate culture, in organizational structure and on how top management views the job of the CIO.

The concept of the CIO today can be characterized as follows:

- reports to the chief executive officer and is part of the senior management team;
- is directly involved in corporate-wide strategic planning and policies;
- is market-driven;
- has broad business and managerial experience and considers himself or herself a business professional rather than a technical expert;
- has superior communication skills;
- selects computer technology most appropriate to meet and enhance corporate goals;
- is concerned with all areas of technology, including computers, communications and office automation.[9]

In many corporations, the CIO functions as an inhouse consultant to senior management; in others, as a true information czar, with real influence over the actions of top management. Although all CIOs must be able to handle line responsibilities, not all are actively involved in the daily operations of the computer and communications departments. There is evidence that many of the most successful CIOs began their careers in technical positions and then moved into line management, thus combining technical competence and broad business expertise.[9] Indeed, a survey of new CIOs conducted in the United States between 1986 and 1989 revealed that 70 per cent or more had at least five years of general management experience; 37 per cent had both strong business and technical backgrounds; and that only 30 per cent reached their position through the traditional information systems function.[10]

There has been some speculation that the growing practice of outsourcing could have an adverse effect on the position of the CIO, with outside companies taking over an organization's computer operations. However, where the idea has originated with the CIO and is successful, then the outcome need not necessarily be negative.[9] In any case, no matter how much companies begin to outsource their operations, they still cannot abdicate their responsibility for managing technology within the organization. Indeed, it is likely that the CIO will have to assume even greater responsibilities both as regards strategic partnerships in outsourcing and in helping to advance the processes of organizational change.[10]

STRATEGIC INFORMATION MANAGEMENT

In today's increasingly complex business environment, where networking and desktop technologies combine with organizational change to empower individuals and challenge long-established hierarchies, the so-called information czar cuts an even more unlikely figure. With extensive decentralization of responsibility and authority and the emergence of flatter organizational structures, the role of line management has been strengthened. Information systems and services are consumer products, whose success depends upon customer involvement in their development.[11] Consequently, information management is now emerging not just as an integrated management function involving corporate executives, information technology managers, business and human resources managers, but also the users of their services in the creation of strategies that will maximize intelligent use of information to achieve such corporate objectives as cost minimization, quality improvement and customer responsiveness.[3]

Consequently, businesses and other organizations do not need information technology strategies. They need clear business strategies where the use of information and knowledge are included as central elements.[11] Increasingly the focus is on the integration of all the information assets of an organization – strategy, people, systems, operations and technology – using business needs as the primary driver to create a value-added, synergistic approach to information management. One variant of this approach, known as *information value management* (IVM), stresses the unique characteristics of every organization and highlights the importance of shifting the perspective from one based on costs and their control, to one that looks for realizing the value of an organization's total information assets. It considers the strategic and operational goals and objectives of the organization and how their information assets can be integrated into achieving these goals and principles.[12]

Although based in the information systems function, IVM is dependent upon close liaison with senior and non-technical management and their involvement in the process. This activity is based upon certain clear principles of information management:

- management direction of information assets to meet the goals and objectives of the organization;
- integration of plans for using information assets into the strategic business plans of the organization;
- justification of expenditures for information assets based upon economic effectiveness and value to the organization;
- allocation of information assets to meet prioritized organizational needs;
- matching of needs for information and information assets;
- linking the organization's users with information asset functions to accomplish approved objectives and profits.[12]

Central to the concept is the need for a comprehensive data architecture – a detailed analysis of data flows and interrelationships – and recognition that a wider approach than the traditional return on investment (ROI) must be taken to the justification of information expenditures, including qualitative and intangible factors as well as those of business fit and support for critical success factors. Under an IVM process, executives, managers, information users and information professionals at all levels of the organization are held accountable for not only assessing needs, but also for deciding the prioritized utilization of information expenditures and assets in their areas of responsibility. They are held accountable for managing the use of these

175

expenditures and assets to ensure that they are integrated and utilized to meet the desired goals and objectives of the organization.[12]

The IVM approach refocuses attention on some of the basic principles of information management. It also touches upon certain fundamental problems which are common to information management projects and environments. These problems have been identified in the field of computer integrated manufacturing by Marchand, but they are in fact common to the information management discipline:

- Information excess: there is frequently either too much information or too little information.
- Poor definition of information costs, with the result that it is difficult to establish a baseline for evaluating existing or future resources.
- Inadequate definition of information needs, thus increasing the risks and costs of information management.
- Underutilization of existing information resources owing to lack of awareness or of access to the facilities.
- Inadequate information locator tools, for helping to trace relevant information and provide linkages to information analysis and simulation facilities.
- Inadequate information architecture, leading to the fragmentation of information sources, services and systems.[3]

As most of these problems are virtually perennial, they may seem insoluble and thus, clear indication that the information resource cannot really be managed as are other resources. It could also be argued that in the age of the laptop computer and the Internet, information management is no longer necessary at the institutional level, and that technology is making everybody, in effect, their own information manager. On the matter of costs, it is worth pointing out that even critics of the concept acknowledge that information is a resource at least some of the time. Where this resource is acknowledged in the market, costs can be recovered through the price mechanism, and this applies in internal markets within organizations as well as on those in the wider world. The fact that this mechanism may not be perfect does not mean that it should be abandoned, nor in the real world is it likely to be.

As for the technology, while useful, it never has provided the complete solution to the problems of information management, nor is it likely to in the future. In fact, Marchand found that, in manufacturing industry, the availability of electronic systems for informal communication, while useful, were also time consuming for all concerned, and a major contributor to information overload.[3] Current developments involving personal digital assistants or electronic agents, while helping with day-to-day routines are still likely to be little more than advanced support tools for the manager. However, the very availability and bewildering array of information and communication technologies, if not controlled, is a recipe for ad hoc development, system incompatibilities and the worst excesses of information overload. In order to mitigate these problems, to keep costs under control and support the business objectives of the organization, there is likely to be a need for more information management rather than less. As a consequence, there is a continuing need for tools and methodologies that will assist information managers in planning, programming, budgeting and accounting for the information resource.

TOOLS FOR INFORMATION MANAGEMENT

In attempting to come to grips with the practical problems of managing information, managers have employed a range of standard tools including, for example, Porter's industry structure analysis model and value chains, the Boston Consulting Group's growth-share matrix and a number of strategic-alignment models emerging from the MIT Management in the 1990s programme.[13] These and similar approaches will continute to be employed but there is also a range of communication and information audits which offer the additional advantage of being designed for use in information management situations. These have received comprehensive coverage in a recent paper by some of the people responsible for the design and creation of the audits.[14] In this chapter the intention is merely to refer to the main thrust of this activity and to highlight any major differences between the approaches taken.

Information audits

Information audits tend to fall into the category of *advisory audits*, that is they are more concerned with the assessment of existing systems and strategic planning, than with reporting the financial performance or legal compliance of the system as happens with *compliance audits*. The different approaches to information auditing have been characterized as follows:

- cost-benefit methodologies
- geographical approach
- hybrid approach

177

- management information audits
- operational advisory audits.[14]

Cost-benefit audits compare lists of options on the basis of their cost and perceived benefit. The more effective versions are systems-oriented, seeking to review the existing information management environment in an organization, to identify problems and recommend solutions to them.

Geographical audits seek to identify the major components of a system and to map them in relation to each other.

Hybrid approaches combine aspects of the other systems as, for example, David Worlock's attempt to relate the mapping of needs and resources, but also to consider possible solutions to problems, thus combining aspects of the cost-benefit and the geographical approaches.

Management information audits can frequently involve the somewhat narrower field of MIS, although they do exist for management information as such, for example, audits of reporting systems within organizations.

Operational advisory audits determine the purpose of the system and its success in meeting its objectives in accordance with the philosophy of the organization. One of the weaknesses identified in these approaches is the fact that they fail to address the compliance aspect, that is conformance with obligations, regulations and standards. Barker has devised a model for information audit which addresses this key weakness.[14]

Communication audits

Communication audits are intended to facilitate comparisons of the state of communication within organizations as measured against a set of criteria. The practice embraces a broad spectrum of activities including:

- a means of assessing the effectiveness of the introduction of information technology into an organization
- a measure of interpersonal communication
- a measure of management/employee communications
- a means of assessing the effectiveness of organizational communications
- a measure of public relations activity.[14]

All of these are relevant to the concerns of information management, and their frequently overlapping boundaries can help draw necessary connections between the *harder* technological considerations and the *softer* human variables.

Information mapping

Although this relatively new concept means different things to different people, a common theme running through a number of approaches is that of discovering the information resources of an organization and *mapping* these out in some form. One such approach which has been well-received for its breadth of coverage, which includes that of the use of the system, is that of Pridgeon. It involves the following steps:

- Identify the need for an information map.
- Choose the information mapping project.
- Plan: define and agree purpose, scope and methodology.
- Prepare: team preparation and preparation with the group.
- Gather information: by interviews, documentation and observation.
- Collate and evaluate information in parallel with further information gathering.
- Format map.
- Feedback to the group.
- Produce and release report.[14]

The purpose of information mapping is to relate managerial effectiveness to the acquisition and use of information in the organization. A recent addition to the field has been Burk and Horton's Infomapper which inventories all information resource entities (IREs) according to their characteristics as services, sources or systems, enabling assessment of individual entities and comparisons of their value to the organization. The Infomapper software package facilitates the mapping process and the various stages of the exercise can be useful in themselves, as well as in their totality. These stages are:

- surveying
- cost and valuing
- analysis
- synthesis.[14]

THE CONTEXT OF ORGANIZATIONAL CHANGE

The development of systems such as Infomapper are part of a much greater movement whereby information activities are shifting from

179

being primarily a support function in organizations to becoming a management function. In the new, flatter organizational structures of the 1990s, it is claimed, priority will be placed on information sharing among workers and on the targeted use of expertise and knowledge in support of work tasks and a market-driven approach to business. A critical factor will be the extent to which management can enhance the effectiveness of knowledge workers as key leverage points for achieving quality and flexibility in production or service delivery.[15]

There is already plenty of *prima facie* evidence for the transformative effect of new technology on both organizational structure and the nature of the work performed within these structures. An obvious example is the impact of computer networking on traditional hierarchical structures. In many cases, the outcome appears to be the destruction of hierarchy, with the emergence of widely-dispersed teams of professionals sharing information across the network without it first being filtered through a managerial hierarchy.[16] Executives are claiming that working in so-called *wired organizations* produces at least three major benefits. The first is that of time and money saved, with examples of simple electronic delivery of mail and files speeding product-development projects by as much as 25 per cent. The second is the short-cutting of communications across functional boundaries between departments, because moving information laterally between departments, rather than up and down the hierarchy saves time. The third is a facility to see the company's markets more clearly, with information available in real time and without first being filtered internally and perhaps inevitably being coloured by the inside culture of the organization.[16]

For each of these benefits, of course, there must be tradeoffs in the need for a looser, more co-operative style of management which puts more emphasis on leadership than on management, and on communication than on control. In networked organizations, the authority of management no longer rests on an ability to control information, but on being able to empower the workforce through information-sharing and in trusting employees to use their new freedoms responsibly.[16] As the pace of organizational change continues to pick up, management is turning to a range of solutions in the form of methodologies designed to add value to their business and increasingly to help transform it.

Benchmarking, total quality management and business process reengineering

In response to such challenges, leading companies around the world have recognized the importance of knowledge and learning to organizational change and development. This entails not just attention to detail and to the demands of the market, but also to core business and the nature of the processes involved. All the methodologies concerned are heavily dependent on information and are directly relevant to the interests of information managers.

Benchmarking

Benchmarking is based on the premise that customer satisfaction can be achieved by continuously improving processes that support the customer. It is an important activity in helping organizations towards Total Quality Management (TQM). Basically, benchmarking is a tool – a means of measuring and comparing performance – a search for industry best practices that lead to superior performances. It is the formal process of measuring and comparing an existing process, product or service against that of recognized top performers, both within and outside an organization. Benchmarking helps a company focus its efforts in areas where it achieves the most improvement. If it is to be implemented, a well-structured methodology must be employed.[17] One example of such a methodology, at Sandia Laboratories in the United States, entails taking the following steps:

1. Identify the process to be benchmarked.
2. Establish a management commitment for the benchmarking effort.
3. Identify and establish the benchmarking team.
4. Define and understand the process to be benchmarked.
5. Identify metrics and collect process data.
6. Identify, rank and implement internal process improvements.
7. Identify benchmarking partners.
8. Collect process data from benchmarking partners.
9. Analyse benchmarking partners' process data and compare against internal process data.
10. Site visits, interviews and reanalyse data.
11. Implement improvements and monitor results.
12. Continue to conduct benchmarking of this process, or other aspects of this process, as appropriate.[17]

TQM

Total Quality Management (TQM) emerged in the 1950s with the pioneering efforts of W. Edwards Deming. During the last couple of decades it gained acceptance as the way to correct defects in production and hence to boost productivity and increase customer satisfaction. The TQM approach, so successful in manufacturing industry, has now been adopted by service organizations, largely because customers' expectations have risen sharply, and because quality improvement programmes can be adapted to service industries.[18]

TQM offers no single blueprint for success, but all successful quality programmes are characterized by commitment, ingenuity and employee empowerment, linked to the placing of responsibility for achieving improvement with frontline staff. However, commitment is essential to what is usually a lengthy and painstaking process, in which quick results are unlikely. Nevertheless, some companies are moving towards *breakthrough* techniques which produce substantial improvements to smaller segments of an operation in a short amount of time.[18]

TQM and organizational learning

TQM can be more than a means of improving quality; it can also lead to the expansion of organizational thinking and learning capabilities. As the quality improvement effort bore fruit, organizations began to search for truly different levels of service, with leading edge firms aspiring to meet *latent needs*, to deliver the kinds of service which users had not even asked for, but in which they might be interested. To make this kind of transition requires a measure of organizational flexibility and adaptability or, in other words, that ability to learn.[19]

Organizations that are capable of this level of production and service delivery must have a profound understanding of their own structure, operations and stakeholders. Where TQM is to be adopted it must *fit* with the way things are done in an organization and with its particular culture. TQM should be implemented not for its own sake, but to enhance the learning capability of the organization.[19]

Business Process Reengineering

A survey of US organizations reported by Booz Allen & Hamilton Inc. in 1993 concluded that organizations embarking on Business Process Re-Engineering (BPR) could expect potential productivity improvements of the order of 30 to 40 per cent. For the sceptics, there was the persuasive example of the Ford Motor Company in the United States, which by re-engineering its accounts payable section, reduced an unwieldy organization with 500 people to the point where they perform the same function with only 25 per cent of the staff.[20]

BPR seeks to obtain the same results for very much less cost, or to gain much better results for similar cost. The business process is a set of related tasks which provide a useful outcome for a customer. Moreover, as each process includes all the activities necessary to produce the desired outcome, BPR affords an end-to-end view. BPR is the task of reconstructing processes in order to achieve radical improvements in business effectiveness.[20]

The nature of such improvements is important. Whereas, TQM is also a means of producing improvements, the essential focus is on *how well* things are done. The underlying assumption is that the process is essentially correct, and that many small refinements will lead to its optimization. BPR is different in that it challenges the process itself by questioning *what* it is that is being done. BPR operates by taking an outcomes-oriented approach to the total business process, which relentlessly pursues those elements which customers might value. In seeking to achieve its aims, BPR typically involves the setting of extremely unrealistic goals, such that would seriously challenge the status quo and hold the promise of truly radical outcomes.[20]

The prospect of this level of change poses a potential threat to a variety of stakeholders in the organization, and will meet both open and covert resistance. Once again there is no recipe for success, and what is needed is a good idea and the will to see it through. However, certain principles identified by Michael Hammer, one of the leading authorities on BPR, are applicable to the general implementation of this methodology. These are:

- Organize the process around outcomes, not around tasks.
- Those who need the results should perform the process.
- Include information processing as an integral part of an activity, not as an add on.
- Replace physical movement with the transfer of information.
- Co-ordinate independent processes instead of reconciling them later.
- Put the decision point where the work is performed; build control into the process rather than make a separate activity.
- Capture information once and at source.[20]

BUSINESS TRANSFORMATION AND INFORMATION MANAGEMENT

It is clear that all three of these major methodologies are utterly dependent upon high quality information. It should be equally clear that, in order to provide this information and optimize its value-adding potential, information management must itself be subject to the same processes of improvement, renewal and transformation. Two points *183* immediately become apparent: the need for some means of measuring information quality and the establishment of standards of service against which such measures can be tested. In this case, measurement can have both a quantitative dimension and a more qualitative one related to the perceptions of customers in receipt of that information. The absolutely fundamental requirement in both cases, is for customer focus and a search for measures of effectiveness based firmly on customer perceptions of value in the product or service.[21]

There is also a key role for information technology in the application of change methodologies. However, as with the relationship between information management and information technology, the key drivers must reside in the business organization. Information technology can make a substantial contribution, but as a service provider in the application of change methodologies and in the more general context of its role as enabler. It is important to emphasize this role in which information technology can serve to redefine market boundaries, alter the fundamental basis of competition and redefine business scope. Michael Barrett, a leading Australian authority on BPR, suggests that BPR could lead to a new partnership role between the IT and business areas.[20] There is clearly scope for an enhanced relationship between all these methodologies and information management, as the former depend on the availability of relevant and accurate information and the latter is a source of that vital resource.

Information and knowledge play an increasingly active and prominent role in the value-creating activities of organizations, with competitive position and customer satisfaction largely dependent on the quality of information management. Hence, information and knowledge have to be as much a part of business strategy as such customary elements as finance, human resources, marketing, distribution and research and development. Indeed, in truly information-based organizations the defining characteristics are increasingly, information production, consumption and use.[11]

In developing and enhancing the strategic contribution of information management, three *buzzwords* from the world of business transformation occur with monotonous regularity – customer focus, teamwork and empowerment. The following brief examples should help to emphasize the importance of these three terms.

Customer focus at American Airlines

An acknowledged leader in the use of information technology for competitive advantage, American Airlines is currently working on means of using information obtained from customers at various stages of their journey. The intention is to *empower* the airline's frontline staff by providing them with the kind of information that will enable them to customize their service delivery.

Quality service at Chase Global Securities

Chase Global Securities uses an electronic information system called ASPA (Account Service Planning and Analysis) to identify key service problems, or potential service problems, around the world. The key to success is the system's customer focus and its ability to *drill-down* through countries and customer accounts in any country and solve the problem. Chase claims that the system results in what it calls a truly *win-win* situation in which both the quality of service to customers and its ability to expand its own business are enhanced.

Cultural change at Chrysler Corporation

Chrysler is moving from the position of being a troubled giant in 1991 to one where, today, it is among the most profitable automobile manfucturers in the world. The reason for the transformation is a total change in culture and a strategy that focuses on change towards the goal of being the premier automobile company in the world. The basis of this change is teamwork and empowerment. Chrysler reorganized its engineers, marketers and finance people into four product-focused platform teams, each responsible for a different line of vehicles, drastically reducing its product development cycle and making savings of billions of dollars in the process.

Chrysler is attempting to diffuse this level of teamwork throughout the company by revamping its hiring procedures in a search for employees who can adapt to the team approach. The view is that if people can be empowered and trusted, they will respond innovatively and set new goals for themselves, leading to new breakthroughs for the company.

Teamwork at MetLife

At MetLife Insurance Corporation they have recognized the value of teamwork to employee morale and productivity. By grouping staff into teams they have, in effect, turned them into inhouse *consultants* who are keen to contribute ideas and help improve both the quality of service and the profitability of the company. To this end the company organizes an annual competition for its employees which it calls *Team of the*

Nineties. Much of the focus of these teams is on finding improvements to customer service, seeking to translate customer feedback into actions that will lead to enhanced customer satisfaction.

These highly selective examples could have been duplicated many times by similar illustrations of the strategic and operational value of information management in the business world.

THE IMPORTANCE OF INFORMATION

In all these developments, an extremely critical linkage is that which connects the information management strategy to the strategic business plan of the organization. The problem is that in responding to the need to manage their information resources, organizations tend to put more emphasis on carriers and systems than on content. This is understandable in view both of the enabling characteristics of the technology and the fact that, in most organizations of any size, there is a place for the MIS or the information systems department on the organization chart. While this is necessary given the significance of technology platforms to modern business activity, it can easily lead to a situation whereby *ends* are being confused or, indeed, overshadowed by *means*.

In the haste to computerize or to network operations, how much thought is given to the information and data which resides within such systems, and which flows into and out of the organization? What mechanisms exist to identity the costs of information assets and their contribution to value added within the organization? Are there policies for managing the information life cycle and for integrating information flows into the business plan of the organization? Is the information accurate, relevant, up to date and secure? If not, who, if anyone, will be held responsible? Although in a great many cases these questions will be rhetorical, they need to be asked, because information management still tends to be a *motherhood* concept in many organizations – everybody approves of it, but implementing the practice is another matter.

CONCLUSION

It would be a pity if reservations over the resource attributes of information, or turf battles over ownership of the field, were to cause further delays in the development of information management. It would also be unnecessary and indeed appears increasingly unlikely, with the
global economy and the fortunes of multinational corporations and

entire regions equally dependent upon management of the information resource. In a world that is rapidly becoming a vast network marketplace, the ability to access, exploit, add value to and profit from information has become a core, indeed perhaps the fundamental, survival skill, whether for individuals seeking to make their way in the world or for the companies that employ them. At the corporate level, it is essential that all an organization's information assets – its strategy, people, systems, operations and technology – are integrated in a coherent fashion. This will simply not happen without effective information management.

REFERENCES

1. Forrest Woody Horton (1992) The corporate information management function. *Aslib Proceedings*, **44**, (3), March, pp. 107–14.

2. Rick Tetzeli (1994) Surviving information overload. *Fortune* **130**, (1), 11th July, pp. 26–29.

3. Donald A. Marchand (1988) Strategic information management: challenges and issues in the CIM environment. *Information Management Review*, **4**, (2), pp. 15–23.

4. William J. Martin (1993) Information management in the United Kingdom. In: *Encyclopaedia of Library and Information Science*, Allen Kent (ed), Vol. 51, Supplement 14. New York: Marcel Dekker, pp. 266–76.

5. Cornelius Burk *and* Forrest Woody Horton (1988) *Infomapper*. Englewood Cliffs, NJ: Prentice Hall, 343 pp.

6. J. J. Eaton and D. Bawden (1991) What kind of resource is information? *International Journal of Information Management*, **11**, pp. 156–65.

7. Eric H. Brown, Kirk R. Karwan and John R. Weitzel (1988) The chief information officer in smaller organisations. *Information Management Review*, **4**, (2), pp. 25–35.

8. Eugenia K. Brumm (1990) Chief Information Officers in service and industrial organisations. *Information Management Review*, **5**, (3), pp. 31–45.

9. William F. Emmons (1990) Executive search and the chief information officer. *Information Management Review*, **5**, (4), pp. 47–51.

10. Lynda M Applegate *and* Joyce J. Elam (1991) CIO and SuperCIO. *CIO*, **4**, (7), April, pp. 26–28.

11. Karl Kalseth (1991) Business information strategy: the strategic use of information and knowledge. *Information Services & Use*, **11**, pp. 155–64.

12. John Framel (1993) Information value management. *Journal of Systems Management*, **44**, (12), pp. 16–41.

13. John Beaumont and Ewan Sutherland (1992) *Information resources management*. Oxford: Butterworth Heinemann, 309 pp.

14. D. Ellis *et al.* (1993) Information audits, communication audits and information mapping: a review and survey. *International Journal of Information Management*, **13**, pp. 134–51.

15. Sharon L. Caudle and Donald A. Marchand (1990) Managing information resources: new directions in state government. *Information Management Review*, **5**, (3), pp. 9–30.

16. Thomas A. Stewart (1994) Managing in a wired company. *Fortune*, **130**, (1), 11th July, pp. 16–22.

17. Ferne C. Allen (1993) Benchmarking: practical aspects for information professionals. *Special Libraries*, Summer, pp. 123–29.

18. Crit Stuart and Miriam A. Drake (1993) TQM in research libraries. *Special Libraries*, Summer, pp. 131–36.

19. Christine M. Pearson (1993) Aligning TQM and organisational learning. *Special Libraries*, Summer, pp. 47–49.

20. Michael L. Barrett (1994) Re-engineering as a management practice: if it's not broken, fix it. *Management*, April, pp. 5–11.

21. Guy St. Clair (1993) The future challenge: management and measurement. *Special Libraries*, Summer, pp. 151–54.

9 Global Information Flows: Content and Context

Although there may be those who regret the consequences, there can be little doubting the fact of global information transfer. The examples are manifold and even relatively long after the event, impressive. The mortal blow dealt to the regime of Shah Mohammed Reza Pahlavi by the distribution of audio cassettes taped from off-air telephone messages from the Ayatollah Khomeini then in France, was among the most spectacular. Just as important were the eventual effects on the former Soviet regime of the widespread dissemination of satellite pictures of the Chernobyl nuclear disaster taken by the United States LANDSAT and the French SPOT satellites, and who will forget the drama of the infamous Pentagon tapes?

This chapter is of necessity selective, focusing largely on information flows at the corporate or business level. However, in a global business environment this will entail an overview of such developments in both the developed and the developing world, and the social, economic and cultural implications of their interaction.

NETWORKS AND ORGANIZATIONAL STRUCTURE

Along with the phenomenon of globalization perhaps the most significant dimension to the world of corporate information flow is the networking of organizations both in the technical and the structural sense. With globalization and technological change operating in tandem to transform both the nature of businesses and the basis upon which they operate, networking has become a fact of life in international business. Indeed, the networked firm has been described as a model to which, in the 1990s, companies in Japan, the United States and the European Union all aspire.[1] Communication networks and the information flows which they support, have enabled companies to completely reconceptualize their operation, facilitating new forms of functional structure, new divisions of labour and a new geography of the organization. These networks operate at both intraorganizational and interorganizational levels, the former to control the flow of goods, ideas and capital within the organization, and the latter to facilitate a range of alliances between companies. The networking process exhibits different degrees of iteration between the technology and the organization, depending on such factors as transaction and decision-making patterns, internal and external relations, the decision-making process and the strategies underpinning technological investments.[2]

Although nothing would happen without the technology platform of local and wide area networks, desktop computers and software, the true significance of these networks lies in their organizational impact and in the information they make available. Corporate networks now routinely extend not just to the operations of the parent organization, its divisions and branches, but to customers and suppliers and, in some cases, even to competitors as well. Initially introduced to rationalize resources and reduce costs, communications networks have become the basis for radical restructuring and in many cases have developed into value-added marketplaces on which completely new services have emerged, with for example retail organizations such as Sears Roebuck in the United States and Marks & Spencer in the United Kingdom using their networks to provide financial services.[3]

GLOBAL MARKETS FOR TELECOMMUNICATIONS

The networking phenomenon carries widespread implications not just for the organizations most directly involved, but for business and the economy as a whole. The market in data communications is expanding at a tremendous rate. In Europe, demand for business data services is growing at about 30 per cent per annum, and public carrier data revenues for 1989 were estimated at around 5 per cent of total revenues. In the United States for the same period, however, the data communication market represented 20 per cent of carrier revenues and by that date around $17 billion had been invested in corporate networks.[1] The potential of the Asian market is staggering, both within the high performing economies of the so-called *little tigers* such as Hong Kong and Singapore and in the enormous market that is erupting in China. Moreover, this is all happening at a time of unprecedented liberalization of trade in data services, most notably in telecommunications and financial services.

The initial response to the need for specialized data communications services came from the private sector, with companies such as IBM, GEISCO and EDS, emerging to provide the kinds of service that was not then available from the public networks. Using the latest technology, including specially created network architectures, they could offer both competitive prices for large volume transactions and increased control over content. This was followed by the development of those major private international networks which have since become household names, for example, SITA in the world airline industry and SWIFT, VISA and Mastercard in the banking and financial services industries. Later, with the onset of deregulation, transnational corporations started to build their own private networks and, for example, by 1988 there were almost 150 private satellite networks in the United States operated by companies such as Federal Express and K-Mart.[3]

The public telephone companies are emerging as competitors to private network operators in such areas as managed data network services (MDNS), Centrex, X.25 networks, ISDNs and EDI. As has been mentioned in a previous chapter, a number of international alliances of public and private providers have recently been targeted at the data communications needs of multinational corporations. Although it is still too early to predict the outcome of such developments, there will inevitably be implications for organizational structure and business scope. For example, this could well lead to a refocusing by some of these target organizations back into their core businesses, and changes to the situation whereby they have chosen to bypass not just the local network, but also formal relationships with banks, suppliers or even other parts of the organization.[3] Moreover, with roughly half of all information flows across borders occurring within the private networks of transnational corporations, and with the industrial third of the world spending of the order of $50,000 billion a year on information-related services and the remaining two-thirds of the world hoping to bring their total up to $20 billion, there will also be extremely serious ramifications for telecommunications operators in the developing world. It is unlikely that this will entail removal of the continuing problem of bypass of local telecommunications operators.

DEVELOPMENTS IN TRADE IN SERVICES

World trade in information services is currently subject to two major forces, the development of intelligent communications networks and the shift in trading policy towards competition and the freeing up of markets. Software-based communications functionality now supports the electronic processing of digital signals and global trade in telecommunications services is growing faster than that in any other sector. Moreover, with the competitive marketplace overwhelmingly regarded as the best mechanism for ensuring that the potential of intelligent networks is realized in terms of competitiveness, efficiency and the widespread diffusion of service, there seems little prospect of operators in the developing world emerging as front runners in these markets.

Progress at the GATT

During the recent marathon session of the General Agreement on Tariffs and Trade (GATT), a separate Group of Negotiations on Services (GNS), in parallel with mainstream negotiations on goods, was launched at Punta del Este, Uruguay in 1986. The aim was to establish an overall framework of principles and rules for international trade in services, including within it matters such as Trade-Related Intellectual Property Rights (TRIPs) and Trade-Related Investment Measures (TRIMs).[4] These were complex and delicate negotiations, involving both the developed and the developing world, but dominated by exchanges between the major providers of information services, notably the United States and Europe. The European position was based both on the need to respond to the perceived threat from the United States and Japan, and on its Open Network Directive, which was intended to harmonize network access and use within the European Union. The United States pushed initially for a multilateral agreement that would cover a wide range of services, including telecommunications. This position was based on the belief that the introduction of multiple, competitive service providers, the privatization of monopolistic international service organizations and resale of value added would reduce the costs and improve the quality of telecommunications services everywhere. It was also based on the market strength and technical efficiency of United States companies, many of whom constantly lobbied the negotiators for the exemption of basic services from any subsequent agreement and restrictions on the award of most favoured nation status to foreign telecommunications providers.[5]

Central to the negotiations were such matters as access to and use of networks, standards and pricing. On the matter of standards and of attachments to the network, the consensus was that international standards should ensure network integrity and interoperability and that standards, whether international or proprietary, should not be used as discriminatory barriers to competition. There was also a consensus that pricing mechanisms should not permit discrimination among parties not lead to distortions in trade. Initially, there was only limited support for United States efforts to obtain support for the full resale and shared use of private lines leased from the public telecommunications network, and as the negotiation unfolded it became clear that the general United States position was regarded as somewhat extreme in other countries. Such perceptions were no doubt reinforced by attempts by the United States to engage in bilateral negotiations with countries which it perceived as carrying on unfair trade practices in telecommunications, notably Europe as a whole and Japan.

In the event, Europe, Japan, Korea and a group of developing countries including India, Cameroon, Egypt and Nigeria, all put forward their own proposals. In the case of the developing countries, the intention was largely to *unbundle* the delivery aspects of telecommunications networks from those concerning its sectoral implications for national development. For its part, the United States eventually produced a proposal which entailed amending its position on most favoured nation status and access to its own long-distance markets in return for similar access to those of its major trading partners, particularly the European Union. Europe responded by attempts to assuage American fears on matters of resale and use of leased lines and the use of proprietary as well as international standards.[5]

General Agreement on Trade in Services (GATS)

Agreement on most of these matters was reached in 1994 and formally enshrined as the GATS – General Agreement on Trade in Services. The intention is to open up world markets in services, and within this financial services and telecommunications services are seen as the most significant elements. The agreement commits signatories to the opening up of their markets for value-added telecommunication services to competition. Although coverage does not as yet extend to basic voice communications, there is clearly the intention to introduce this area for consideration in the relatively short-term future. It has to be realized that the signing of the GATS will not end at a stroke all the difficulties of imperfect markets in telecommunications or other services. It is basically a framework within which free trade can operate, and time alone will tell just whether or not the framework and associated arrangements are effective.

The immediate indications are highly favourable, not only because of the relentless pace of technological change and its impact on markets and borders, but also, owing to the business potential of the agreement, *193* with phenomenal levels of cross-trading expected in ancillary services. Inevitably there will be winners and losers in this situation and it is evident that among the former will be numbered multinational corporations and large scale users of business data communications. The impact on small business and on communities is much less certain, and in the developed world will undoubtedly vary from country to country and from market to market. What does seem quite clear, however, is that people living in the developing world are unlikely to be among the earliest beneficiaries of this more liberalized trading regime.

Information flows in the developing world

One has to be careful when referring to the developing world, a term much preferable to *Third World*, in that it allows for the various gradations of development which are to be found in that two thirds of the world that has not yet crossed the threshold of industrialization. On the one hand are included countries such as India, which has a vibrant information industry and many of the human resources so essential to the attainment of informatization. On the other are numerous African countries which are the very epitome of underdevelopment, and where any talk of take off into sustained growth on the basis of judicious mixes of savings, investment and foreign aid and the use of the free market to iron out imperfections in the allocation and use of resources is at best irrelevant.

Quite apart from a lack of resources, in many developing countries the institutional and political structures are totally unsuited to meaningful involvement in a global market economy. What are needed are attitudinal changes, cultural adaptation, a trained and educated workforce and a political structure willing and able to take the inherent risks that the search for development inevitably requires.[6] In the poorer developing countries therefore, the immediate need is not for informatization but for development. At its most basic level, this entails the raising of living standards above subsistence levels towards those considered normal in modern, industrialized societies. It also involves the operation of a wide range of socio-cultural and educational variables, and the implementation of qualitative changes to transform *life chances*, and provide an opportunity to exercise choices and a degree of control over one's own future, free of dependency on internal and external forces.

Development can be an elusive target and is not something for which simple recipes or formulae exist, which, if applied, will lead to success. However, a number of factors have emerged as being necessary to the successful pursuit of development:

- investment in human capital, as embodied in education and basic health services;
- investment in fundamental infrastructure such as water and electrification, transport and communications;
- the removal of institutional barriers to the widespread exploitation of the potential of human resources.[7]

At all times, however, the primary perception of what constitutes development must be that of the developing countries themselves. As Michel Menou has observed, many so-called development indicators and the value judgements based upon them, seem to equate development with the replication of socioeconomic structures found in the northern hemisphere. In searching for more appropriate and, indeed, more accurate indicators, the conceptual framework is critical. In fact, where dimensions such as the quality of life are concerned, gross national happiness may be a more appropriate criterion of development than is Gross National Product.[8]

THE ROLE OF INFORMATION AND ITS ASSOCIATED TECHNOLOGIES IN ECONOMIC DEVELOPMENT

With its demands for skilled workers and a potential to produce high value added goods and services, informatization is seen by many emerging nations as the route to economic development. Nevertheless, the application of technology on its own will not result in development, being heavily dependent upon the uses to which it is put and on the availability of other infrastructure and human resources inputs. Equally important in the 21st century will be positioning the workforce for the production of high value added goods and services in high value markets, and the ability to exploit the technology as a source of organizational innovation and learning.[6]

Computers, telecommunications and developing countries

Although not everyone would agree, there is considerable support for the view that the information and communications technologies can make a positive contribution to development. In a report published in 1988, the United States Board on Science and Technology for International Development (BOSTID), concluded that cutting-edge technologies had, in fact, a special relevance to developing countries, offering the opportunity to shortcut the development process.[9] A   *195* similar study, focusing on Africa and published by the OECD in 1992, argued for a positive impact by investments in computer and telecommunications networking on all economic sectors.[10] In 1991, Gorham cited the emergence of *teleports* as examples of how countries such as the Philippines, India and Jamaica were entering the information economy as dedicated information processing zones for companies located in the developed world.[11] There is also a potential drawback to such developments in that they normally involve only low-level, low-paid employment and are vulnerable to removal to areas with even lower wages levels. Still, for the people finding employment, perhaps for the first time in their lives, all such things are relevant. In any case, as was pointed out in the BOSTID report, staying out of such developments is not really an option, as there could be disadvantageous consequences for those developing countries which remained outside the telecommunications loop.

In the event, few developing countries have deliberately sought to exclude themselves from such opportunities. Most developing countries are aware, for example, that unless they modernize their telecommunications networks to allow innovations such as computer networking, the economic gap between themselves and the developed world will grow wider. In the attempt to catch up, many have received assistance from those international agencies attempting to promote the transfer of new technologies to emerging countries – bodies such as the World Bank, the International Development Research Centre, the United States Agency for International Development and the German Foundation for International Development.

Therefore, in view of the substantial body of empirical evidence that telecommunications investment in developing countries is beneficial both in its own right, and in terms of externalities within the economy as a whole, it is scarcely surprising that there should be such a level of interest in the acquisition and deployment of these and other technologies. It must be reiterated, however, that telecommunications as a form of infrastructure, is not sufficient in itself to lead to economic development. The effectiveness of the investment will be dependent on whether the institutional structures of the specific country stimulate the development activities that can make effective use of the new infrastructure.[7]

It is critically important that the technologies selected as part of the development process be appropriate to the needs and circumstances of the particular country concerned. Broadbent has rightly emphasized the need for developing countries to avoid the *black box syndrome*, in which the technology is somehow viewed as external to the socioeconomic system. Instead, the information and communication technologies should be conceptualized as part of the environment they operate in, and treated as social systems in which technology is merely one dimension. This approach is likely to result in optimal conditions for the transfer of technology which is suitable for conditions in the importing country.[12]

The contribution of information to development

As in the case of information technology, information can only be of real use in the development process when it is appropriate and where it is used effectively. Hence, it has been argued, given the widely acknowledged relationship between information and the decision making process, developing countries should concentrate on the training and creation of skilful producers of information and the creation and consolidation of cost-effective information services appropriate to the local milieu.[13] It has been further argued, that the major obstacles to the implementation of these policies include:

- lack of appreciation of the potential role of information in the development process;
- inadequate nature of existing information services;
- shortages of funds, foreign exchange, technology and trained staff;
- absence of an appropriate *information culture*;
- serious problems of access to information;
- lack of a coherent national information policy.[13]

It is clear that most developing nations face some or all of these problems as they seek to come to grips with the challenges of the development process. Nevertheless, the level of priority and support which is actually granted to information systems and services in most developing countries, sits uneasily with all those ringing declarations about information being a scarce resource.[8] Not of course that countries whose formal mechanisms are inadequate by western standards lack either systems or information. As happens in the economic sphere, there is a great deal of informal information activity, much of which is crucial to the conduct of everyday life. If anything like appropriate information systems are going to emerge in developing countries then they must exploit the potential of these existing channels and embody the kinds of information which they contain. This suggests that at least some of the foreign aid spent on importing outdated or inappropriate technologies to developing countries should be channelled into indigeneously produced information systems. Such systems might avoid the more obvious dangers of cultural bias present in many imported systems and would be geared to the satisfaction of a

197

range of human needs including:

- biological and physiological needs: coping information;
- security needs: helping information;
- social needs: enlightening information;
- ego needs: enriching information;
- self-actualization and fulfilment needs: edifying information.[8]

The role of information policy

One of the more obvious approaches to the development of relevant systems and services would seem to lie in the creation of comprehensive national information policies. However, there can be real problems when it comes to the implementation of such policies, which tend to be couched in quasi-constitutional language and addressed to ideals and aspirations rather than to practical solutions. One means of addressing this problem could be to treat the policy itself as a set of guidelines and supplement it with specific information management plans for particular projects. Thus to be appropriate to the circumstances of a developing country an information system would have to be capable of:

- transferring the precise amounts of information needed;
- presenting information in the user's own language and at levels appropriate to the understanding of different users;
- providing information in a timely fashion without delay;
- providing information in desired forms: print, nonprint;
- providing information at little or no cost.[13]

STRATEGIES FOR DEVELOPMENT

It is clear that all developing countries seeking to provide a better life for their citizens will have to make investments in telecommunications infrastructure and services. Given that in most cases this calls for impossible levels of resource inputs, it is imperative that every avenue for co-operative action be explored, particularly at regional level. The specific elements of such co-operation would be as follows:

- exchange of information and experience;
- joint R&D;
- collaborative training, especially of managers;
- mobilization of local and regional sources of investment capital;
- encouragement of local and foreign investment, for example in joint

ventures;

- co-ordinated approaches to the World Bank, the Asian Development Bank and to other sources of international investment finance;
- provision of advice on the preparation of programmes to upgrade and expand existing networks;
- creation of regional centres for telecommunications development.[14]

It should be obvious by now, however, that what is needed in developing countries is not just science and technology policies but appropriate investment policies. Investment in local R&D, in the education and service sectors in developing countries remains weak because the need to absorb new technology requires a greater proportion of effort in the form of funds for training and R&D.[12] It is also important to devise means by which information and technology reach the ultimate beneficiaries and are not limited to urban elites in developing countries. This suggests finding ways for the widespread dissemination of such appropriate technologies as radio and satellite stations, microcomputers, video and CD-ROM among the poorer sections of the population, particularly to small scale enterprises and farms.[12]

Many developing economies are dualistic economies, with extremely modern sectors co-existing alongside those largely backward sectors which constitute the bulk of their economies. It is essential that the private sector be fully integrated into national development plans, even to the point where a mixed economy of public and private provision is permitted in the telecommunications sector. This is a complex and, indeed, controversial issue, which is obviously subject to a range of differing national perspectives. Nevertheless, with national postal and telephone administrations still regarded as the main impediment to the development of reliable telecommunications services in many developing countries, and hence contributing to the retardation of the economy as a whole, there is an urgent need for fresh perspectives on the subject.[15]

If the new information and communications technologies are to be exploited in the interests of the developing world, it is necessary that we take full account of the wider social implications of technology transfer and the need to align the resulting infrastructures and services to local needs and priorities. There is clearly scope here for creative interaction between the nations of the South, for co-operation between developing countries. This will not of course detract from the level and significance of North–South interaction.

199

NORTH VERSUS SOUTH

Some readers may find it inappropriate to categorize relations between the developed and developing worlds – between the North and the South – in such essentially adversarial terms. In fact, such are the complexities of international trading and political relations in the global, networked society that any such categorization would be a massive oversimplification. It is employed here, partly as a device to facilitate comparison between countries at different stages of development, but also to help focus attention upon issues which, if not attended to, could lead to fresh tensions or to the exacerbation of existing difficulties between countries in the developed and the developing world. Despite the efforts of various aid agencies and of individual governments, it is still possible to regard the current information revolution as something that operates simply to reinforce the long-standing situation of dependency by the South on the North. The enormous disparities in levels of income between the developed and the developing nations show few signs of amelioration. The average level of income in the South is about 6 per cent that of the North, and little progress has been made in alleviating the suffering of that three-quarters of the world's population that lives in the developing countries.[16] Moreover, while in 1991 the per capita Gross Domestic Product of both Switzerland and Sweden was well over US $30,000, and that of Germany and Japan approaching the $30,000 mark, the figure for India was $360 and for Nigeria, $278. Indeed, after five decades of unprecedented economic growth, there were more than a billion people in the world living in poverty – that is, on incomes of less than US $370 a year.[17]

If this situation is to change in any meaningful way, it will inevitably entail compromises on both sides, and these may in turn involve some form of conflict. However, even without such changes, the potential for misunderstanding and polarization over specific issues remains strong. Some of these issues such as privacy and data protection and the abuse of copyright and intellectual laws have been dealt with elsewhere in this volume. Those covered in this chapter are: transborder data flows, sovereignty, the activities of multinational corporations and cultural imperialism.

Transborder data flows

The problems arising in the realm of transborder data flows are not by any means limited to exchanges between developed and developing nations. In fact, there are systematic restrictions on the flow of data across borders all over the world. In some cases, these restrictions can be defended in that they operate within the context of data protection and privacy laws. In others, they are used to shore up protectionism, in the form of requirements to purchase data and equipment in a particular country or to make use of public networks. In Canada, there is a requirement that all data generated by banks in that country be stored in Canadian databases, while in Brazil access to all foreign databases is controlled through the Embratel gateway. Along with restrictions on service industries, obstacles to the flow of data across national boundaries emerged in a 1986 survey of multinational corporations as the most severe impediment to the globalization of business activity.

The other side of the coin is that governments can face destabilization as the result of network-induced changes in the money supply or the triggering of runs on the currency. Companies can face plummeting share prices or worse, as a flood of buying or selling in one country causes panic across the networks.[3] In many instances, the actions taken to guard against such eventualities can be even more damaging to national economies, by restricting consumer choice and increasing the prices of goods and services. In any case, the sheer pace of technological change and business globalization means that it is impossible to exercise complete control over all data flows.

Sovereignty

Indeed, the impact of information and communications technologies has been such as to transform traditional perceptions of national sovereignty. Whereas, hitherto, sovereignty was viewed in territorial or spatial terms, it has now acquired a different dimension with, for example, growing concern over the control of national information resources. In the Philippines, for example, 65 per cent of international telecommunications circuit use is accounted for by British, United States and Japanese companies. There is another dimension to this erosion of informational sovereignty. The US LANDSAT and French SPOT (Satellite pour l'Observation de la Terre) satellites export images of the world's resources, of crop patterns and minerals, without regard to any traditional notion of sovereignty.[3]

The activities of multinational corporations

Another major problem for developing countries arises from the activities of multinational corporations, which, attracted by low wage rates or tax concessions, set up businesses in the developing world but maintain their information or decision-making centres in the home country. Frequently this can involve the bypassing of the local telephone network because the multinationals have their own private networks. Inevitably, however, it has meant that control is imposed from the outside, with those in developing countries remaining in a subservient position and enjoying few of the benefits of the relationship.[18] All such arrangements are vulnerable to the removal of the offshore operation to cheaper or safer locales. In manufacturing industry, moreover, where multinational corporations are adept at switching production from one country to another to take advantage of differences in labour costs, the rapid deployment of robots could be a more viable option than the maintenance of factories in developing countries. This would have devastating effects on the people and countries concerned.[19]

Robert Reich has raised pointed questions about the role of multinational corporations in the developing world, particularly those companies in the financial services and communications industries. Apart from the dangers of speculation on world commodity prices for items such as cocoa, coffee and ores, upon which much of the developing world depends for its livelihood, the multinationals are unlikely to be interested in financing the environmental, health, educational and basic infrastructure investments that are desperately needed if developing countries are to become effective players in the global free market.[20]

Cultural imperialism

Many developing nations fear the increase of cultural, economic and political imperialism by the already powerful developed nations and the loss of indigenous languages and traditional ways of life. These were among the concerns that underlay what was perhaps the most celebrated of disputes between the developed and the developing world, that was launched by publication of the Macbride Report on the New World Information and Communication Order (NWICO), in 1980. The report sought to bring about what its authors regarded as a more equitable system of information flows between the developed and the developing worlds. Nothing came of it, and in fact the free flow of information, which Macbride in effect sought to control, has now reached unprecedented proportions. The ability of foreign broadcasters to beam television programmes into other countries regardless of the wishes of the governments concerned is only one example, albeit a spectacular one, of the perceived threat to cultural integrity. It will be fascinating to watch the impact of other advances in communication, for example in use of the Internet, in countries where an advanced technological infrastructure co-exists with traditional and authoritarian forms of government, for example in Singapore or Taiwan.

GLOBAL TRANSFORMATION

Although the world is still awash with exploitation and injustice, much of which stems, both directly and indirectly, from unequal trading and other relationships between developed and developing countries, it is not the same place as it was even 10 years ago. Hence it is no longer possible to talk simply in terms of dependency relationships or of the exploitation of the South by the North. It is necessary to be specific both in terms of the relationships and countries concerned, and above all to recognize the nature of the transformation that has occurred at the global level. To take just one example, the attitudes underlying NWICO and the view that the South's plight was the result of exploitation by the North are no longer in vogue. Such views may still be encountered on the periphery, but even the former Soviet Union and China are embracing the market system, while in Latin America, once in the vanguard of anti-imperialist thought, there is incipient privatization of telecommunications monopolies and a growing acceptance of the need for competition. It may just be possible, for example, that in the telecommunications sector, the contribution of infrastructure enhancements to development may well match the benefits obtained by exporters from the developing countries. Moreover, lacking both the capital and the infrastructure to operate on their own, most developing countries will have to go to the private sector for help. This could result in opportunities for global *win-win* situations such that what is good for the North is good for the South and vice versa.[7]

There is undoubtedly a kind of cultural overlay to these developments, which has to be recognized as part of the cost of development. Privatization, the emergence of multiple competing carriers in telecommunications and the convergence of once distinct and separate media, are simply rolling over national borders and, in the process, many of the attitudes and policies of their governments. In this very real sense, the global information society is already a fact of life.

REFERENCES

1. Robin Mansell (1992) Multinational organisations and international private networks. In: *Telecommunications in transition*, Steinfield *et al.* (eds). Newbury Park, California: Sage, pp. 204–31.

2. Roberta Capello and Howard Williams (1992) Computer network trajectories and organisational dynamics. In: *The economics of information networks*, Cristo Antonelli (ed.). Amsterdam: Elsevier Science Publishers, pp. 347–61.

3. Geoff Mulgan (1991) *Communication and control: networks and the new economics of communications.* Cambridge, England: Polity Press, 302 pp (chapter 11).

4. Kenneth W. Bleakley (1992) Global information in transition: new technologies and competitive forces. *The Information Society*, **8**, pp. 97–99.

5. R. Brian Woodrow and Pierre Sauve (1994) Trade in telecommunications services: the European Community and the Uruguay Round Services Trade Negotiations, In, Chapter Six, pp. 97–117.

6. Herbert S. Dordick and Georgette Wang (1993) *The information society: a retrospective view.* Newbury Park: Sage, pp. 8–30.

7. Edwin B. Parker (1992) Developing Third World telecommunications markets. *The Information Society*, **8**, pp. 147–67.

8. Michel Menou (1993) *Measuring the impact of information on development.* Ottowa: International Development Research Centre, pp. 37–61.

9. United States Board on Science and Technology for International Development (1988) *Cutting edge technologies and microcomputer applications for developing countries: Report of an ad hoc panel on the use of microcomputers for developing countries.* Boulder, Colorado: Westview Press.

10. Scott Tiffin and Fola Osotimehin, with Richard Saunders (1992) *New technologies and enterprise development in Africa.* Paris: OECD.

11. Sydney Gorham (1991) Teleports as catalysts for international trade. In: *Accessing the global network: weaving technology and trade in the Pacific*, Proceedings of the Pacific Telecommunications Conference (January 13–16 1991). Dan J. Wedermeyer and Mark. D. Lofstrum (eds), pp. 2–24.

12. Kieran P. Broadbent (1990) New information-communication technologies in scientific communication: implications for Third-World user. *The Information Society*, **7**, pp. 203–32.

13. J.A. Boon (1992) Information and development: some reasons for failures. *The Information Society*, **8**, pp. 227–41.

14. Sir Donald Maitland (1992) The 'missing links' revisited. *Transnational Data & Communications Report*, **15**, (6), Nov/Dec., pp. 15–18.

15. Heather Hudson (1991) Two solitudes: bridging the gap between telecommunications planning and regional development planning. In: *Accessing the global network: weaving technology and trade in the Pacific*. Proceedings of the Pacific Telecommunications Conference (Jan 13–16, 1991). Dan J. Wedermeyer and Mark D. Lofstrum (eds), Honolulu, pp. 84–94.

16. William E. Halal (1993) World 2000: an international planning dialogue to help shape the global system. *Futures*, **25**, (1), pp. 5–21.

17. Robert B. Reich (1991) *The work of nations: preparing ourselves for 21st Century capitalism*. New York: Alfred A. Knopf, 331 pp.

18. Carolyn Woody and Robert A. Fleck (1991) International telecommunications: the current environment. *Journal of Systems Management*, **42**, (12), pp. 32–36.

19. Paul Kennedy (1993) *Preparing for the 21st Century*. London: Harper Collins, 428 pp.

20. Reich (1991) *op. cit.*, p. 58.

Bibliography

Adonis, Andrew (1993) A brief encounter, now line is engaged: the Franco-German telecoms pact was prompted by growing global competition. *Financial Times*, 9th December, 23.

Adonis, Andrew (1993) Global links down the line: BT's venture with MCI is a pricey but plausible strategy. *Financial Times*, 5th June, 11.

Adonis, Andrew (1993) 6000 km under the sea: a transatlantic breakthrough for fibre optic cables. *Financial Times*, 17th August, 11.

Adonis, Andrew (1993) Survey of IMF, world economy and finance (43): Stuff of dreams a decade ago. *Financial Times*, 24th September, xxv.

Adonis, Andrew (1993) Survey of international telecommunications (1): Era of explosive growth. *Financial Times*, 18th October, 1.

Adonis, Andrew and Tait, Nikki (1993) Mobiles break into the big times: Can cellular communications replace traditional networks? *Financial Times*, 19th August, 15.

Allen, Ferne C. (1993) Benchmarking: practical aspects for information professionals. *Special Libraries*, Summer, 123–29.

Amidon, Stephen (1994) Lost in cyberspace. *Sunday Times: Arts and Culture Section*, 17th July, 8–10.

Antonelli, Cristiano (1992) The economic theory of information networks. In: *The economics of information networks*, C. Antonelli (ed.). Amsterdam North Holland, 5–27.

Applebaum, Herbert (1992) Work and its future. *Futures*, **24**, (4), May, 36–50.

Applegate, Lynda M. and Elam Joyce J. (1991) CIO and SuperCIO. *CIO*,

4, (7), April, 26–28.

Babe, Robert E. (*ed.*) (1994) *Information and communication in economics.* Boston: Kluwer Academic Publishers, 347 pp.

Babe, Robert E. (1994) The place of information in economics. In: Babe (1994), *op. cit.*, 41–68.

Baker, Richard H. (1991) Physical security techniques, In: *Managing Information Technology*, Delran, NJ: Datapro, 6030, 1–14.

Bankes, Steve, Builder, Carl *et al.* (1992) Seizing the moment: harnessing the information technologies. *The Information Society*, **8**, 1–59.

Barkvens, Jan and Schauss, Marc (1992) New EC Data Protection era. *Transnational Data & Communication Report*, **15**, (6), November–December, 43–45.

Barrett, Michael L. (1994) Re-engineering as a management practice: if it's not broken, fix it. *Management*, April, 5–11.

Bearman, Toni Carbo (1992) Information transforming society: challenges for the Year 2000. *Information Services and Use*, **12**, 217–23.

Beaumont, John and Sutherland, Ewan (1992) *Information Resources Management.* Oxford: Butterworth Heinemann, 309 pp.

Bell, Daniel (1973) *The coming of postindustrial society.* New York: Basic Books, 507 pp.

Black, George (1993) Survey of A-Z of computing (17): testing the limits of silicon chips: multimedia, one more milestone. *Financial Times*, 26th May, vi.

Blake, Virgil L.P. and Surprenant, Thomas T. (1990) Electronic immigrants in the information age: some policy considerations. *The Information Society*, **7**, 233–44.

Bleakley, Kenneth W. (1992) Global information in transition: new technologies and competitive forces. *The Information Society*, **8**, 97–99.

Bloombecker, Jay (1990) US computer crime legislation: a review. In: *Managing Information Technology*, Delran, NJ: Datapro, 1430, 1–28.

Boon, J. A. (1992) Information and development: some reasons for failures. *The Information Society*, **8**, 227–41.

Bradley, Stephen P., Hausman, Jerry A. and Nolan, Richard L. (eds) (1993) *Globalization, technology and competition: the fusion of computers and telecommunications in the 1990s.* Boston: Harvard Business School Press, 392 pp.

Braman, Sandra (1989) Defining information: an approach for policymakers. *Telecommunications Policy*, **13**, (3), 233–42.

Braman, Sandra (1994) Commentary: Commodities as sign systems. In: Babe, (1994), *op. cit.*, 92–104.

Branscomb, Anne W. (1991) Common law for the electronic frontier.

Scientific American, **265**, 3 September, 112–16.

Brier, Soren (1992) A philosophy of science perspective on the idea of a unifying information science. In: *Conceptions of library and information science*, Pertti Vakkari and Blaise Cronin (eds). London: Taylor Graham, 97–108.

Broadbent, Kieran P. (1990) New information-communication technologies in scientific communication: implications for Third World users. *The Information Society*, **7**, 227–41.

Brown, Eric H., Karwan, Kirk R. and Weitzel, John R. (1988) The chief information officer in smaller organisations. *Information Management Review*, **4**, (2), 25–35.

Brumm, Eugenia K. (1990) Chief information officers in service and industrial organisations. *Information Management Review*, **5**, (3), 31–45.

Buckeridge, Roger and Cutler, Terry (1994) *Commerce in context: building Australia's future in interactive multimedia markets*. Melbourne: Cutler & Company, 45pp.

Buckland, Michael (1991) Information as Thing. *Journal of the American Society for Information Science*, **42**, (5), 351–60.

Burch, John G. (1992) *Systems analysis, design and implementation*. Boston: Boyd & Fraser, 854 pp.

Burk, Cornelius and Horton, Forrest Woody (1988) *Infomapper*. Englewood Cliffs, NJ: Prentice Hall, 343 pp.

Bushell, Sue (1994) The story in pictures. *Informatics*, **2**, (2), March, 37–39.

CAIRO (1994) *Datamation*, **40**, (6), 1st March, 30–33.

Cane, Alan (1994) Fingers crossed as Digital gets to grips. *Financial Times*, 26th July, 17.

Cane, Alan (1994) Microsoft signs up ICL for servicing. *Financial Times*, 8th August, 15.

Cane, Alan (1993) Survey of A-Z of computing (8) : Teamwork via a PC network – for groupware. *Financial Times*, 20th April, viii.

Capello, Roberta and Williams, Howard (1992) Computer network trajectories and organisational dynamics. In: *The economics of information networks*, C. Antonelli (ed.) Amsterdam: North Holland, 5–27.

Capurro, Rafael (1992) What is information science for? In: Vakkari and Cronin, *op.cit.*, 97–108.

Caudle, Sharon L. and Marchand, Donald A. (1990) Managing information resources: new directions in state government. *Information Management Review*, **5**, (3), 9–30.

Coffin, Stephen (1991) UNIX:- history, philosophy, future. In: *Managing Information Technology*, Delran, NJ: Datapro, 1217, 1–10.

Cole, Charles (1993) Shannon revisited: information in terms of uncertainty. *Journal of the American Society for Information Science*, **44**, (4), 204–11.

Coleman, Richard (1992) International communications: constraints and issues. In: *Managing Information Technology*. Delran, NJ: Datapro, 1238, 1–9.

Conners, Emma (1993) The paperless dream. *Informatics*, **1**, (8), October, 23–27.

Data Protection (1993) *Transnational Data & Communication Report*, **16**, (2), March–April, 39–42.

Deutschman, Alan and Tetzeli, Rick (1994) Your DES in the year 1996. *Fortune*, **130**, (1), 11th July, 46–51.

Development futures (1993) *Informatics*, **1**, (7), September, 33–34, 67.

Dibbell, Julian (1994) Data rape: a tale of torture and terrorism online. *Good Weekend, The Age Magazine*, Melbourne, 9th February, 26–32.

Dickson, Martin(1993) Survey of international telecommunications (9) : Whirlwind of change developments in the United States. *Financial Times*, 18th October, viii.

Dordick, Herbert S. and Wang, Georgette (1993) *The information society: a retrospective view*. Newbury Park. California: Sage, 166 pp.

Drucker, Peter F. (1988) The coming of the new organization. *Harvard Business Review*, **66**, (1), January–February.

Dunning, Thad (1993) Data Protection. *Transnational Data & Communication Report*, **16**, (1), January–February, 26–29.

Dunphy, Edward P. (1992) Standards and the UNIX industry. *In*: *Managing Information Technology*, Delran, NJ: Datapro, 8430, 1–12.

Eaton, J. J. and Bawden D. (1991) What kind of resource is information? *International Journal of Information Management*, **11**, 156–65.

EC Data Protection (1993) (Special Report). *Transnational Data & Communication Report*, **15**, (6), November–December, 31.

Elliott, Philip (1986) Intellectuals, the information society and the disappearance of the public sphere. In: *Media, culture and society: a critical reader*, Richard Collins *et al.* (eds). London: Sage, 105–15.

Ellis, D. *et al.* (1993) Information Audits, Communication Audits and Information Mapping: a review and survey. *International Journal of Information Management*, **13**, 134–51.

Emmons, William F. (1990) Executive search and the chief information officer. *Information Management Review*, **5**, (4), 47–51.

Firebaugh, Morris W. (1988) *Artificial Intelligence: a knowledge-based approach*. Boston: PWS-Kent Publishing Company, 740 pp.

Fischer, Margaret T., Feder, Judith and Gurnsey, John (1990) The electronic information industry and forecast: in Europe, North America and Japan. In: *Online Information 90: Proceedings of the*

International Online Conference, London, 11–13th December, 515–25.

Fist, Stewart (1994) Why ATM is the mode of the 90s. *Informatics*, **2**, (1), February, 37–41.

Flood, Gary G. (1993), Cutting through the NT mania. *Informatics*, **1**, (6), August, 29–32.

Foremski, Tom and Kehoe, Louise (1993) Strong feelings on patent dispute. *Financial Times*, 2nd December, 20.

Forester, Tom (1992) The electronic cottage revisited: towards the flexible workstyle. *Urban Futures*, **2**, (1), February, (Special Issue 5), 27–33.

Forester, Tom (1992) Megatrends or megamistakes? What ever happened to the information society? *The Information Society*, **8**, 133–46.

Forester, Tom (1993) Japan's move up the technology 'food chain'. *Prometheus*, **11**, (1), June, 73–94.

Forester, Tom and Morrison, Perry (1990) Computer crime: new problem for the information society. *Prometheus*, **8**, (2), December, 257–72.

Framel, John (1993) Information value management. *Journal of Systems Management*, **44**, (12), 16–41.

Frazier, Donald and Herbst, Kris (1994) Get ready to profit from the Infobahn. *Datamation*, **40**, (9), 15th May, 50–56.

Frohmann, Bernd (1992) Knowledge and power in library and information science: towards a discourse analysis of the cognitive viewpoint. In: Vakkari and Cronin (1992) *op. cit.*, 135–48.

Gershuny, Jay and Miles, Ian (1983) *The new service economy*. New York: Praeger, 281 pp.

Gooding, Claire (1993) Detectives of the database. *Financial Times*, 26th August, 12.

Gorham, Sydney (1991) Teleports as catalysts for international trade. In: *Accessing the global network: weaving technology and trade in the Pacific*. Proceedings of the Pacific Telecommunications Conference, Dan J. Wedermeyer and Mark D. Lofstrum (eds), January 13–16, Honolulu, 2–24.

Gottinger, Hans W. and Weinmann, Hans P. (1990) Fundamentals of Artificial Intelligence and Expert Systems. In: *Managing Information Technology*, Delran, NJ: Datapro, 7620, 1–8.

Graham, George (1994) US telecoms reform bill abandoned in Senate. *Financial Times*, 24/25th September, 26.

Green, Daniel (1993) Minding your own business: software that shifts the furniture. *Financial Times*, 24th July, vii.

Green, Daniel (1993) Survey of personal and portable computers (4): every variety from Apple on display. *Financial Times*, 19th February, iii.

Grewlich, Klaus and Pedersen, Finn (eds) (1984) *Power and participation in an information society*. Luxembourg: Commission of the European Communities, 289 pp.

Halal, William E. (1993) The information technology revolution: computer hardware, software and services into the 21st century. *Technological Forecasting and Social Change*, **44**, 69–86.

Halal, William E. (1993) World 2000: an international planning dialogue to help shape the new global system. *Futures*, **25**, (1), January–February, 5–23.

Hald, Alan and Konsynski, Benn R. (1993) Seven technologies to watch in globalization. In: Bradley *et al*. (1993), *op. cit.*, 335–58.

Hall, Peter (1992) Cities in the informational economy. *Urban Futures*, **2**, (1), February, (Special Issue 5), 1–12.

Harnett, Julie (1993) Survey of information and communications technology (14): Faster and cheaper data links – Wide Area Networks. *Financial Times*, 23rd March, vi.

Hawkins, Donald T. (1994) Electronic advertising on online information systems. *Online*, **18**, (3), March, 26–39.

Hayes, Robert (1992) The measurement of information. In: Vakkari and Cronin (1992) *op. cit.*, 268–85.

Hepworth, Mark (1994) The information economy in a spatial context: city states in a global village. In: Babe (1994) *op. cit.*, 211–29.

Hertzoff, Ira (1992) Voice network fraud. *In*: *Managing Information Technology*. Delran, NJ: Datapro, 1434, 1–9.

High Level Group on the Information Society (1994) *Europe and the global information society: recommendations to the European Council*. Brussels, 26th May, 35 pp. (The Bangemann Report).

Hoey, John (1994) Waking up to the new economy. *Fortune*, **129**, (13), 27th June, 22–28.

Horton, Forrest Woody (1992) The corporate information management function. *Aslib Proceedings*, **44**, (3), March, 107–14.

Hubley, Mary I. (1993) Moving to UNIX and Open Systems. In: *Managing Information Technology*. Delran, NJ: Datapro, 4237, 1–7.

Hudson, Heather (1990) Two solitudes: bridging the gap between telecommunications planning and regional development planning. In: *Accessing the global network: weaving technology and trade in the Pacific*. Proceedings of the Pacific Telecommunications Conference (January 13–16, 1991). Dan J. Wedermeyer and Mark D. Lofstrum (eds), Honolulu, pp. 84–94.

The importance of computer industry standards (1991). In: *Managing Information Technology*. Delran, NJ: Datapro, 8010, 1–12.

Industry ratings: Computers (1993) Australia, Sydney: Standard & Poor, 27 pp.

Industry ratings: Telecommunications (1993) Australia, Sydney: Standard & Poor, 28 pp.

Inglis, Andrew F. (1991) *Satellite technology: an introduction.* Boston: Focal press, 110 pp.

ISO reference model for Open Systems Interconnection (1991) In: *Managing Information Technology.* Delran, NJ: Datapro, 8440, 1–6.

Jackson, Carl B. (1992) The need for security. In: *Managing Information Technology.* Delran, NJ: Datapro, 6010, 1–12.

Johnson, Craig (1992) Wireless data: high growth in the 1990s. *Transnational Data & Communication Report,* **125**, (4), 7–8.

Kalseth, Karl (1991) Business information strategy: the strategic use of information and knowledge. *Information Services & Use,* **11**, 155–64.

Kapor, Mitchell (1991) Civil liberties in cyberspace. *Scientific American,* **265**, 3 September, 116–20.

Kavanagh, John (1993) Survey of A-Z of computing (22): A key role in commercial computing – for UNIX. *Financial Times,* 20th April, xx.

Kehoe, Louise (1993) Apple faces up to decline in PC profits. *Financial Times,* 22nd June, 30.

Kehoe, Louise (1994), Apple to allow Macintosh clones. *Financial Times,* 19th September, 21.

Kehoe, Louise (1994) Compaq but it's perfectly formed. *Financial Times,* 25th July, 15

Kehoe, Louise (1993) Gerstner sees no place for a *vision* at IBM. *Financial Times,* 28th July, 24.

Kehoe, Louise (1994) More on the *vision* thing. *Financial Times,* 13th May, 17.

Kehoe, Louise (1993) US moves one step nearer the 'information highway'. *Financial Times,* 14th December, 26.

Kehoe, Louise *and* Cane Alan (1994) Chips are down for PC partners, *Financial Times,* 20th September, 21.

Kelly, Hugo (1988) Law aims to hunt computer hackers. *The Age,* Melbourne, 7th December, 12.

Kennedy, Paul (1993) *Preparing for the 21st century.* London: Harper Collins, 428 pp.

Kiernan, Casey (1993) Faces users can relate to. *Informatics* **1**, (7), September, 75–79.

Kling, Rob *and* Dunlop Charles (1993) Controversies about computerization and the character of white collar worklife. *The Information Society,* **9**, 1–29.

Koesler, Marina and Hawkins, Donald T. (1994) Intelligent agents: software servants for an electronic information world and more. *Online,* **18**, (4), July, 19–32.

213

Kupfer, Andrew (1994) Augmenting your desktop with telecom: phones and PCs to merge. *Fortune*, **130**, (1), 11th July, 54–58.

Lamberton, Donald McL. (1994) The information economy revisited. In: Babe (1994) *op.cit.*, 1–33.

Larsen, Judith K. and Rogers, Everett M. (1989) Silicon Valley: a scenario for the information society of tomorrow. In: *The information society: economic, social and structural issues*, J.L. Salvaggio (ed.). Hillside, NJ: Lawrence Erlbaum Associates Inc., 51–62.

Laurence, Les (1994) Client/server security *Australian Communications*, May, 127–35.

Leeflang, Karel J. (1994) Is Europe's position in the information market weakening? *Information Services & Use*, **14**, 1–8.

Lettice, John (1993) Survey of personal and portable computers (20) : IBM poised to compete – Personal Digital Assistants. *Financial Times*, 19th February, x.

Lincoln, Adam (1994) Dawn of a new information age? *Managing Information Systems*, **3**, (3), April, 70–73.

Lloyd, Peter (1993) Survey of using computers in business (14): Expectations are high – multimedia. *Financial Times*, 21st September, xv.

Losee, Stephanie (1994) Watch out for the CD-ROM hype. *Fortune*, **130**, (6), 19th September, 89–94.

Lucas, Henry C. (1991) A guide to computer systems. In: *Managing Information Technology*. Delran, NJ: Datapro, 7210, 1–9.

Lyon, David (1988) *The information society: issues and illusions*. Cambridge, England: Polity Press, 196 pp.

MacDonald, Stuart (1992) Information networks and information exchange. In: *The economics of information networks*, C. Antonelli (ed.). Amsterdam: North Holland, 51–69.

Machlup, Fritz and Mansfield, Una, (*eds*) (1983) *The study of information*. New York: Wiley, 743 pp.

Maitland, Donald (1992) The *Missing Links* revisited. *Transnational Data & Communication Report*, **15**, (6), November–December, 15–18.

Manchester, Philip (1993) Survey of A-Z of computing (4) : Doorway for innovative applications for client/server. *Financial Times*, 20th April, v.

Manchester, Philip (1993) Survey of personal and portable computers (16): A general purpose toolbox, applications software *Financial Times*, 19th February, viii.

Manchester, Phillip (1993) Survey of international telecommunications (14) : A new breed of communications, multimedia, *Financial Times*, 18th October, vi.

Manchester, Philip (1993) Survey of A-Z of computing (3): A measure of how data is transmitted – for bandwidth. *Financial Times*, 20th April, iv.

Mansell, Robin (1992) *The new telecommunications*: a political economy of network evolution. London: Sage Publications, 260 pp.

Marchand, Donald A. (1990) Infotrends: a 1990s outlook on strategic information management. *Information Management Review*, **5**, (4), 23–32.

Marchand, Donald A. (1988) Strategic information management: challenges and issues in the CIM environment. *Information Management Review*, **4**, (2), 15–23.

Martin, William J. (1993) Information management in the United Kingdom. In: *Encyclopaedia of Library and Information Science*, Allen Kent (ed.). Vol. 51, Supplement 14. New York: Marcel Dekker, 266–76.

Marx, William (1993) Building the broadband society. In: Bradley *et al.* (1993) *op. cit.*, 359–70.

Massey, Judith (1993) Survey of A–Z of computing (23) : Still at the stage of baby talk – voice technology. *Financial Times*, 20th April, xx.

Meley, Mimi S. (1992) Scanners: overview. In: *Managing Information Technology*. Delran, NJ: Datapro, 7260, 1–9.

Menou, Michel (1993) *Measuring the impact of information on development*. Ottowa: International Development Research Centre, 188 pp.

Miles, Ian (1988) *Information technology and information society: options for the future*. London: Economic and Social Research Council, 31 pp.

Mitchell, Ben (1994) Workforce of the future stays home. *The Sunday Age*, Melbourne, 20th February, 18.

Morris, Michelle D. (1991) RISC vs CISC. In: *Managing Information Technology*, Delran, NJ: Datopro, 1215, 1–5.

Mosco, Vincent (1994) The political economy of communication. In: Babe (1994), *op. cit.*, 105–24.

Mulgan, Geoff (1991) *Communication and control: networks and the new economies of communications*. Cambridge, England: Polity Press, 302 pp.

Netmap: database visualisation and analysis (1994) 12 pp. (Promotional literature)

Newton, F. W. (1993) Australia's information landscapes. *Prometheus*, **11**, (1), June, 3–39.

Nolle, Thomas and Haggerty, Charles (1992) Data communications standards: overview. In: *Managing Information Technology*. Delran, NJ: Datapro, 8410, 1–12.

Olson, Jack (1994) Defining a new state of databases. *Informatics*, **2**, (3), 41–45.

Organisation for Economic Cooperation and Development (1986) *Trends in the information economy*. Paris: OECD, 42 pp.

Organisation for Economic Cooperation and Development (1992) *Convergence between communications technologies: case studies from North America and Western Europe*. Paris: OECD, 147 pp. (Information Computer Communications Policy, 28).

Overview of mainframes (1991) In: *Managing Information Technology*. Delran, NJ: Datapro, 7220, 1–8.

Paquet, Gilles (1994) Commentary : From the information economy to evolutionary cognitive economics. In: Babe, (1994). *op. cit.*, 34–40.

Parker, Edwin B. (1992) Developing Third World telecommunications markets. *The Information Society*, **8**, 147–67.

Patton, Robert (1994) Cutting the cord. *Financial Times*, 1st September, 19.

Pearson, Christine (1993) Aligning TQM and organisational learning. *Special Libraries*, Summer, 47–49.

Perone, Giovanni (1992) Close up on CASE. In: *Managing Information Technology*. Delran, NJ: Datapro, 7615, 1–11.

Philipson, Graeme (1993) In search of client/server. *Informatics*, **1**, (6), August, 23–28.

Pickering, Wendy (1994) Computer: take a memo. *Datamation*, **40**, (1), 7th. January, 51–52.

Poirier, Rene (1990) The information economy approach: characteristics, limitations and future prospects. *The Information Society*, **7**, 245–85.

Porat, Marc Uri (1978) *The information economy: definition and measurement.* Washington D.C., US Department of Commerce, Office of Telecommunications, 9 vols.

Potter, Ben (1994) Waiting for directions on the technological superhighway. *The Age*, Melbourne, 11th February, 14.

Prescott, Michael and Foster, Howard (1994) Police get new powers to fight computer porn. *Sunday Times,* July.

Quayle, Michael (1990) Value Added Services: applications, acceptability and politics, the case of teleconferencing. *Prometheus*, **8**, (2), December, 273–87.

Quinn, Sherry (1993) Australian databases and information services: summary of developments, 1988 to 1992. In: *Information Online & On-Disc*, Proceedings of the 7th. Australasian Online & On-Disc Conference, Sydney, 19–21 January, 49–69.

Quinn, Tony (1993) Survey of A-Z of computing, systems, software and services (13): Myth of the panacea interface–Human Machine Interaction. *Financial Times*, 26th May, v.

Radosevich, Lynda (1994) Users want better messaging tools. *Computerworld*, **16**, (38), April, 3.

Ravetz, J. R. *and* Funtowicz, S.O. (1992) *Total Information Quality*. (Pre-publication draft of seminar paper).

Rees, David W.E. (1990) *Satellite communications: the first quarter century of service*. New York: Wiley, 329 pp.

Reich, Robert (1991) *The work of nations*. New York: Alfred A. Knopf, 331 pp.

Ricciuti, Mike (1994) The mainframe as server : is IBM totally bonkers or brilliant? *Datamation*, **40**, (10), 61–64.

Rosenberg, Richard S. (1993) Free speech, pornography, sexual harassment and electronic networks. *The Information Society*, **9**, 285–331.

Ruben, Brett D. (1992) The communication-information relationship in system-theoretic perspective. *Journal of the American Society for Information Science*, **43**, (1), 15–27.

St. Clair, Guy (1993) The future challenge: management and measurement. *Special Libraries*, Summer, 151–54.

Salvaggio, Jerry L. (ed.) (1989) *The information society: economic, social and structural issues*. Hillsdale , NJ: Lawrence Erlbaum Associates Inc., 143 pp.

Salvaggio, Jerry L. (1989) Is privacy possible in an information society? In: Salvaggio (1989) *op. cit.*, 115–29.

Saracevic, Tefko (1992) Information science: origin, evolution and relations. In: Vakkari and Cronin (1992) *op. cit.*, 5–27.

Savolainen, Reijo (1992) The sense-making theory : an alternative to intermediary-centred approaches in library and information science? In: Vakkari and Cronin (1992) *op. cit.*, 149–64.

Schement, Jorge Reina (1989) The origins of the information society in the United States: competing visions. In: Salvaggio (1989) *op. cit.*, 29–50.

Schoeffel, Penelope, Loveridge, Alison and Davidson, Carl (1993) Telework: issues for New Zealand. *Prometheus* **11**, (1), June, 49–60.

Schoonmaker, Sara (1993) Trading on-line: information flows in advanced capitalism. *The Information Society*, 39–50.

Schreibman, Vigdor (1994) Closing the *values gap* : the crisis point. *Federal Information News Syndicate*, **11**, (18), 29th August (taken from the Internet).

Schrifeen, Robert (1993) Freefone lines set of spate of *data rape*. *Sunday Times*, 14th November, 11.

Schroeder, Ralph (1993) Virtual reality in the real world: history, applications and projections. *Futures*, **25**, (9), November, 963–73.

Schutzer, Daniel (1991) The latest technological trends. In: *Managing*

Information Technology. Delran, NJ: Datapro, 1272, 1–19.

Semich, J. William (1994) Surprise. OS/2 is taking off. *Datamation*, **40**, (8), 15th April.

Sim, Philip (1994) Telecommuting, still a long way off. *Computerworld*, April, 29.

Shannon, Claude E. (1948) A mathematical theory of communication. *Bell System Technical Journal*, **27**, July, 379–423.

Simitis sees improvement in EC data protection revision (1992) *Transnational Data & Communication Report*, **15**, (5), November–December, 42.

Slaughter, Richard A. (1993) Looking for the real *megatrends Futures*, **25**, (8), 827–49.

Smart, Barry (1992) *Modern conditions, postmodern controversies.* London: Routledge, 241 pp.

Smith, Doug (1992) Getting involved with communications standards. In: *Managing Information Technology.* Delran, NJ: Datapro.

Standards and the UNIX industry (1992). In: *Managing Information Technology.* Delran, NJ: Datapro, 8430, 1–12.

Steinfield, Charles and Salvaggio, Jerry L. (1989) Towards a definition of the information society. In: *Salvaggio* (1989) *op. cit.*, 1–14.

Steinfield, Charles, Bauer Johannes, M. and Caby, Laurence, (eds) (1994), *Telecommunications in transition: policies, services and technologies in the European Community.* Newbury Park, California: Sage, 307 pp.

Stevens, Larry (1994) Are you ready for the desktop of the future? *Datamation*, **40**, (11), 1st June, 60–63.

Stewart, Thomas A. (1994) Managing in a wired company. *Fortune*, **130**, (1), 11th July, 16–22.

Stonier, Tom (1991) Towards a new theory of information. *Journal of the American Society for Information Science*, **17**, 257–63.

Strauss, Paul (1994) Welcome to client/server PBX computing *Datamation*, **40**, (11), 1st June, 49–52.

Stuart, Crit and Drake, Miriam A. (1993) TQM in research libraries. *Special Libraries*, Summer, 131–36.

Tannenbaum, Andrew S. (1992) *Modern operating systems.* Englewood Cliffs, NJ, Prentice Hall,

Targowski, Andrew S. (1990) Strategies and architecture of the electronic global village. *The Information Society*, **7**, 187–201.

Taylor, Jonathan (1993) A kick start for multimedia – technologically speaking. *Financial Times*, 7th September, 15.

Taylor, Paul (1993) Survey of information and communications technology (6): Plenty of surprises ahead. *Financial Times*, 23rd March, iii.

Taylor, Paul (1993), Survey of technology in the office (14) : Small is beautiful. *Financial Times*, 26th October, vii.

Temby, Ian (1993) Australia exposes illegal data sales. *Transnational Data & Communication Report,* **16**, (1), January–February, 26–29.

Tetzeli, Rick (1994) Surviving information overload. *Fortune*, **130**, (1), 11th July, 26–29.

Tiffin, Scott and Osotimehin, Fola, (with Richard Saunders) (1992) *New technologies and enterprise development in Africa.* Paris: OECD, 54 pp.

United States Board on Science and Technology for International Development (1988) *Cutting edge technologies and microcomputer applications for developing countries: Report of an ad hoc panel on the use of microcomputers for developing countries.* Boulder, Colorado: Westview Press,

Vakkari, Pertti and Cronin, Blaise (eds) (1992) *Conceptions of library and information science: historical, empirical and theoretical perspectives.* London: Taylor Graham, 314 pp.

Ware, Willis H. (1993) The new faces of privacy. *The Information Society*, **9**, 195–210.

Wark, McKenzie (1994) Mass media races down the infobahn. *The Australian*, Melbourne, 18th May, 26.

Webster, Frank (1994) What information society? *The Information Society*, **10**, 1–23.

Wedermeyer, Dan J. and Lofstrum, Mark D. (eds) (1991) Accessing the global network: weaving technology and trade in the Pacific. Proceedings of the Pacific Telecommunications Conference (Jan 13–16, 1991), Honolulu.

Weilerstein, Kenny (1992) Optical storage: overview. In: *Managing Information Technology.* Delran, NJ: Datapro, 7265, 1–7.

Wersig, Gernot (1992) Information science: origin, evolution and relations. In: Vakkari and Cronin, (1992) *op.cit.*, 201–17.

Wheelright, Geoff (1993) Homing in on a new market: Microsoft plans for PCs in the home. *Financial Times*, 21st December, 8.

Whittle, Robin (1994) ADSL: bridging the superhighway gap? *Australian Communications*, May, 81–90.

Williams, Martha E. (1994) The Internet: implications for the information industry and database providers. *Online & CD-ROM Review*, **18**, (3), 149.

Williams, Martha E. (1994) The state of databases today. In: *Gale Directory of Databases*, Vol. 2. Detroit: Gale Research Inc., x.

Womack, Audrey (1992) Videoconferencing services: overview. In: *Managing Information Technology.* Delran, NJ: Datapro, 1219, 1–5.

Woody, Carolyn and Fleck, Robert A. (1991) International telecommunications: the current environment. *Journal of Systems Management*, **42**, (12), 32–36.

Yacco, Wayne (1992) GUIs: a general perspective. In: *Managing Information Technology*. Delran, NJ: Datapro, 7658, 1–3.

Young, Peter (1994) Internet shake-out looms. *Computerworld*, 1st August, 8.

Index